EUROPEAN COMMISSION

The Single Market Review

IMPACT ON SERVICES

TRANSPORT NETWORKS

The Single Market Review

SUBSERIES II: VOLUME 11

OFFICE FOR OFFICIAL PUBLICATIONS
OF THE EUROPEAN COMMUNITIES

KOGAN PAGE . EARTHSCAN

Table of contents

List of tables

List of figures

List of abbreviations

ATC	air traffic control
ATT	advanced transport telematics
BR	(former British Rail)
CC	congestion charging
CEEC	Central and Eastern European country
CFMU	central flow management unit
CTP	Common Transport Policy
DB	Deutsche Bundesbahn (the German state-owned railway company)
EATCHIP	European Air Traffic Control Harmonization and Integration Programme
EC	European Community
ECMT	European Conference of the Ministers of Transport
ECU	European currency unit
EEC	European Economic Community
EFTA	European Free Trade Association
ELA	European Logistics Association
ESA	European system of integrated accounts
EU	European Union
EUR-12	Belgium, Denmark, Germany, Greece, Spain, France, Ireland, Italy, Luxembourg, Netherlands, Portugal, United Kingdom
Eurocontrol	European Organization for the Safety of Air Navigation
Eurostat	Statistical Office of the European Communities
feu	forty foot equivalent unit
FI	full integration
FPIV	IV Framework Programme (for Research and Development)
FRG	Federal Republic of Germany
FS	(former Ferrovie dello Stato)
GDP	gross domestic product
GDR	German Democratic Republic
GPS	global positioning system
HGV	heavy goods vehicle
Horeca	hotel, restaurant and catering
HST	high speed train
IC	inter-city (conventional train)
ICAO	International Aviation Civil Organization
IOT	input-output table
IT	information technology
JIT	just in time
M&As	Mergers and acquisitions
n.a.	not available
NUTS	nomenclature of territorial units for statistics (Eurostat)
O–D	origin–destination
OECD	Organization for Economic Co-operation and Development
p.a.	per annum
pcu	passenger car unit
PI	partial integration
p-km	passenger-kilometre
PTRC	Planning and Transport Research and Computation
R&D	research and development
RDS	Retrieval Data System
RENFE	Red Nacional de Ferrocarriles Españoles (the Spanish state-owned railway company)
RPI	rail price increase
RQI	rail service quality improvement
RTI	road traffic information
TEE	Trans-Europe Express
TEN	Trans-European transport Network

TEU	twenty foot equivalent unit
tkm	tonne-kilometre
TMC	Traffic Management and Control
SMEs	small and medium-sized enterprises
SNCF	Societé Nationale des Chemins de Fers (the French state-owned railway company)
UIC	Union Internationale des Chemin de Fer
UNECE	United Nations Economic Commission for Europe

Acknowledgements

Project director/Steering Committee Chairman: Prof. Marco Ponti (TRT Trasporti e Territorio).

Members of the Steering Committee: Prof. David Newbery (Marcial Echenique & Partners), Roberto Crapelli (AT Kearney), Dario Inti (FS).

External assessor: Prof. Dr S.J.G. van Wijnbergen and Prof. C. Peeters.

Project coordinator: Silvia Maffii (TRT Trasporti e Territorio).

Model application: Ian Williams (Marcial Echenique & Partners), Ying Jin (Marcial Echenique & Partners) and Angelo Martino (TRT Trasporti e Territorio).

Scenario design: Chiara Borgnolo (TRT Trasporti e Territorio).

Analysis of inefficiencies: Silvio Beccia (AT Kearney).

The project team wish to thank particularly members of Eurostat and of UN Economic Commission for Europe staff for their professional guidance and swift data provision during the course of the project.

1. Summary

1.1. Scope and study process

The aim of this study is to assess the impact of the existing transport barriers on the functioning of the single market. Much of the benefits of the single market programme stem from increased competition due to liberalization of the regulatory framework and more efficient allocation of resources as a result of the removal of non-tariff barriers to free intra-EC trade. However, physical barriers, either natural, such as geography, or artificial, due to costly interfaces and poor connections between countries, are limiting competition and continue to impede the free flow of goods, services and persons in the European Union.

The study is carried out in two stages. In the first stage the sources of inefficiency in the present transport network are investigated. This is done through a review of existing surveys on the transport system, and a new survey which is implemented to collect the views of a sample of large European manufacturers and freight shippers.

In the second stage, a base case and some policy scenarios are prepared for the year 2005. The base case, which is a 'minimum' scenario of the transport system, is compared with alternative policy scenarios of differing degrees of integration, using a simulation model. Operating statistics are produced for each transport mode. The cost, time and other indirect savings are estimated for each type of transport user. The effects are also evaluated at a macro-economic level in terms of regional growth and change. Direct and indirect effects on the economy are distinguished and a number of quantitative indicators are produced. The study provides a limited set of environmental indicators such as energy use and emissions by mode for each scenario; these indicators, together with other transport operating statistics, may be used in further analysis to assess the benefits of improving environment-friendly transport modes.

1.2. Present and foreseen inefficiencies

In order to identify the more critical existing and foreseen transport inadequacies and their impact on the single market, a survey was completed, exploring the attitude and the point of view of large European manufacturers and freight shippers. The results were partially unexpected: the transport costs are perceived as declining in past years, and are foreseen as further declining also in the future, albeit at a slower rate.

Contradicting the 'common wisdom' of the increasing burden of congestion, the combined effect of improved logistics ('just in time' etc.) and of the increasing value of the goods exchanged more than counterbalances the increased transport costs related to congestion, inadequate infrastructure, etc.

Another crucial inefficiency of transport in Europe, which is outside the scope of this study, is its environmental impact. Being an externality, it is by definition not directly perceived by the firms (and the private motor vehicle drivers) that generate it. It is, however, a critical factor in the sense that improving the environment-friendly transport mode is, together with enhanced competition, a major goal of the Common Transport Policy, potentially generating important economic trade-offs.

Figure 1.1.   Logistics costs reduction (European average)

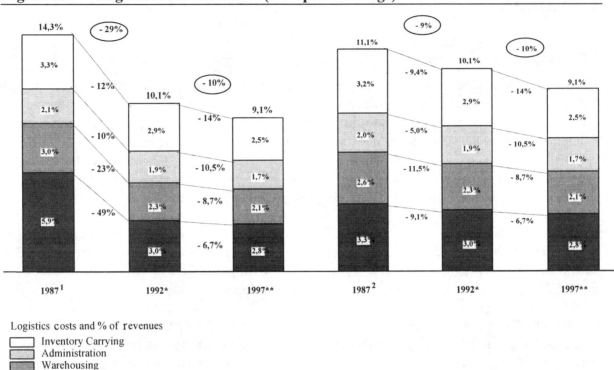

Logistics costs and % of revenues

☐ Inventory Carrying
▨ Administration
▦ Warehousing
■ Transportation

Source: A.T. Kearney
1   1987 actual values obtained from the European Logistics survey 1988
2   1987 estimated values obtained from the European Logistics survey 1993
*   1992 actual values obtained from the European Logistics survey 1993
**   1997 forecast values obtained from the European Logistics survey 1993

1.3.   The base and policy scenarios

In order to pinpoint the impact of different possible policies, a base (or 'minimum') scenario is compared with two main policy scenarios (partial integration and full integration) and two sensitivity tests based on the full integration scenario.

The contents of the alternative scenarios, partial integration and full integration, are defined in such a way as to allow for separate assessment of the impact of infrastructure investment and of policy actions on the performance of transport systems in the single market.

To do so, policy actions are assumed to vary between scenarios. The partial integration scenario includes all infrastructure projects but only a minimum number of policy measures. The full integration scenario, on the other hand, assumes that a set of policies are successfully implemented to enhance competition and to achieve cost reduction and larger scale, integrated transport operations in the Union by 2005.

The main assumptions on **infrastructure** are:

(a)   In the base scenario, only limited components of the Trans-European transport Network (TEN) priority projects are put into operation by 2005. The projects comprise those which are already under construction and due for completion by 2005, and those already committed by the Member States to be completed by 2005.

(b)   The partial and full integration scenarios include all the remaining parts of the TEN priority projects that are expected to be completed by 2005.

The main assumptions about **policies** are:

Harmonization measures

(a)   As far as policy measures are concerned, both the base and the partial integration scenarios describe a situation in which an increase in qualitative environmental and safety standards is the only area for harmonization.

(b)   The full integration scenario describes a situation in which Common Transport Policies to integrate and make transport services competitive in Europe are fully implemented. This would result in significant changes in relative prices, fares and tariffs of different transport modes.

Liberalization and competition

(a)   In both the base and the partial integration scenarios in the absence of a strong European commitment to remove price distortions, the liberalization of transport industries will be only partially achieved.

(b)   The adoption of a wide set of harmonization measures in the full integration scenario is assumed to complement the establishment of a full set of regulatory powers by the year 2005 to regulate monopolistic practices in the transport sector and guarantee competition in the European Union.

Two further sensitivity tests have been designed based on the full integration scenario. These deal with two critical issues in the European transport sector. The first sensitivity test examines the impact of an extensive introduction of congestion pricing on the main roads throughout Europe. The second explores the effect brought about by a quality improvement in rail services.

1.4. Costs and prices

The different policy scenarios have been translated, for modelling purposes, into changes in the transport costs and tariffs perceived by the firms and the general public. The base scenario assumes that present costs and tariffs regimes continue with no more than minor variations. In the other scenarios each policy action or infrastructure implementation generates specific transport cost and price changes which affect the users' choice of modes and routes. In addition to the consideration of direct cost accounting, efforts have been made to quantify 'disutility functions', i.e. the indirect transport costs.

Values have been identified for critical factors such as the willingness of different users to pay for better levels of service, and for determinants in modal choice in terms not only of costs but also of line haul and terminal times and, in particular, the quality of transport services. Validation data have been prepared in order to estimate model parameters to represent the interaction between economic sectors and activity distribution, the choice of transport modes made by each type of passenger and for each type of freight, and the network congestion effects.

1.5. Model structure and implementation

The assessment of the scenarios has been carried out by the implementation of the Meplan model, a set of integrated regional-economic and transport models explicitly designed to consider the demand for transport services as an economic input and to disaggregate between transport costs and attributes that enter the production costs of different economic industrial sectors located in different regions.

The implementation of the model has been completed successfully. Data structures for the regional economic and transport modules have been determined. An extensive data analysis has been carried out in order to define the categories of economic sectors and trade, the types of transport flows and the transport modes. All the data have been classified in terms of the zoning system. The strategic multimodal transport network has been implemented representing all modes of transport for both passengers and freight for 1991 and for the different scenarios in 2005. Based on macro-economic and demographic projections the model has been run and provided estimates of transport demand in 2005 for the different scenarios.

1.6. Assessment of the scenarios

As far as the two main scenarios are concerned, the model results highlight differences of some interest between partial and full integration: the impact of Common Transport Policies seems to be more significant, both on travel demand and on regional economies, than pure infrastructure improvement.

The partial integration scenario which is essentially an infrastructure improvement scenario, appears to stimulate the overall demand for transport. This results from an expansion of capacity as well as an improvement in service quality. Both in terms of passenger-km and tonne-km there is a growth in comparison with the 2005 base run. There is a marked increase in the use of high speed trains, in response to the major projects included in the TENs, with passengers attracted both from conventional trains and cars (for the medium-distance trips) and aeroplanes (for longer distance trips). For freight, the overall changes in modal share are small, given that the majority of the TEN projects are mainly concerned with passenger services.

In the full integration scenario the impacts are more evenly distributed between freight and passenger flows, and there seems to be a more sustainable use of different transport modes: road losing out on longer distances to rail and air for passengers, whilst for freight, shipping and inland waterways increase their share. Passenger travel sees a reduction of road travel as a result of motorway tolling; air captures some of the medium-distance travel from road modes, a limited amount of the high speed train market, owing to a further reduction in air tariffs, and a small increase of the high speed train fares overall. On the other hand, passenger trains gain in the short to medium distance where air cannot compete effectively. On the whole there is a slight decrease in passenger travel demand within the EU, compared with the 2005 base scenario. In all scenarios, substantial growth is forecast from 1991.

Freight transport sees a small yet significant increase in total tkm as a result of some freight being diverted to non-road modes, which generally involve an increase in travel to transfer points. Lorry use reduces slightly in volume yet significantly in tkm, shedding some of the medium- and long-distance movements to the other modes.

By extending congestion charging also to non-motorway links, there is a further decrease in road modes in favour of rail both for passengers (high speed trains and conventional trains) and for freight. Finally, the sensitivity tests on railways show that there is a potential for rail service improvement; both freight and passengers respond positively to the modification of terminal costs and times.

An overall economic appraisal of the scenarios and sensitivity tests has been carried out showing the user's benefits and the operator's revenues.

Table 1.1.   Annual savings against 2005 base (million 1991 ECU)

	Cost savings	Time savings	Total cost & time savings	Total savings (including other indirect costs)
Partial integration (PI)				
Annual savings	2,089	1,546	3,635	10,268
Full integration (FI)				
Annual savings	53,407	13,118	66,525	92,467
Congestion charging (CC) (based on FI)				
Annual savings	60,812	24,738	85,550	119,321
Rail service quality improvement (RQI) (based on CC)				
Annual savings	66,893	27,674	94,567	128,965

Source: A.T. Kearney

Notes:

1   Annual savings include passengers, freight and operator revenue. The last column is a composite sum of cost savings, time savings (i.e. hours converted into monetary units using the values of time) and savings on modal constants.

2   For passengers, all times are included in the calculations; for freight, only the times involved in general freight are included. For bulk freight, time and disutility savings are excluded, since for planned, regular bulk transport transit time would not seem to be a main consideration, so long as reasonable punctuality is maintained. Note the times include access, transfer and waiting at the terminal. Thus for some policies where passengers and freight are shifted from road to other modes, the actual door-to-door time may lengthen: this is then shown as a disbenefit. Such losses of time, however, should be taken with caution.

The results obtained from the regional economic model are important for us to gain insight into the potential impact of the transport policy scenarios. In fact the output from the regional economic model and the transport model offer parallel and consistent stories of what is going on in the interaction of regional economic activities and transport.

Compared with 2005 base, under the partial integration scenario there is a small relative reduction in total production in the peripheral countries, due to improved access of other countries to the local markets in the peripheral regions. The pattern of relative strength is, however, somewhat uneven across the sectors. It seems that in agriculture and heavy industries the peripheral countries and regions are more likely to grow under infrastructure improvements, whereas light manufacturing and services tend to concentrate on the centrally located regions, by a small margin.

There is virtually no impact on direct monetary cost of the goods and services, whilst both production and consumption are likely to benefit from the improvement of infrastructure and intermodal operations in disutility terms. This is consistent with what is shown in the transport evaluation.

Under the full integration scenario, the model projects a stronger trend of growth in the centrally located countries and the new Member States. The peripheral cohesion countries, on the other hand, appear to grow somewhat less. It has to be remembered, however, this slight reduction in growth strength is shown comparing with a base case, where the cohesion countries are expected to grow substantially more than the centrally located countries. Across the sectors, agriculture and light manufacturing are expected to grow more strongly in the cohesion countries in the full integration scenario than in the base case. Services, however, tend to grow less. In the model, the trade of services is directly related to the ease of business travel, and since in full integration the air tariffs are assumed to fall substantially more than in partial integration, those outlying regions are able to import more business services from the major metropolitan centres, resulting in slightly weaker growth. When reaching a definitive projection for the service sector, it is necessary to take full account of the factors other than business travel that are not considered in the model.

Under congestion charging, the locational impact in general seems to be similar to that of full integration. One noticeable change appears to be a tendency for the centrally-located countries and the new Member States to reduce their overall level of production in all primary and secondary industries. Tolling on long-distance traffic results in a rise in production cost. However, in disutility terms (i.e. when indirect transport costs are taken into account), the cost rise does not seem to be as severe. Note that none of the cost and disutility signals include the redistribution of the toll revenue as well as the benefit of increased revenue for the non-road modes.

A major difference that can be identified in the rail quality improvement run is the reduction of production and consumption disutilities, which demonstrates the potential benefit of rail service quality improvement to the economy as a whole. Heavy industries and services see the largest fall of production disutility, indicating the areas where rail has a natural advantage over other modes, i.e. bulk and semi-bulk freight and business travel.

1.7. Main impacts and results

Given the short time span of the study, the indicators produced by the model are suggestive rather than conclusive, and they need to be interpreted with caution in the policy context. In summary, the main results of the study suggest the following considerations:

(a)   The review and survey carried out in the study show that transport costs need to be examined systematically. Apart from direct monetary costs incurred in course of the line haul, which were not identified as a crucial issue for the economic development of the European market, there are many extremely important factors such as travel time, reliability, flexibility, and interoperability. As the European industries develop and personal mobility rises, the above-mentioned factors (which represent indirect transport-related costs) are gaining more and more importance in interregional passenger and freight transport. In many instances the indirect cost component may outweigh the direct monetary outlay in transport.

(b) Using the study methodology in accounting for direct and indirect transport costs, it is shown that the impact of the planned European policies and infrastructure construction is positive by comparison. The cost and pricing policies that apply to the whole of the EU have a far more profound impact than the localized infrastructure improvements such as the TEN links.

(c) This impact is widely differentiated for the various transport industries: it is limited for road freight transport (the dominant mode), which is already fairly competitive; the potential impact is far greater with air services, given the wide opportunities for liberalizing the sector and reducing the tariffs; a similar potential exists for the rail sector.

(d) Medium- to long-distance passenger travel stands to benefit from the policies included in the scenarios, particularly through developments in air services and high speed rail. This will bring benefits to the service industry and those sectors of manufacturing which are founded on a highly skilled labour force. On the other hand, intra-EU tourism will gain from this. These benefits would lead to further social and political benefits, such as cohesion of the EU.

(e) For freight transport there are trade-offs to be expected between the European policy objectives of reducing congestion and pollution, and the costs that road users will have to face. It is useful to bear in mind the fact that, in the future, higher monetary costs for firms (through road tolls and other congestion charges) should be translated into larger transport investments, a reduced overall fiscal burden for the state, and an improved quality of life.

(f) A number of important issues deserve further analysis:

   (i) the perspectives of rail transport: as stated in a recent White Paper, railways can either enter a virtuous circle of growing efficiency through competition, or the burden of the required subsidies will be considered unbearable by the major states resulting eventually in a contraction of their role;

   (ii) the role of transport costs for peripheral regions: for industries, improving the links with the more developed areas can have both positive impact (resulting from improved accessibility) and negative effects (due to increased competition). The exact extent of the impact would depend much on the local industrial structure. Close investigation is needed for each branch of industry;

   (iii) congestion and pollution due to urban traffic probably needs stronger public action than those due to long-distance transport, while often public attention is focused on the latter;

   (iv) the impact of the Common Transport Policy and of new infrastructures on specific regions and industrial sectors would benefit from further more detailed analysis.

Please note that throughout this study, where tables or figures provide no sources, they have either been originally prepared by TRT for the work in object, or are the output of the model supplied.

Figure 1.2.   Analytical framework of the study

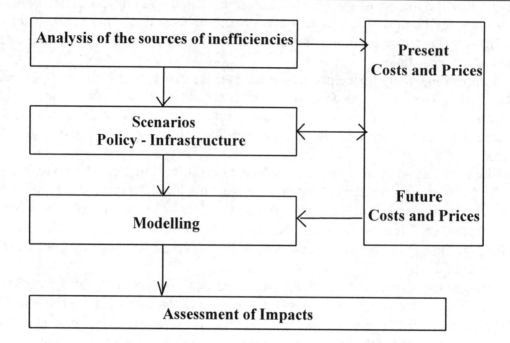

2. Analysis of the inefficiencies

Sources of inefficiencies have been identified from the point of view of European firms. Following an outline of main changes in mobility patterns and requirements for both passenger and freight in Section 2.1, Sections 2.2 to 2.7 concentrate on freight transport. In order to assess the present situation and foreseeable trend of goods transportation within the single market different levels of analysis/different perspectives have been considered:

(a)   the logistics perspective as a general frame regarding requirements to be satisfied and how companies are approaching transportation within the logistics process: this explains why, despite longer distances, transportation costs are declining as a percentage of companies' turnover (Sections 2.2 to 2.5);

(b)   the point of view of a number of industrial sectors described through case studies: this shows the increasing level of European integration for significant industry sectors and the trade-off between production cost/investments related to plant specialization and transportation costs for distributing products (Section 2.6);

(c)   the identification of sources of inefficiency that still represent elements of inadequacy of the transportation system as in the evaluation of a sample of selected manufacturers and shippers: this indicates how many opportunities for improvement exist in the different areas of transportation (Section 2.7).

The detailed results of these sections are presented in Appendix A.

2.1. Transport demand in Europe

2.1.1. Passengers

It is well known that passenger transport demand rises with income. This in turn relates to both a corresponding increase in leisure time and the shift of work content toward professional activities that imply more travelling than traditional factory or office work. This phenomenon is compounded by the increasing ageing of the population: retired persons travel more.

Table 2.1.   Passenger and freight transport growth (1970–91)

Index 100 = 1970	1991
GDP	168
Industrial output	160
Passenger transport (passenger-kilometres)	188
Cars	200
Coaches	150
Rail	130
Freight transport (tonne-kilometres)	160
Road	220
Rail	94
Inland waterway	98

Source: ECMT (ECMT member countries excluding CEECs).

Besides the demand expressed by the consumers, there are aspects of passenger mobility that are also relevant from the firm's point of view. While traditionally the firms were advocating good passenger systems in order to enlarge their potential labour markets, there are growing symptoms of a new aspect of passenger mobility of interest for the firms, at least for the more service-oriented ones: good passenger mobility is a factor of the overall quality of life that a firm can offer to its most qualified workforce as a fringe benefit. This factor can become substantial for firms competing for scarce technical skills.

2.1.2. Freight

A parallel process is also going on in freight demand: quantities are increasing with industrial production and distances with the opening-up of the European market. This phenomenon, in turn, is compounded by the increasing role of just-in-time logistics (to substitute stocks with freight flows), a factor related to the reduction of relative transport costs (see below). Since transport is relatively less expensive, it is *not* the cost that has to be minimized in the first place; if a dispersed, transport-intensive production chain shows advantages in terms of better access to markets, flexibility, etc., it will be favoured against a compact, transport-minimizing scheme.

Also, the qualitative aspects of freight transport are concerned, where their monetary costs will be a declining factor against time and reliability. Goods with high 'value-density' (i.e. with high value per unit of weight) have, by definition, a lower percentage of transport monetary cost and a higher percentage transport time cost (i.e. the monetary value attached to transport time).

2.1.3. Common aspects

The main common characteristic of transport demand for freight and passengers is their trend toward a 'rich' market, in which monetary costs decline in importance compared with qualitative aspects (comfort, speed, reliability, punctuality, flexibility, etc.). This phenomenon is evident by the relative growth of 'expensive' transport modes (private cars, air transport, trucks) against 'cheap' ones (rail, inland waterways). High speed trains are confirming this rule: the only successful rail service is an expensive but rapid one.

Obviously 'poor' demand still exists, and will continue to exist; but its relative role is declining.

2.2. The business environment and the logistics to the year 2000

An analysis was completed to understand the importance of transport by focusing on the changes in the business environment and the evolution in the logistics process. This analysis is based on the A.T. Kearney research on these subjects and particularly on the last term of the 'European Logistics – Quality & Productivity Survey' completed in 1994.[1]

---

[1] This study is the third in a series of research studies conducted by A.T. Kearney on logistics management in Europe. The series began in 1982 with a study of logistics productivity measurement and improvement in 500 companies across six European countries. The research, conducted in 1992 and completed in 1994, involved 1,000 major European companies and parallels similar research carried out in North America and Japan. The majority of respondents had manufacturing as a primary business activity: 21% were wholesalers and 13% retailers.

The study looks at the entire logistical process and points out how transportation proceeds in its trend of performance improvement. The main trends can be summarized as follows:

(a)   service level is vital in order to match market expectation of service improvement with regards to all service dimensions. Transportation is a key element for punctuality and lead time while for other dimensions, like invoice accuracy and order fill rate, its contribution is not the most significant;

(b)   transportation cost remains the biggest part of the logistical costs, but it continues to decrease despite increasingly longer hauls associated with the fact that source and distribution markets are becoming geographically wider;

(c)   even if the transportation performance is expected to continue to improve, the trend will be lower than in other logistic areas, like inventory and administration, as it is generally considered that transportation has already shown most of its potential for improvement.

A company's ability to grow, compete and survive depends on different forces which have a high impact on the logistics process and can raise the standard against which goals and results are measured.

2.2.1. Escalating customer demand

Customers, who represent the main asset of a business, have become more demanding. High quality products and excellent service are required. They expect not only a basically flawless delivery, but also cost reductions or higher revenue. In order to be competitive in such a changing environment, companies will be forced to redesign their productivity. The supplier's mandate is therefore the following:

(a)   product design must be right and products have to perform as expected, the first time;

(b)   service must be appropriate and reliable in order to have the right product for the right customer at the right time for the right price.

Logistical issues pervade all three areas, but especially the third one. Materials management and physical distribution practices affect product availability and delivery reliability.

2.2.2. Cycle time compression

Companies have reduced their development times, brought new products and services to the market months before, assumed a major responsibility for production and service quality, enhanced the order integrity and cut days and weeks from purchasing, production and distribution cycles. The lever for many of these gains remains information technology. This allows a company to adopt new approaches and to improve the use of the traditional ones by identifying gaps, selecting options to obtain a strategic service advantage and offering the required service.

2.2.3. Globalization of markets

One of the forces which is currently reshaping business and certainly has a significant impact on the logistics process is the globalization of markets. Globalization means targeting the best markets world-wide. Transportation, handling, inventory, damage, time, and paperwork increase with distance. Companies look for less expensive sources of materials and components on an international level and domestic markets are no longer safe. Despite rapid economic integration, Europe in 2000 will not be a single unified logistical market; companies must therefore remain sensitive to a country's specific needs in order to respond to different requirements and expectations. Success will heavily depend on how well the logistics process can cope with such complexity and link global operations together.

2.2.4. Corporate restructuring

In the European market, many companies are expanding, acquiring, or merging with, other firms. The focus shifted to increasing shareholder value by bringing together businesses that are natural partners. This is to achieve economies of scale and above all long-term pay-off. Others are repositioning themselves, breaking chains of integration and divesting non-core business and activities.

2.2.5. Supply chain partnership

If globalization becomes the norm only a few companies will be able to cover the entire logistics supply chain by themselves. To get the right product in the hands of the final consumer and provide an efficient service, there is a need for many partners along the logistics flow. Trends to reduce complexity mean selecting and working closely with suppliers, procuring partnerships between shippers and carriers, providing access to research and developing new thinking.

2.2.6. Productivity pressure

Economic integration gives European companies a major opportunity to improve productivity, but in a global market providing high level service to customers is not sufficient to gain or sustain a competitive advantage. To be a major player, a company must be at least as productive as any other in its industry.

2.2.7. Environmental awareness

In order to limit the impact on the environment, governments have adapted regulations, and many of these affect logistics. Refuse must be recycled or eliminated, and all decisions regarding packaging design, materials, transportation and manufacturing locations have to be considered from an ecological point of view.

2.3. The response: logistics excellence

Changes described above imply a strong evolution in the way companies design and manage their logistics. The new approach has three main components:

(a)   establishing strong connections with customers, suppliers and service providers through strategies that meet customer requirements, synchronizing product and information flows;

(b)   satisfying customer needs, providing a defect-free service by integrating planning and procedures internally across functional areas and locations;

(c)   providing effective management capabilities and achieving a continuous quality improvement process.

Not many European companies are ready to understand customer service requirements and support a strategy to meet them using a total supply quality approach. The main shortfalls which have been pointed out are the following: insufficient connection between customers and suppliers, lack of integration between operations and internal planning, insufficient externally orientated information systems and poor implementation of quality improvement initiatives.

2.3.1. Weak links between customers and suppliers

Having strong links between suppliers and customers is a necessary condition to attain leadership in excellence. This means effectively communicating in order clearly to identify customer requirements and achieve customer satisfaction. Through the survey it was found that only 6% of the companies have leadership characteristics when dealing with customers and 21% with suppliers.

2.3.2. Limited integration for internal planning

At many companies, the chief executive officer or chief operating officer is responsible for the integration of all elements of the process in order to keep a continuous link between the different functions of the company. Real integration is measured by how well the organizational units, which report to the executives, develop plans that link with, support and complement one another.

2.3.3. Lack of externally orientated information system

Even if a company recognizes the need for closer relationships between suppliers and customers, imperfection in information capabilities may limit success. Systems that link suppliers with customers are still in their early stage and information technology is often under-utilized as a support to logistics integration.

2.3.4. Poor implementation of quality improvement initiatives

Total supply quality evolves around a series of incremental and/or fundamental changes. In order to achieve total supply quality, companies that have formal processes for driving change and securing improvements are certainly better positioned. Having a formal quality improvement initiative is not enough. Shortfalls in implementing programmes must be avoided. To achieve total supply quality, it is necessary to attain excellence across the eight dimensions of the logistical process.

2.4. Measuring excellence in logistics

In order to know the company's status against the eight dimensions, A.T. Kearney has developed a framework called the 'stages of excellence' which also helps to identify correct action (Table 2.2).

Companies that excel in all eight dimensions of logistical quality obtain better results than others. Service performance and goals of leading companies were confirmed by the survey results on the following service dimensions:

(a)   on-time delivery,
(b)   order completeness,
(c)   invoice accuracy,
(d)   damage-free delivery.

Table 2.2.   Characteristics of the stages of logistics excellence

	Stage I	Stage II	Stage III
Customer orientation	• Handle each transaction as a separate situation • Keep 'noise level' down	• All customers are treated the same • Attain internally set goals	• Provide differentiated service • Meet/exceed customer requirements
Integrated long-range planning	• Not formally carried out • Fragmented planning	• Narrow scope (e.g. distribution) • 1- to 3-year horizon	• Full logistics scope, all departments • 3- to 5-year horizon
Supplier partnerships	• Crisis-driven • Unmanaged • Adversarial	• Cost-driven • Multiple sources • Competitive bid orientated	• Result -driven • Partnership • Joint improvement
Cross-functional operations	• Today • Transaction based	• Period (e.g. monthly) • Budget-period based	• Rolling periods • Integrate all functions
Continuous improvement process	• Quick-fix 'stop the bleeding'	• Formal process • Cost reduction • Average quality	• CEO commitment • Continuous improvement toward goals • Quality and productivity
Employee empowerment	• Employees versus management	• Limited employee involvement	• Training • Empowerment • Shared goals/rewards
Integrated IT systems	• Process transaction • Little or no data • No analysis capabilities	• Report period's financial results • Fragmented data • Limited analysis capabilities	• Support planning with operational data • Easy-to-use shared data • Flexible analysis capabilities
Measurement, comparison & action	• Cost versus last year • Cost as percent of sales • Service 'noise level'	• Cost versus budget • Productivity versus past levels • Service versus competition	• Cost versus standard • Productivity versus goal • Service versus customer requirement

Source: A.T. Kearney.

By comparing cost levels of stage III companies with the survey average, it appeared that leading companies have cost levels that are 36% lower than the average company, and they plan further cost reduction.

A continuous migration of companies from lower stages (I–II) to higher stages can be measured by comparison with similar previous surveys. They form the bigger part of productivity improvement in logistics and specifically in transportation.

2.5. Transportation effectiveness

Companies wanting to expand their quality and productivity improvement process consider transport as a key element.

Companies that have partnerships with carriers measure their business not only on rates, but also on service quality, which plays a fundamental role.

Transport represents the main element of the logistics costs. In 1992, according to the 'European Logistics – Quality and Productivity Survey', this cost was equal to 3.0% of companies' turnover and the forecast for 1997 is 2.8%.

In the past, transport has contributed in a significant way to increasing productivity (despite the increased distance of the sourcing and sales markets) and, in the future, it will increase further because of several improvement actions already identified and in place (Table 2.3).

The expected productivity improvement will in general overcome the higher cost for longer distances.

Table 2.3a. Improvement actions in transportation

Transportation strategy	Strategy in progress (%)[1]	Extent of improvements[2]	
		Productivity	Quality
A. Increase leverage in negotiations by reducing number of carriers	70	66	62
B. Capitalize on volume discounts, backhaul rates and other discounts	63	62	46
C. Develop long-term contracts with carriers	61	62	62
D. Establish cost-plus based rates with carriers (open-book)	27	50	41
E. Develop customized price structures	44	67	43
F. Integrate long-distance trucking with deliveries at transit terminals	34	73	54
G. Establish transportation service standards for own fleet and carriers	36	55	65
H. Use more cost/time effective transportation mode mix	35	54	47
I. Increase use of non-national carriers	29	36	27
J. Establish electronic data linkages with carriers for capacity planning/workload scheduling	35	68	62
K. Establish formal partnership relations with selected carriers to achieve improved customer service and productivity	62	73	79
L. Develop a transportation-flow database and analysis model	31	62	53
M. Outsource fleet operations to a third-party contractor	40	67	51
N. Outsource transportation management to third-party contractor	27	53	45

Source: European Logistics – Quality and Productivity Survey.
Notes: [1]Percentage of respondents having implemented the strategy in their firms.
        [2]Percentage of respondents evaluating the strategy in terms of productivity/quality.

Table 2.3b.   Improvement actions in transportation

Transportation operations	Operations in progress (%)[1]	Extent of improvements[2]	
		Productivity	**Quality**
A. Consolidate or pool outbound shipments to customers	67	80	58
B. Capitalize on volume discounts, backhaul rates and other discounts	40	60	44
C. Develop long-term contracts with carriers	40	60	39
D. Develop customized price structures	45	69	46
E. Unitize to reduce individual piece handling	51	73	63
F. Pre-schedule deliveries into specific market area with scheduled dispatch dates	58	72	59
G. Use incentive programmes to encourage higher service/productivity	18	37	38
H. Use specialized equipment which complements the type and size of load to be transported	48	63	69
I. Concentrate deliveries into specific market areas on selected days to reduce inter-stop distance	37	67	50
J. Reduce drivers' time 'at depot' to maximize time spent en route and delivering	41	60	44
K. Review routes regularly to minimize distance travelled	36	66	45
L. Improve equipment procurement and retirement methods	21	45	45
M. Apply standard times to plan routes better	20	53	42
N. Measure service performance	46	57	66
O. Improve maintenance effectiveness	12	44	46
P. Use computer-based vehicle routing and scheduling	23	61	47

Source: European Logistics – Quality & Productivity Survey.

Notes: [1]Percentage of respondents having implemented these operations in their firms.

[2]Percentage of respondents evaluating the operations in terms of productivity/quality.

In the past, productivity and quality improvements in transportation as well in warehousing have been achieved by traditional, internally orientated actions.

These typically include:

(a)   using specialized equipment that complements the loads to be transported;
(b)   co-ordinating and optimizing back haul and round-trip scheduling;
(c)   regularly reviewing routes and drops to minimize distance travelled;
(d)   using computerized warehouse operations;
(e)   training personnel in handling methods;
(f)   incorporating engineering analysis of warehousing methods.

Major productivity and quality gains in areas such as system and inventory management, however, can no longer be accomplished by traditional internally orientated improvement actions. These actions are no longer sufficient to gain other improvements in areas such as inventory management and systems. Under various names – quick response, efficient consumer response or supply chain integration – shippers in Europe are increasingly focusing on total product cycle time as the key driving force of logistical quality and productivity.

In order to have tangible results, these efforts must include computer assisted ordering, continuous replenishment systems, automated account-payable systems, electronic store receiving systems, item price and promotion databases and integrated purchase order management systems, along with redesigned distribution systems to enable rapid continuous movement of products.

For these reasons, even if the transportation performance is expected to continue to improve, the trend will be lower than in the past and in other logistic areas (Table 2.4).

Figure 2.1.   Respondents' reported expectation of productivity improvements.

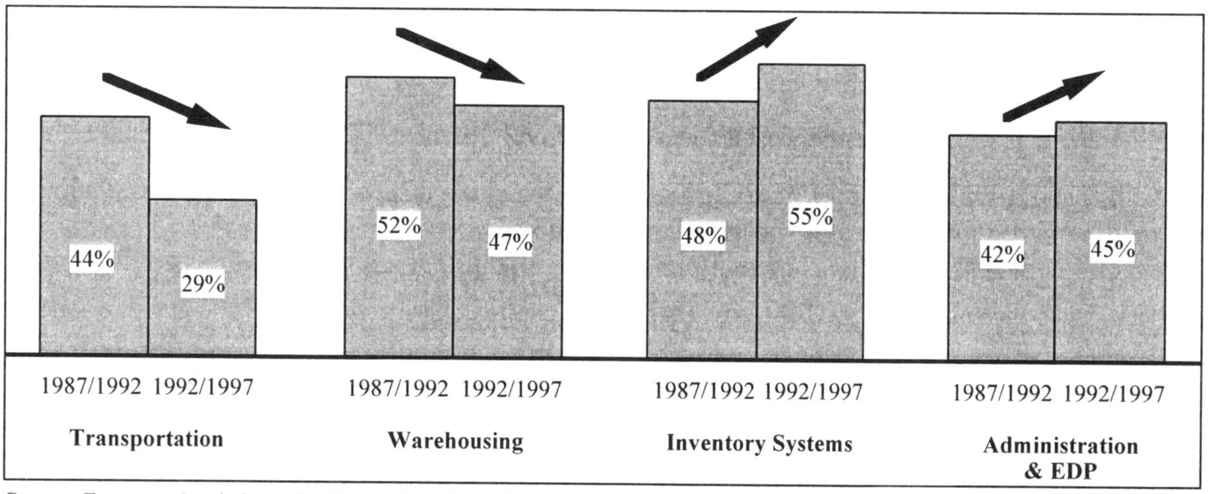

1987/1992 1992/1997	1987/1992 1992/1997	1987/1992 1992/1997	1987/1992 1992/1997
Transportation	**Warehousing**	**Inventory Systems**	**Administration & EDP**

44%   29%   52%   47%   48%   55%   42%   45%

Source: European Logistics – Quality and Productivity Survey.

The increasing transport productivity must be understood also through specific changes in liberalization and in the removal of barriers within the single market.

Similar to the US transport sector in the 1980s, in the late 1990s the logistics industry in Europe will go through a period of deep restructuring.

A dual market will develop; on one side, there will be a small group of leading providers closely integrated with their customers, and on the other side, there will be a large group of subcontracted road transporter, terminal and warehousing companies and air, sea and rail operators. The consequence will be a wave of consolidations, divestments and new entrances.

In order to be a leading provider, the operator needs to be closely linked with the customer's supply chain which requires massive investments in information technology systems, hubs and networks. The trend is to integrate the transport in wider logistical services.

Logistics service companies have succeeded in increasing their productivity from 1987 to 1992 and plan to improve it again. However, the productivity improvement focus is shifting towards the area of value added service. The expectations of decreasing costs and service performance improvement are due to clearly identified or ongoing actions. These can be grouped in two main categories of strategy:

(a)   to achieve a high professional level in transportation management;
(b)   to increase the number of long-term partnerships between shippers and carriers.

2.6. Transportation and increasing level of European integration

An in-depth description of the role and cost of transportation in four case study companies is also enclosed. The selection focused on those industries where concentration is high and European global companies have, in place, significant plans for increasing their level of efficiency in terms of European operations: beverages; automotive; appliances; petrochemical.

Major conclusions include the following:

(a)   the integration of intra-European flows is still at an early stage;
(b)   the integration of flows is a slow process because it implies the integration at higher business levels and the restructuring of the manufacturing network;
(c)   while the 'spontaneous' trend is slow, a breakthrough in the regulatory framework might accelerate the evolution;
(d)   transportation is not considered a major constraint, as the present level of integration is relatively low and most of the intra-European flows concern close/contiguous countries.

2.7. Stated inefficiencies of European transportation

This section analyses constraints and inefficiencies external to the companies that significantly limit transportation performance.

To verify the preliminary set of sources of inefficiency identified in the Terms of Reference of the European Commission's Directorate-General for the Internal Market and Financial Services (DG XV) and to identify possible additional items, a number of interviews with opinion leaders were completed in January 1996 (see Appendix A).

Revealed inefficiencies were also explored by extracting and analysing relevant information from work completed in recent years by A.T. Kearney in the fields of Management Consultancy and European Logistics.

The main objectives of the survey were to identify the major relationship among the stated sources of inefficiency, productivity and adequacy of transportation infrastructures, structure and/or productivity of carriers, logistics and/or other factors of shippers, logistics and/or other factors of the channel/sector.

Even if similar weights were attached by respondents to different inefficiency sources in the functioning of the single market, the survey confirmed a great expectation of new investments in infrastructure. Relative differentiations between European regions, shippers and carriers were also highlighted.

As for shippers' and carriers' segmentation, shippers confirmed the high impact of capacity constraints with regard to the productivity of transportation infrastructure and the low weight of barriers on their international trade. They also see a lack of clarity in the pricing policy of carriers.

Carriers consider shippers a constraint to their efficiency increase. They seem to judge the market sufficiently accessible and transparent, especially in terms of their industry supply and productivity. Another constraint for the carriers' productivity increase is the high fragmentation of supply and demand: suppliers are very fragmented in terms of company structure, especially with regard to certain regions and service supply segments. Different manufacturers have different needs in terms of transportation, warehousing operations, handling equipment, etc.

By comparing the opinions of carriers and shippers, it appears that they do not know each other well enough.

Inefficiencies in transport – and especially infrastructural problems – are perceived to have a higher impact in southern and eastern Europe than in the centre and north. Furthermore, it must be considered that in the south, companies are smaller and less organized than in the north with direct consequences in terms of economies of scale.

The leading problem of the East is that the market is not yet well interconnected with the one in the West. The majority of the products are not competitive in terms of quality, image, design and there is a consistent lack of technological innovation as well as of skilled workers and qualified employees. There is a high perception of monopoly protection, particularly, limiting the carriers' activity and productivity. The pricing policy is not considered relevant for the intra-European trade increase.

3. Scenarios

3.1. Summary

The impact of transport policies and infrastructures on the functioning of the single market is assessed by comparing two alternative scenarios – partial integration and full integration – with a base scenario. The three scenarios are designed using a common set of assumptions about the likely evolution of macro-economic variables and demographic developments in Europe. Common assumptions are also made about a number of current trends in transport demand and supply, and the likelihood that they will continue into the future.

Within a time horizon of 10 years, each scenario is characterized as a specific combination of infrastructure investments and transport policies. Investment schemes are selected from those in the agenda of both the EU and Member States that may be realistically implemented by the year 2005 to upgrade and to integrate the Trans-European transport Networks (TENs).

As far as policy measures are concerned, each scenario should be considered as an attempt to combine, in a coherent package, the *horizontal* measures in the agenda for a Common Transport Policy (CTP) with the *vertical* ones that are currently being implemented by means of adopting European directives aimed at re-introducing market guidance in the development of main transport industries namely road haulage, civil aviation and the railways.

The benefits from deregulation and commercialization – in terms of lower prices and better service for customers – as well as the degree of integration of transport services in the single market, are both expected to vary significantly as a function of the degree of success in implementing CTP to remove present distortions and/or differences in national regulations that are affecting competition within and among transport modes in the European Union.

To take into account both the type of investment schemes engaged in the TEN programme and priorities and targets in EU policy and regulatory agendas, particular attention is devoted to changes in competition between air and high speed train for passenger transport and between rail and road for freight transport.

The base scenario describes a situation in which only those investment schemes are completed that Member States would have completed in the absence of a supranational commitment towards the completion of the TEN programme. Without a fully implemented CTP action programme, national constraints and points of view are assumed to prevail also in the adoption of liberalization/regulatory policies.

Within the same policy framework assumed in the base scenario, the partial integration scenario describes a situation in which all the TENs priority projects are in operation by the year 2005.

A further increase in the performances of European transport systems is explored in the full integration scenario in which the same TENs priority projects are completed as in the partial integration scenario in combination with the adoption of the full set of measures envisaged in the CTP action programme.

With the main difference between the partial integration and the base scenarios being in infrastructure – and the differences between the partial and full integration scenarios being in policies – the impacts of an overall increase in the capacity and infrastructure performance of Trans-European transport Networks are assessed as separate from the impacts of integration policies in the single market.

The full integration scenario has been used as the base to design a third scenario to assess the impacts of introducing congestion charges on a number of selected non-motorway road links: congestion charging scenario.

To take into account the importance assigned to the goal of inverting the decline of the European railways in both transport strategies and TENs, a rail quality improvement sensitivity test has also been designed in which significant improvements are exogenously introduced in the quality of rail services in the congestion charging scenario.

Figure 3.1.   Scenarios

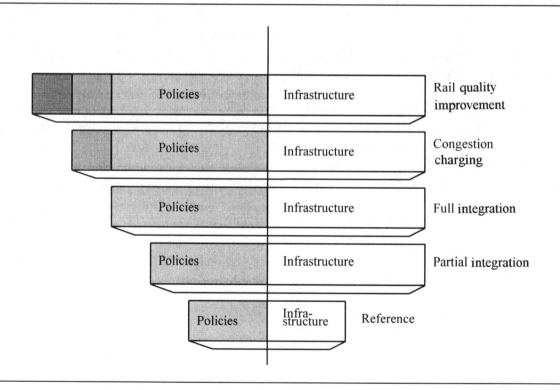

3.2. Common assumptions

Common assumptions – i.e. not scenario specific – are made on macro-economic and demographic projections up to 2005. A number of current trends in transportation demand and technology are also assumed to continue up to the year 2005.

3.2.1. Macro-economic assumptions

The purpose of macro-economic projections in this study is to establish a setting of overall economic development up to 2005 in the EUR-15. The macro-economic projections have been mainly used in the regional economic model, though certain components, such as the expected

GDP growth, also affected a limited number of inputs to the transport model (e.g. the increase in the value of time savings).

The regional economic model required the following macro-economic projections from a source external to the model to set up the 2005 run:

(a)   investment,
(b)   private consumption,
(c)   public consumption,
(d)   exports to outside the EU,
(e)   imports from outside the EU.

The Directorate-General for Economic and Financial Affairs' short- and medium-term forecasts (European Commission DG II, 1996a; 1996b) formed the basis of the macro-economic projections that have been implemented in the model. Data used in this process are listed in Table 3.1.[2]

An important assumption in addition to the illustrated indicators concerned the geographical distribution of import and export in the rest of the world. Some growth rates of import and export, with their geographical breakdown, are listed in Table 3.2. The rates 1994–97 are taken from material recommended by DG II, and the projections 1997–2005 are assumed by this study.

For export, additional data concerning the growth rates by goods type have been extracted from Eurostat's TREX database. The export projection makes use of these differentiated growth rates, whilst applying the overall growth rates above as a guide. In the model, growth of import for intermediate consumption is generated directly by the input-output model; the difference between overall growth projected above and that of intermediate consumption is assumed to be for finished products of final consumption.

Country-specific GDP growth rates are not reported here, following the practice of the DG II Medium Term Forecast.[3] Given the growth rates of private and public consumption, investment, and export, the regional economic model generates a rate of production growth by sector which is consistent with the input-output tables in use. For this reason, the GDP growth rates have not been applied as external constraints to the model; rather, they have been used to compare the results with the model-generated rates of total production after the model run, as benchmarks, to check the consistency of the model.

---

[2]   With reference to Table 3.1, please note that the 1975–92 data are taken from Eurostat's New Cronos Database EUR2_01. These are the National Accounts data (ESA-harmonized) in ECU (historic data for the new Member States are not available). For the data 1975–92 Germany denotes the former West Germany only. Differentiated growth rates were used for private consumption, investment, and public consumption in the former East Germany, where the growth is assumed to be at 5.9% per annum, the rate of GDP growth in the region as projected by ECMT (1994).

[3]   It is useful to note some of the pitfalls of the country-specific growth rates of GDP. First, the bases upon which the GDP forecasts are made may not be compatible between the Member States. For example, the country GDP assumption includes assumptions about its neighbouring countries, which may not be what is assumed by those neighbouring countries themselves. Secondly, assumption of GDP is often related to assumptions already made for transport development.

Table 3.1.   Macro-economic indicators: historic trends and projections (% p.a.)

		Trend						Forecast	
		1975–80	1980–85	1985–90	1991–93	1994	1995	1995–2000	2000–05
GDP	EU			3.30	0.70	2.8	2.5	2.5	2.5-3.5
Investment	Austria				2.10	10.8	2.4	3.8	3.8
	Belgium	1.70	-4.18	9.38	-2.7	0.5	2.7	4.4	4.4
	Denmark	0.11	2.28	0.87	-4.9	3.0	11.0	5.4	5.4
	Finland				-18.8	0.3	8.1	9.5	8.0
	France	1.84	-1.26	5.90	-3.0	1.3	2.8	4.5	4.5
	Germany	4.09	-1.52	4.95	1.2	4.3	1.5	3.3	3.3
	Greece	4.43	-2.34	7.61	0.1	1.0	6.3	8.9	8.0
	Ireland	8.74	-2.90	4.42	-3.7	7.3	12.2	6.9	6.9
	Italy	3.12	-0.88	4.44	-4.8	0.2	5.9	5.8	5.8
	Luxembourg	2.50	-5.93	13.89	3.7	-7.3	6.0	5.3	5.3
	Netherlands	1.25	-0.31	3.75	-0.8	3.0	5.0	4.2	4.2
	Portugal	1.84	-4.31	10.49	0.9	3.5	4.0	6.6	6.6
	Spain	-1.64	-0.83	11.67	-4.5	1.4	8.4	6.6	6.6
	Sweden				-12.2	-1.2	10.6	6.1	6.1
	United Kingdom	0.01	2.60	5.53	-3.5	3.0	-0.7	5.6	5.6
Private consumption	Austria								
	Belgium	3.25	0.35	2.89	1.7	1.3	1.4	2.0	2.0
	Denmark	1.42	1.98	0.54	1.8	2.6	2.3	2.5	2.0
	Finland				-3.8	1.8	4.2	3.8	2.3
	France	3.10	1.98	3.16	1.0	1.4	1.8	1.4	2.0
	Germany	3.29	0.59	3.36	3.1	0.9	1.7	2.1	2.0
	Greece	3.65	2.35	2.45	1.6	1.6	1.6	2.3	5.0
	Ireland	4.67	0.34	4.98	2.1	4.3	3.5	3.4	2.0
	Italy	4.87	1.68	3.98	0.2	1.5	1.7	2.4	2.0
	Luxembourg	2.80	1.34	4.02	2.4	2.3	2.4	2.6	2.0
	Netherlands	3.56	0.05	2.77	2.2	2.1	2.1	2.3	2.0
	Portugal	3.52	0.64	5.12	3.0	0.0	1.8	2.8	5.0
	Spain	1.96	0.43	4.64	0.9	0.8	1.8	2.8	3.0
	Sweden				-1.1	0.8	0.3	2.3	2.1
	United Kingdom	1.94	2.28	4.66	0.1	2.7	2.3	2.9	2.0
Public consumption	Austria				2.6	2.2	2.1	0.1	0.1
	Belgium				1.2	1.5	0.6	0.5	0.5
	Denmark				1.1	1.4	0.2	0.8	0.8
	Finland				-1.7	0.9	1.1	1.5	1.5
	France				3.2	1.1	0.9	0.5	0.5
	Germany				0.1	0.7	2.1	0.7	0.7
	Greece				-0.5	1.1	1.4	0.2	0.2
	Ireland				2.1	3.9	3.0	2.0	2.0
	Italy				1.1	0.0	-0.5	0.6	0.6
	Luxembourg				3.0	1.2	2.3	1.6	1.6
	Netherlands				1.1	0.9	0.2	1.7	1.7
	Portugal				1.5	1.4	2.5	1.2	1.2
	Spain				4.0	-0.3	0.9	0.8	0.8
	Sweden				1.1	-0.5	-2.3	-0.1	-0.1
	United Kingdom				0.9	1.7	0.9	0.6	0.6

Source: GDP data taken from European Commission (1996b), the growth rates under 1991–93 cover the period 1990–93; Eurostat New Cronos for data 1975–90; European Commission (1996a) for data 1991–93; European Commission (1996b) for projected data 1994–95 and projections 1995–2000; the growth rates for 2000–05 were estimated by this study.

Table 3.2. **Geographical breakdown of import and export growth rates (p.a.)**

Import	1994–95	1995–96	1996–97	1997–2000	2000–05
USA	12.3	7.7	7	7	7
Japan	11.4	10.5	12.6	10	7
Canada	13.5	7	8.2	8	7
Norway	8.3	4.3	3.7	4	4
Switzerland	7.5	2.6	4.2	4	4
Iceland	0	1.8	1.8	2	2
Turkey	15	16	16.5	15	12
Australia	10	6	6	5	5
New Zealand	12	5.6	5	5	5
Eastern Europe and the former USSR	7.3	9	8.5	10	10
Dynamic Asian economies	14.4	12.4	11.7	10	10
Other Asia	10.4	13.8	13	10	10
Latin America	16.5	9.2	7.9	10	10
Africa	4.2	5	5.4	5	5
Export	**1994–95**	**1995–96**	**1996–97**	**1997–2000**	**2000–05**
USA	13.5	9	9	9	7
Japan	6	6	8.5	8	7
Canada	13.9	6.9	7.5	8	7
Norway	6.7	6.6	5.8	6	4
Switzerland	3.1	3	5.1	4	4
Iceland	0.5	1.8	1.8	2	2
Turkey	12	14	15.5	15	12
Australia	5	5.5	5	5	5
New Zealand	6	4	4.2	5	5
Eastern Europe and the former USSR	6.4	9.5	10.2	10	10
Dynamic Asian economies	13.6	12.1	11.8	10	10
Other Asia	17.6	14.9	13.1	10	10
Latin America	8.5	8.2	7.9	10	10
Africa	4.3	4.6	5	5	5

Source: European Commission DG II for projections 1994-97; the rest of the projections were done by this study.

In addition to the private consumption data, demographic projections for the Member States have been used for the purpose of estimation of personal travel demand. As regional demographic forecasts were not available at the time of writing, the European Commission's low growth forecast has been used as published in the *Fifth Periodic Report on the Social and Economic Situation and Development of the Regions of the Community* (1994). This forecast indicates that for the period of 1991–2005, the overall growth of population will be 0.7%. This growth rate has been applied to all zones in the study area. Although a regionally differentiated growth forecast would have been desirable, the difference it makes in a study area wide projection would be relatively small. This is the case particularly because private consumption (i.e. consumer final demand for goods and services) was already projected at a country-specific rate. The growth rates assumed are well within the commonly received forecast ranges and are fully compatible with data provided by the Commission services.

3.2.2. Trends in transportation demand and supply

Common assumptions are made on trends that are expected to affect the evolution of transport demand (freight and passengers) and transport supply, technology and organization.

Main trends have been derived from published technical literature.[4] Expert judgement has been intensively used to reduce their type and number to those from which most significant changes are expected to take place in the structure and performance of transport systems in the next 10 years. With a broader discussion in Appendix B, a categorization of past trends and driving forces is presented in Table 3.3.

3.3. Transport investments

3.3.1. The Trans-European transport Network

In December 1994, the Essen European Council endorsed the recommendation of the Group of Permanent Representatives of the Heads of State or Government which included establishing 14 Trans-European transport Network (TEN) projects as Union priorities. Priority projects were selected from a more comprehensive investment scheme of some ECU 400 billion. The group's choice was determined by four criteria: the size of the project, its economic viability, its potential attractiveness to private investors and whether it could be launched within two years.

The projects of common interest also reflect the priority attached to strengthening alternatives to road transport. About 80% of their estimated total ECU 91 billion investment is on rail links (including new, dedicated HST links and combined transport) and a further 9% on rail/road links. Only 10% is earmarked for new road building, most of which aims to complete motorway networks in peripheral countries.

Within a time horizon of 10 years, the impact of inadequate transport infrastructures on the functioning of the single market is assessed by comparing transport performances that are likely to be achieved if *all* the 14 TEN priority projects are open to traffic in 2005. The comparison is done with a base scenario in which only the individual TEN components that are either already under construction or already decided by Member States are considered.

A short description of the 14 TEN projects is given below. Divisible investment components that were identified for each project are shown in Table 3.4.

The 14 TEN priority projects

1. *High Speed Train/Combined Transport North-South (Berlin-Nürnberg-München-Brenner-Verona)*
    The Berlin-München-Verona axis forms part of a strategic European rail corridor which links Scandinavia, Austria and Italy. The project is composed of two parts: the Berlin-Nürnberg line and the Brenner axis München-Verona, which comprises the base tunnel under the Brenner Pass.

2. *High Speed Train PBKAL (Paris-Brussels-Köln-Amsterdam-London)*
    The PBKAL high speed train project consists of the following sections: Paris-Lille-Calais-London, Brussels-Lille, Brussels-Amsterdam and Brussels-Köln. A noticeable reduction in travelling time between capitals and other important cities in northern Europe would be obtained.

---

[4]   See Chapter 7.

3.   *High Speed Train South (Madrid-Barcelona-Montpellier and Madrid-Vitoria-Dax)*
     The project will link the Iberian peninsula with the French high speed train network and
     consists of two parts: the Mediterranean branch, Madrid-Zaragoza-Barcelona-Perpignan-
     Montpellier and the Atlantic branch, Madrid-Vitoria-Dax. The lines will be used for
     both passenger and freight traffic, except for the Madrid-Barcelona section.

4.   *High Speed Train East (Paris-eastern France-southern Germany and Metz-
     Luxembourg)*
     This line links important centres such as Paris, Reims, Strasbourg, Saarbrücken,
     Karlsruhe, Mannheim, Frankfurt-am-Main and Köln. The project is to be set in a larger
     context: the northern branch is intended to arrive at Berlin, and the southern at Stuttgart
     and Basel. The project can be split into two different parts: the French part, which is
     composed only of newly constructed lines, and the German part, the result of an upgrade
     of the existing lines.

5.   *Conventional Rail/Combined Transport: Betuwe line (Rotterdam-Emmerich – German
     border)*
     This conventional line, thought to be run practically only by freight traffic, will be 75%
     newly constructed and aims to improve the combined transport inland waterway/railway.

6.   *High Speed Train/Combined Transport France-Italia (Lyon-Torino and Torino-Milano-
     Venezia-Trieste)*
     This line consists of two parts: the Lyon-Torino axis and the Torino-Milano-Venezia-
     Trieste axis. The line is projected with the possibility for handling both passenger and
     freight trains. The project involves the construction of a 54 km tunnel under the Alps.

7.   *Greek Motorways PATHE and Via Egnatia*
     This project consists of two axes: the north-south axis Rion/Antirion-Patras-Athina-
     Thessaloniki-Promahon (PATHE), and the west-east corridor, Igoumenitsa-
     Thessaloniki-Alexandroupolis-Ormenio-Kipi (Via Egnatia). The project will form the
     backbone of the Greek road network.

8.   *Lisboa-Valladolid Motorway*
     This project concerns the connection between Portugal and Spain. In Portugal the project
     will be implemented as a dual-carriageway expressway with 2x2 lanes (3 lanes per
     direction near Lisboa) and will include the construction of the tunnel of Gardunha. Spain
     has planned the construction of an expressway with two lanes per direction.

9.   *Conventional Rail Link (Cork-Dublin-Belfast-Larne-Stranraer)*
     The line already exists, but is equipped with poor signalling systems and track assets,
     and improvements are urgently called for. The line plays the particular role of spine in
     the network of Ireland's transport, also connecting Ireland with Northern Ireland.

10. *Milano – Malpensa Airport*
     Malpensa airport is part of the existing Milano airport system, which also comprises
     Linate airport and the relatively small airport of Orio al Serio (Bergamo). The main
     features of this extension of Malpensa Airport are the doubling of the runway capacity,
     the construction of a completely new terminal, the development of new apron and cargo
     areas and the construction of technical buildings to increase safety systems.

11. *Fixed Rail/Road Link Between Denmark and Sweden (Øresund fixed link)*
     The project includes a four-lane motorway and a double-track railway line and consists
     of three main parts: a 4-km-long tunnel under the sea (starting from the Danish coast), a
     4-km-long artificial island and a 7.5-km-long bridge starting from the Swedish coast;
     both on the Swedish and Danish side, four-lane motorways and double-track railways
     will ensure the connection with Copenhagen and Malmö, respectively.

12. *Nordic Triangle*
     This is a proposal put forward by Norway, Sweden and Finland, in order to create new
     opportunities for economic and political development within the extended European
     Union. This multimodal corridor is divided into four sections: Oslo-Copenhagen, Oslo-
     Stockholm, Copenhagen-Stockholm and Turku-Helsinki-(Russian border).

13. *Ireland-United Kingdom-Benelux Road Link*
     The link starts in Ireland, where it connects the three main cities – Belfast, Dublin and
     Cork – to each other; a ferry links Ireland to the United Kingdom, where it is possible to
     move diagonally towards the south-east, in the direction of Dover and the Channel
     Tunnel, which provide the connection with the network of the Benelux countries. The
     project involves new constructions, sometimes realignments or road widening.

14. *UK West Coast Main Line*
     This is an upgrade of an existing railway Intercity network: the axis running from
     Glasgow to Birmingham serves a catchment area of about 15 million people. Besides
     enhanced conditions for passenger traffic, the project will bring significant advantages
     for freight traffic, too.

Table 3.3. Common assumptions

Past trends to continue to 2005 and driving forces	Impacts on transport demand and supply
(1) Freight demand Steady move from basic industries to manufacturing Concentration on core business and outsourcing of specialist sub-activities Manufacturing strategies to improve the utilization of resources over space diffusion of the role of logistic management	Increased proportion of high value goods Increased proportion of value added by services in the manufacturing and commercialization of goods Smaller delivery size and more frequent deliveries for high value goods (over shorter distances)
(2) Passenger transport demand Income increase Increase in available income Steady development of service sectors and production patterns becoming more complex Income increase Increase in available income and ageing society Services and industrial location and internationalization of both production and markets	*Local /regional* [1] Increase in car ownership Increase in mobility Further dispersion of commuter demand over time and space *Long distance* Increase of the value of time Increase in the number and average distance of leisure trips Increase in business travel
(3) Transportation technologies Tighter regulation for environmental safety and security at both national/local and European levels	Introduction of more environmentally friendly and energy efficient vehicles Upgrading of transport infrastructure standards and mitigation measures Increase in both efficiency and road construction and maintenance costs
(4) Advanced Transport Telematics (from R&D to the market also in road transport) Increased possibilities of exchanging accurate, real-time information between vehicles and both infrastructure service operators and transport firms as well as between shippers and carriers	Tracking of commercial fleets in road haulage (Global Positioning System (GPS)) Increased service reliability and reduced proportion of empty trips Improved off-line (pre-trip) and on-line information about traffic conditions (Radio Data System (RDS)/Traffic Management Control (TMC), Variable Message Signs) Automatic Vehicle Identification and Debiting
(5) Organizational Further world-wide integration of production and trade Standardization and interoperability in the rail industry Internalization and liberalization of civil aviation	Consolidation of logistics mega-carriers and alliances of shipping lines to extend market control from port-to-port to door-to-door operations Increased unitization of transport (such as containers and swap bodies) Increase in the size of containers Improved industrial practices at port and inland terminals More cost effective intermodal operations and reduced loading time and costs Standardization of signalling systems and multicurrent locomotives Central Flow Management Unit (CFMU) to become operational Hub-and-spoke strategies

[1] Within a model application at European scale in which short-distance travel demand for roads is treated as a 'background noise', while regional rail passenger services are not considered. See also Section 3.3.2.

Table 3.4.   TEN priority projects

Project sections	State of maturity at 1995	Expected situation at 2005	Implementation	
			In the base scenario	In the two integration scenarios
1. Brenner				
Berlin-Halle/Leipzig	under construction since 1993	operating	operating	operating
Halle/Leipzig-Erfurt-Nürnberg	to be started in 1995	operating		operating
München-Innsbruck	to be started in 1995	under construction		
Innsbruck-Fortezza (Brenner tunnel)	to be started in 2001	under construction		
Fortezza-Verona	in stages from 2002 onwards	under construction		
2. High Speed Train PBKAL				
Belgian section	under construction	operating	operating	operating
Dutch section	to be started in 1997	operating		operating
German section	to be started in next few years	operating		operating
Calais-London	operating	operating	operating	operating
3. High Speed Train South				
Madrid-Barcelona-Montpellier	to be started in next few years	operating		operating
Madrid-Valladolid-Dax	to be started in 1997	under construction		
4. High Speed Train East				
French section	going to be started	operating		operating
German branch	going to be started	operating		operating
5. Betuwe line				
Rotterdam-Emmerich	going to be started	operating		operating
6. High Speed Train Lyon-Torino				
Lyon-Montmélian	to be started in next few years	operating		operating
Montmélian-Torino	to be started in next few years	under construction		
Torino-Milano-Venezia	to be started in next few years	operating		operating
Venezia-Trieste	to be started in next few years	n.a.		
7. PATHE				
Patras-Athina-Thessaloniki-Promahon	under construction	operating	operating	operating
Via Egnatia	under construction	operating	operating	operating
8. Lisboa-Valladolid				
Lisboa-Torres Novas (P)	operating	operating	operating	operating
Torres Novas-Vilar Formoso (P)	under construction	operating	operating	operating
Fuentes de Oñoro-Salamanca (E)	to be started in next few years	operating		operating
Salamanca-Tordesillas (E)	to be started in next few years	operating		operating
Tordesillas-Valladolid (E)	operating	operating	operating	operating
9. Cork-Dublin railway line				
Cork-Dublin-Belfast	under construction	operating	operating	operating
10. Milano Malpensa Airport				
Runways, aprons, passenger terminal	under construction	operating	operating	operating
Runways, aprons, passenger terminal, cargo area	to be started in next few years	operating		operating
11. Øresund fixed link				
Danish access routes	under construction	operating	operating	operating
Fixed link	under construction	operating	operating	operating
Swedish access routes	under construction	operating	operating	operating
12. Nordic Triangle				
East-West axis (Oslo-Helsinki)	to be started in next few years	partially operating		
North-South axis (Oslo-Malmo)	to be started in next few years	partially operating		
North-South axis (Stockholm-Malmo)	to be started in next few years	partially operating		
13. Ireland-United Kingdom-Benelux				
English section	to be started in 1996	operating		operating
Irish section	to be started in 1996	operating		operating
Welsh section	to be started in next few years	operating		operating
Northern Irish section	to be started in 1996	operating		operating
Scottish section	to be started in next few years	operating		operating
14. UK West Coast Main Line				
Glasgow-Liverpool-Birmingham-	to be started in next few years	operating		operating

Source: TRT processing on data provided in 'Réseaux Transeuropéens, Tableau de Bord', Version 1.3, European Commission, 1995.

3.3.2. The base scenario for investment

The base case against which the impacts of inadequate transport infrastructure on the single market have been measured is a 'minimum' scenario. In terms of investments, the base scenario includes only individual sections or components of the TEN projects:

(a)   that are already under construction;

(b)   that have already been short-listed by the Member State concerned for reasons other than European integration (such as the upgrading of existing standards);

(c)   for which a single Member State or international agency has already engaged the required financial provision for works to start in the 1990s.

The list of the investments which have been identified according to the above set of criteria is shown in Table 3.4.

In addition to the completion of a limited number of TEN sections, it is also assumed that single Member States will be able and willing to complete a number of investment projects either already under construction or to balance transport demand and capacity on national transport networks. In the absence of a detailed analysis of national investment plans – clearly out of the scope of this study – such a partial and gradual removal of bottlenecks, has been considered both a realistic assumption in terms of investment priorities and a fair one in order to allow for a conservative treatment of congestion levels in the modelling and evaluation of impacts.

3.3.3. The partial and full integration investment scenarios

In both the partial integration and the full integration scenarios, all the investment components of the 14 priority TEN projects that are forecast to be completed by 2005 are open to traffic as shown in Table 3.4. Where the completion of TEN schemes is freeing capacity on conventional rail links – as is the case when dedicated links are built for high speed passenger and combined transport – the upgrading of rail freight terminals is also expected to take place.

3.4. Transport policies

As far as policy measures are concerned, each scenario should be considered an attempt to combine in a coherent package (a) *horizontal* measures in the agenda for a Common Transport Policy (CTP) with (b) *vertical* ones that are currently being implemented within the European competition and regulatory framework designed to achieve a competitive single market also for transport services.

For the purpose of scenario writing, combined transport is *not* considered as a specific transport industry and its future evolution is implicitly dealt with in this section in terms of the likely evolution of international freight rail undertakings in different scenarios as well as in terms of trends in intermodal technologies and operations (Section 3.5). Nor is the evolution of different waterborne transport industries discussed in this section as it was assumed to be a trend (i.e. non-scenario-specific).

Based on an intensive review on EU transport policies objectives and targets and analysis of current trends and perspectives in the evolution of different transport industries – whose results are presented in Appendix B – assumptions made to design policy scenarios are

summarized in Table 3.5 in which the degree of achievement of objectives set in different
policy areas and relationships between horizontal and vertical policies are shown in the year
2005. Tables 3.6 and 3.7 summarize how the impacts from policies adopted in different
scenarios are passed through transport costs and performances for passengers and freight
services respectively.

**Table 3.5.   Degree of achievement of European transport policies in different
scenarios (year 2005)**

	Reference scenario	Partial integration	Full integration
(1) TENs			
Completion of 14 priority TENs	X	XXX	XXX
(2) Common Transport Policy			
Harmonization measures			
(a) *environment and safety*	XX	XX	XXX
(b) *social standards*	X	X	XXX
(c) *external dimension*		X	XX
(d) *fair and efficient pricing*			XXX
(3) Liberalization and competition			
Road freight	XXX	XXX	XXX
Rail	X	X	XX
Air	XX	XX	XXX
Water	XX	XX	XX
Consolidation of EU regulatory powers .	X	X	XXX

Notes: X = low degree of achievement;
XX = medium degree of achievement;
XXX = high degree of achievement.

3.4.1. The base scenario and the partial integration scenario

Harmonization measures

As far as policy measures are concerned, both the base scenario and the partial integration
scenario describe a situation in which an increase in qualitative environmental and safety
standards is the only area for harmonization. A steady adoption is assumed of measures that
are already also pursued by Member States to increase:

(a)   standards and targets for CO_2 emission levels;
(b)   standards and targets for transport safety;
(c)   standards and requirements for transport infrastructure.

As far as the external dimension is concerned, the achievement of the CTP's objectives is only
considered in terms of reduced border delays in the partial integration scenario.

Liberalization and competition

In the absence of a strong European commitment to remove distortions, the liberalization of
transport industries will be only partially achieved. For political reasons – including resistance
by state-owned companies and transport lobbies – transport deregulation is kept to a
minimum, i.e. only the policies which are already due to be adopted by the end of the 1990s
will be adopted by year 2005. These include the introduction of unrestricted cabotage for road

haulage as well as the completion of the third stage to introduce freedom of establishment and unrestricted cabotage in European commercial aviation.

Road haulage

On the assumption that the commitment of the Commission to establish market forces in the transport sector is not supported by effective harmonization policies, full liberalization will only be achieved in the road haulage industry. Other than internationalization, deregulation of cabotage will promote (further) competition within the industry. Based on evidence from international experiences, competition will benefit European consumers in terms of lower prices and better services. It will also push producers toward cost reductions by means of adopting a mix of measures to increase productivity and to lower costs (i.e. lower driver's wages).

Civil aviation

Within increasingly world-wide markets and scales of operations, a significant degree of integration is also achieved in the European civil aviation, but failure to re-regulate the air industry at European level is assumed to result into monopolistic practices.

In line with experience in the USA after air deregulation, both the base and the partial integration scenarios describe a situation in which cartelization, slot control and enduring barriers to the entry of low-cost new entrants may reduce the impact of air liberalization in Europe in the years to come. As a result of liberalization of cabotage in 1997, a reduction in air transport costs is, however, assumed to be partially passed on to air fares.

The railways

As far as the railways are concerned, national constraints and points of view will continue to be the leading forces behind restructuring policies that will be implemented by Member States in the adoption of Directive 91/440/EEC.[5] Despite a trend in the fragmentation of nationalized companies into line-of-business organization schemes, each Member State will adopt a different approach toward state subsidies and past debt and therefore to the restructuring of rail companies and separation of responsibility for infrastructure and operations.

Other things being equal in terms of structure and potential of different regional and national markets, an important reason for assuming that a slow, fragmented process in reforming European railways may be an obstacle in the achievement of integrated rail operations in Europe is identified in the difficulty of raising rail fares in competition with deregulated industries and in particular with road freight and air transport.

In a context in which any increase in rail fares could negatively affect the possibility of consolidating and extending the markets for rail services, a vicious circle is expected to take place that can be described in the following sequence:

---

[5]   Council Directive 91/440/EEC of 29 July 1991 on the development of the Community's railways (OJ L 237, 24.8.1991, p. 25).

(a)   incentives for rail managers to concentrate on cost reduction and to set discriminating, profit-seeking prices are likely to become less strong in the presence of governmental intervention to provide subsidies;

(b)   the gap is not reduced between (the few) commercially oriented rail undertakings that were already established in the 1990s and (the large majority of) national, heavily subsidized rail companies;

(c)   in a context in which different European railways will continue to have different financial objectives and different degrees of commercial freedom, international rail undertakings are likely to remain quite similar to current arrangements between national rail companies, therefore reducing the possibility of establishing truly competitive rail operations at European scale, from which most of the benefits from the adoption of Directive 91/440/EEC are expected in terms of exploiting economies of density and scale of operations.

3.4.2. The full integration scenario

Harmonization measures

The scenario describes a situation in which CTP policies to integrate and make transport services competitive in Europe are fully implemented.

Figure 3.2.   Possible policy instruments for efficient and equitable pricing

	Short/medium term		Long term	
	Road	**Other modes**	**Road**	**Other modes**
Infrastructure costs & congestion	– more differentiation according to use and damage in existing charging systems – kilometre tax for HGV (axle based) – tolls	– infrastructure-use related charges	– electronic road pricing for congestion and infrastructure costs	– track charges and other infrastructure-use related charges
Accidents	– progress in gearing insurance systems to the desired long-term structure – labelling		– insurance systems covering full social costs and differentiating according to risk (e.g. bonus/malus)	
Air pollution & noise	– for cars: emission (and possibly mileage) dependent annual taxes – for HGV: surcharges on kilometre tax – differentiated excises according to environmental characteristics of fuel –CO_2 tax for global warming – identical across modes	– introduction of emission based charges, e.g. landing charges in aviation based on noise emissions	– fees based on actual emission/noise with differentiated costs according to geographical conditions (and, possibly, time of day)	

Source: European Commission, *Towards fair and efficient pricing in transport,* 1995b.

The harmonization of a pricing policy in transport sectors is considered a key option in the full integration scenario. In accordance with the Commission Green Paper *Towards fair and efficient pricing in transport* (1995b), the adoption of measures in the EU concentrates on the road sector with three types of measures, the first two to capture environmental externalities through motor fuel taxation, the third one to introduce the territoriality principle by means of direct charges at point-of-use:

(a)   an increase in truck taxation rates and their harmonization across Europe to the highest national rates charged in the 1990s (i.e. in the UK), using diesel and vehicle tax to approximate the costs lorries induce on road infrastructural and maintenance standards;

(b)   an increase in car taxation rates and their harmonization across Europe to the highest rates charged in the 1990s (i.e. in Italy) to approximate the adoption of a CO_2 tax for global warming;

(c)   the adoption of a pan-European toll scheme to be levied only on road TENs and on the most congested links of European motorway networks (congestion pricing) and its harmonization to the weighted European average of tolls currently levied on trucks (and to the Austrian level for cars).

With reference to road charges at point-of-use, the full integration scenario is implemented within the model to reflect two different options. The first option implies the extension and harmonization of charges currently levied on European tolled motorways, while in the second one charges are levied also on non-motorway road sections in which, on average, the volume to capacity ratio is over 50% (congestion charging scenario). Both options are considered feasible, but a separate treatment of their likely impacts has been deemed useful in order to identify possible discrepancies between relevant targets set in the TEN programme to involve private finance and those set in the Commission Green Paper *Towards fair and efficient pricing in transport* (1995b).

As far as the external dimension is concerned, the achievement of the CTP's objectives in this area is considered by means of abolishing cross-border fees currently levied on Western lorries entering Eastern countries. In the absence of an EU framework to sustain, in financial terms, the upgrading and further development of transport infrastructure in neighbouring countries – which may be a particularly acute requirement in Eastern European countries – such an option has been considered an acceptable proxy for the establishment of fair patterns in trade.

Liberalization and competition

The adoption of a wide set of harmonization measures in the full integration scenario is assumed to complement the establishment of a full set of regulatory powers by the year 2005 to monitor monopolistic practices in the transport sector and to guarantee free competition in the European Union.

Road haulage

Other things being equal in terms of both competition and technical standards – such as weight and dimension of vehicles and emission standards – the full integration scenario describes a situation in which a set of measures is adopted in the Union to harmonize operating conditions in road haulage. In a deregulated competitive industry, these include measures designed to increase quality and social standards, such as those designed to strengthen drivers' skills and to increase control over driving hours and working conditions. An increase in operating costs of road haulage is therefore assumed to take into account both the increase in taxation and charges and the fact that part of the increase in productivity is transferred into drivers' wages.

Civil aviation

A substantial degree of competition is assumed as a result of deregulation of cabotage and the strengthening of regulatory powers against protection of national industries and monopolistic practices. Non-discriminatory schemes to allocate airport slots and capacity are also considered to be satisfactorily implemented in the Union by the year 2005. In a competitive European market, most of the benefits are expected to materialize in terms of reduced rates and a larger variety of air services becoming available to consumers.

Table 3.6.   Transport policies implemented in the scenarios – Passengers

	Base scenario	Partial integration scenario	Full integration scenario
Car tolls	No change	No change	Unified tolls on TEN road projects and on the most congested EU motorways – more than 50% of the capacity in the base scenario; tolls are currently in use in Austria
Car operating costs	No change	No change	Increased operating costs (fuel tax) to the highest level in the EU (Italy)
Coach fares	No change	No change	No change
IC train passengers	All countries tend towards EU average increase (or decrease) of 50% of the difference between each country and EU average	All countries tend towards EU average increase (or decrease) of 50% of the difference between each country and EU average	Fares in all EU countries unified to the EU average
High speed train passengers	In each country fares are 25% higher than conventional (IC) trains	In each country fares are 25% higher than conventional (IC) trains	In each country fares are 35% (25% + 10% of infrastructure costs) higher than conventional (IC) trains
Air passengers	20% reduction of fares	20% reduction of fares	35% reduction of fares

Note: Changes are expressed in terms of increases and reductions in comparison with the base year, 1991.

The railways

In the context described in this scenario, railways are in a position to exploit competitive advantages at a European scale. The main reason for this is to be found in the adoption of harmonization measures 'to level the field' for competition within and among transport modes in the European Union by means of establishing conditions for actual transport costs to be passed through prices (including those imposed on other users and society). In a context of fair competition between transport modes, the process of reforming national railways into commercially-oriented companies is expected to be both faster and more transparent, once different business lines are able to recover their production costs by charging commercial rates in competition with other modes.

To describe this process, average rates are harmonized in the EU for commercial rail services – IC passengers and different freight services – in the assumption that a reduction of production costs will follow rail liberalization costs to allow for break-even and reflect competitive pricing, including the cost of using conventional rail infrastructures and track.

By sharing financial objectives and degree of commercial freedom, rail companies will also be able to set up international undertakings to further explore competitive advantages on long-haul high-density European corridors, where both theory and empirical evidence suggest that, in the short run, returns to scale are constant for both freight and passenger services. Commercial companies will also be set up to operate passenger services in the dedicated high speed rail networks in Europe by the year 2005. Also in this case, commercial rates will be charged to recover the costs of the newly constructed infrastructure.

Table 3.7.   Transport policies implemented in the scenarios – Freight

	Base scenario	Partial integration scenario	Full integration scenario
Truck operating costs **(1) Distance based**	Change of empty back-flow for general cargo and high value cargo due to cabotage	Change of empty back-flow for general cargo and high value cargo due to cabotage	Change of empty back-flow for general cargo and high value cargo due to cabotage Increase in operating costs (diesel tax and vehicle tax) to the highest in Europe (UK)
(2) Time based	10% reduction of personnel costs due to the use of non-EU drivers	10% reduction of personnel costs due to the use of non-EU drivers	5% increase in personnel costs due to increase in qualitative standards
Truck tolls	No change	No change	Unified tolls on TEN road projects and on the most congested EU motorways – more than 50% of the capacity in the base scenario [1]; truck tolls are set at the EU weighted average
Delays at border links	No change	Abolition of delays at EU border links for trucks and cars	Abolition of delays at EU border links for trucks and cars; 50% reduction of delays at EU-Eastern countries border links
Truck costs at Eastern countries' border links	Same costs as in 1995	Same costs as in 1995	No costs as in 1991
Rail fares	All countries tend toward EU average increase (or decrease) of 50% of the difference between each country and EU average	All countries tend toward EU average increase (or decrease) of 50 % of the difference between each country and UK fares	Fares in all EU countries unified to the EU average level
Rail terminal times	No change	10% reduction in all nodes involved in rail TEN projects	10% reduction in all nodes involved in rail TEN projects
Rail terminal costs for containers	No change	10% reduction in all nodes	10% reduction in all nodes
Inland waterway	No change	No change	No change
Short sea shipping	20% reduction of port costs and times	20% reduction of port costs and times	20% reduction of port costs and times
Ocean shipping	10% reduction of port costs and times	10% reduction of port costs and times	10% reduction of port costs and times

Note: Changes are expressed in terms of increases and reductions in comparison with the base year, 1991.

3.4.3. Sensitivity test

Given the importance of railways in European transport policies and investments, a sensitivity test has been designed to appreciate the consequences of a rail service quality improvement for both freight and passengers.

The test explores the potential for rail service quality improvements which are represented in the model through modifications of rail terminal costs and times (owing to improved service frequencies, better information, and increased handling volume which tends to reduce average costs) and modal constants for rail (a proxy, in the model, for the service quality not represented by cost and time). The test was run on the basis of the congestion charging scenario.

4. Structure and implementation of the Meplan model

Meplan is a computer software package designed to facilitate analyses of the interaction between economic activities and transport within a single, integrated framework. The software is used to forecast the effects of changes in transport on the regional economy and vice versa. The implementation is designed in such a way that it allows costs and benefits of different investment decisions to be calculated in a consistent manner.

Both the transport and the regional economic modelling capabilities of the software are used to quantify the impact of improvements in transport cost and service quality on the efficient functioning of the single market. An earlier version of this model was used in 1991 for the Directorate-General for the Internal Market and Finanical Services (DG XV) of the European Commission to analyse the regional economic effects in the European Community of the opening of the Channel Tunnel.

In this section, a very brief description is given of the model and its implementation and calibration procedure. Details of the mathematical structure, data use, parameter calibration and validation are provided in Appendix C.

4.1. A brief description of the model structure

The model structure has been designed to represent the regional economic and interurban transport context in Europe, particularly in the Member States.

Technically, the Meplan model consists of four main modules:

(a)   The *regional economic module* implements macro-economic constraints in the base year as well as each future policy period, and estimates the location of production/ consumption and the pattern of trade generated in commodities, business travel and personal travel.

(b)   The *multimodal transport module* builds and validates a multimodal transport network, and, given total transport demand and transport infrastructure supply, estimates the loads of passenger and freight on each mode and route.

(c)   The *interface module* connects the two main simulation blocks above, feeding the transport module with demand matrices from the regional economic module, and passing through cost and disutility information in the reverse direction. It also does all necessary conversions of units, in order to make the information fully compatible before use by the two principal modules.

(d)   The *evaluation module* extracts simulation output from the modules above and estimates the costs and benefits associated with one policy scenario compared with those of an alternative policy, using user-defined formulae.

The regional economic module consists of a regionalized input-output structure representing all sectors of primary, secondary and service industries. It also estimates the demand for personal trips. All types of economic activities are included such as industries, investment, and the value added, and the model calibration procedure can take into account any potential constraints to economic growth as well as historic locational patterns. On the one hand, the regional economic module serves as a procedure to estimate demand for freight transport (based on the interregional trade of the freight-generating industries), business travel (based on the trade of services), and personal travel. On the other hand, it estimates the impact of transport accessibility on the cost of production and consumption, and hence the location of industries in each region. This module is illustrated in the left half of Figure 4.1.

The multi-modal transport module includes all modes of transport. It also represents intermodality in a logical and flexible fashion. The transport module has an explicit representation across Europe of the actual supply of transport (through use of a multimodal strategic transport network) available to each line haul mode and intermodal operations. Moreover, the module represents the demand for transport at a level of disaggregation of freight and passenger flow types that retains explicitly the important differences in their sensitivities to cost and quality of service. It takes into account any possible trade-offs between direct monetary cost, time, and service quality. Constraints on capacity, such as missing links and bottlenecks, are reflected in the module through times and uncertainties of travel. This module is represented on the right half of Figure 4.1.

The two principal components depend on each other in that the regional economic module provides travel demand estimates for the transport module, and the transport module provides feedback on costs and disutilities (i.e. a composite sum of monetary costs, times and service quality) under each policy scenario. This interdependence makes it possible to analyse the impact of transport policies and projects in a consistent way. Between the regional economic and transport modules an interface module is set up to facilitate the two-way information flow.

The model structure has been designed to take account of changes in both passenger and freight transport demand resulting from:

(a)   changing economic and demographic circumstances in different countries and regions;
(b)   redistribution of activities, owing to the introduction of major transport infrastructure;
(c)   redistribution of trips made in response to changes in the costs and quality of service as experienced by users.

The model parameters are calibrated in a base year, in this case 1991, when observed data are obtained for calibration. The actual and forecast changes of macro-economic and demographic circumstances between the calibration year and the policy year (i.e. 2005) are represented through an incremental mechanism set up within the regional economic module. The actual and policy changes in transport supply between 1991 and 2005 (including operating costs, user tariffs as well as infrastructure) are represented for the 2005 base case and each policy scenario through an incremental mechanism set up within the transport module.

The evaluation module is a flexible data extraction and comparison system which works according to a set of formulae defined by the user. It has been used to obtain the regional economic and transport results.

There are three steps in developing the simulation model. They are implementation, calibration and validation. In the implementation phase the data structures are determined for the regional economic and transport module, such as zoning, the categories of economic sectors and trade, the types of transport flows, modes and network links. In the calibration phase extensive data analysis is carried out, and model parameters are estimated to represent the behaviour of the industries and population in terms of their choices of location, transport mode, and route through the network. In the validation phase the model output is compared against not only observed data, but also known sensitivities to change, to ensure, as far as possible, that the model not only reproduces adequately a cross-section of the known patterns in industrial location and transport, but also reacts in a sensible way to changes in the economy, especially further changes in transport policies and infrastructure.

Figure 4.1.   Meplan model structure

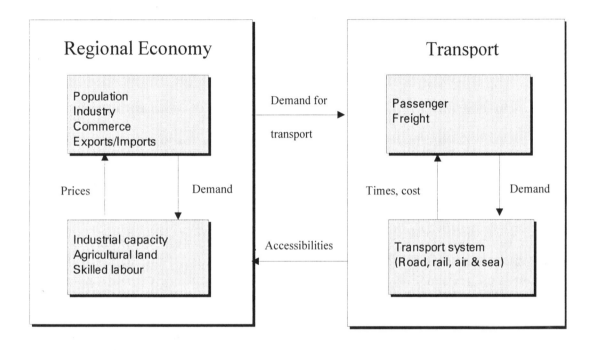

A substantial amount of data is required to develop the simulation model. In the first stage of the present study, efforts are made to collect information from a variety of sources, as identified in the Inception Report. They include:

(a)   information from Eurostat databases, including socio-economic and transport data;
(b)   information from the Directorate-General for Transport's database on transport growth in the EU;
(c)   ECMT (European Conference of Ministers of Transport) studies;
(d)   statistics published by the UN Economic Commission for Europe;
(e)   OECD statistics;
(f)   studies and statistics from modal organizations such as the UIC and ICAO;
(g)   studies and statistics from some Member States;
(h)   transport costs and tariff information from some Member States.

The details of the modules are described below.

4.2. The regional economic module

4.2.1. Theoretical structure

The regional economic module estimates the location of activities of production and consumption, and the pattern of movements of commodities and persons generated by production and consumption. It deals with location in terms of zones, i.e. a scheme of geographical division of the study area (see Table 4.1 and Figure 4.2). The main inputs to this module are:

(a)   location of final demand, including population-based final consumption, investment and export;

(b)   external inputs, such as import expected from outside the single market;

(c)   a set of technical coefficients that describe the input-output structure of the industries in each country or region;

(d)   in the calibration year only, the existing level of production output in each sector and location;

(e)   transport costs and disutilities between any two given locations of interest, of moving goods and people.

The main outputs include:

(a)   for the calibration year, a set of estimated residual attractors which explain the existing location patterns of industries in conjunction with the cost of production and transport; in future policy years, the level of economic activity in each sector and location;

(b)   factory gate producer prices for goods/services of each industrial branch at each location;

(c)   producer disutilities for goods/services of each industrial branch at each location;

(d)   selling prices for goods/services of each industrial branch at each location;

(e)   disutilities associated with sales for goods/services of each industrial branch at each location.

A change in transport costs in any mode, resulting from, for example, infrastructure investment or increased competition or productivity, will feed through directly into the costs of inputs faced by producers in each location. The input-output structure passes the cost changes consistently through the chain of demand and supply so that the second order effects are also captured. In this way the complete impact of transport improvements on the European economy is measured with considerable precision and can be disaggregated both by sector and location zone.

Transport improvements also affect the regional trade pattern. Based on these changes, together with other exogenous economic changes that are forecast, the pressure for changes in the regional economic structure in future years can be analysed to see the possible impacts on the growth and decline in employment in different locations. The regional economic module produces the pattern of trade for commodities and services and the pattern of passenger movement between regions within the EU and to and from the rest of the world. To do this, it incorporates a number of economic theories including a spatial adaptation of the Leontief input-output model and the random utility theory.

Use of Leontief input-output tables

The Leontief input-output framework provides a consistent approach to representing economic linkages between different economic sectors (Leontief, 1986). The basic concept is that the production of some economic activity or sector, an output, consumes a range of economic activities as inputs. These inputs, in the process of being produced, in turn consume further inputs, etc.

The economy of the study area is represented by a number of industrial branches which generate the demand for freight movements, and of service sectors which generate the demand for passenger movements either for business or tourism/social purposes. The starting point for the economic system in the Meplan model structure is final demand. This includes population-based consumption, consumption by government and private non-profit-making institutions, investment, and export of goods and services to countries outside the single market. Import to the single market is treated as exogenous input. For countries which are divided into more than one model zone, these totals have been estimated for each zone.

The final demand consumes inputs in a way that is defined by demand coefficients obtained from existing input-output tables. Some of the inputs may be drawn from imports; yet since there is always a practical limit to how much can be imported, the bulk of inputs needs to be produced inside the study area. Such inputs, in order to be produced, demand further inputs to facilitate their own production. Production demanded in this process is called intermediate production. If the input-output coefficients are estimated correctly, increments down the demand chain will become smaller in each subsequent iteration, and the procedure will always converge to a stable level of consumption for each sector.

Use of random utility theory and the spatial allocation process

The original development of input-output models was mainly concentrated on macro-economic applications with little reference to the spatial issues. However, for regional modelling purposes it is the relationship between production and consumption, or inter-regional trade, that is the focus of the matter. The choice of inputs from different locations is simulated through use of a spatial allocation model.

The spatial allocation model is based on random utility theory, and the functional form is a single level, multinomial logit model of discrete choice. The allocation procedure is analogous to a destination-constrained trip distribution model, taking the demand for the factor in consumption zones as given and distributing the demand amongst the supply zones according to the level of disutility (generalized cost) of production in each zone.

Direct incorporation of transport costs in the spatial input-output model

A particularly important issue in regional economic modelling is the treatment of direct and indirect transport costs in simulating locational choice behaviour and in accounting correctly the costs in the regional economic module.

A first issue to resolve when combining the spatial input-output model with a network-based multimodal transport module is to eliminate as much as possible the double counting of transport costs. Conventionally, input-output tables are set up in monetary value terms of industrial branches, each of which has a unit input cost of 1.0. The Eurostat 1985 country tables, for example, were implemented in monetary units, where the national economy is represented through 59 branches of industries, including six separate branches of transport services (i.e. railway, road, inland waterways, maritime transport, air transport, and auxiliary services). In order to make use of the transport costs estimated from the transport module, and to avoid double counting, the input costs of the transport services branches in the input-output tables are set to 0.0. The technical coefficients of and final demand for these branches are maintained in order to retain the integrity of the input-output tables.

Once the costs of the transport branches are set to zero, model-based transport costs and disutilities are fed into the regional economic module instead. At present, the method offers only an approximation; nevertheless, the articulation of the regional economic module to the transport module in this way has for the first time made it possible to utilize effectively the cost estimates from a multimodal transport model in production cost accounting (for details, see Appendix C).

The role of cost and disutility in accounting direct and indirect transport costs

In regional economic and transport evaluation, it is important to take account as accurately as possible of the costs related to transport which are incurred by producers and consumers. This is a complex issue, not least because there are often implicit or indirect costs, in addition to direct transport costs. For example, the costs involved in freight transport may be summarized as:

(a)   direct costs incurred in the course of transport, including transit and loading/unloading at terminals and transhipment sites;

(b)   costs associated with transport service quality, which include time-related inventory costs, operation-related inventory costs, and costs incurred for providing a high quality of service.

In business travel, there are also indirect costs which are associated with the travel times, service quality and flexibility.

As pointed out in Appendix A of this study and elsewhere (Ernst & Young, 1996), there is ample evidence to suggest that in production and logistics optimization, the industries tend to focus on the overall cost savings in which transport is only an (albeit important) element. However, not all of the objectives are complementary, and under particular sets of circumstances a combination of, and possibly trade-offs between, the components have to be worked out. For example, tighter scheduling of collections and deliveries, which helps with production and logistics optimization in general, would make it 'more difficult for some firms to arrange return loads' (FTA, 1995b). Also, time sensitive delivery systems depend on a highly reliable transport network, and the cost will be high once it is made unreliable by recurring congestion. In addition to the drive to optimize logistics, producers may also impose higher service quality requirements on transport in order to compete more effectively on the sales market. Increasing pressure in sales competition tends to exert higher requirements not only on the quality of the product itself, but also on its delivery to retailers or other customers. A reliable and flexible transport service often provides opportunities for a producer to optimize production scheduling, as well as to deliver products as and when the customers require them. In such cases transport costs are weighed against savings that are to be achieved elsewhere in the production chain, and in marketing benefits.

In the model, transport cost for freight transport represents direct monetary cost for the user, whilst transport disutility represents the sum of direct and indirect costs. The costs and disutilities are then accounted for in the regional economic module through the following four definitions:

(a) production cost, i.e. factory gate cost of products in the zone of production, which include only direct transport costs;
(b) production disutility, i.e. an indicator of factory gate cost of products in the zone of production, which include the impact of both direct and indirect transport costs;
(c) consumption cost, i.e. selling price of products in the zone of consumption, which include only direct transport costs;
(d) consumption disutility, i.e. an indicator of selling price in the zone of consumption, which includes the impact of both direct and indirect transport costs.

In summary, whilst production and consumption costs reflect the impact of the direct monetary costs of transport, production and consumption disutilities may be formulated in such a way as to highlight the potential trade-offs between cost, time and service quality which have become increasingly important in European freight transport. This formulation will become particularly meaningful in policy and project assessment where industries are offered opportunities to use reliable, high quality yet more expensive transport services to optimize logistics and production management. The spatial allocation model uses transport disutility in determining the probabilistic distribution of suppliers, which is entirely consistent with this accounting framework.

4.2.2. Implementation of the regional economic module

Implementation of the regional economic module includes the definition of the zoning scheme and the definition of the categories of economic sectors and other demand/supply elements to be modelled (these elements are called, in Meplan terminology, regional economic factors).

Zoning determines the level of spatial and economic details to be modelled. Table 4.1 gives the zoning scheme, together with a description of the regions/areas/countries included in each zone. The zones are classified in two types: those internal to the study area and those external. Input-output economic links are only modelled amongst the internal zones. The trade links between the internal and the external zones are represented through import, export, and passenger travel demand.

The zoning scheme is principally based on the geographical division of NUTS1. In some countries, a lower level NUTS division is used, in order to give sufficient detail for modelling the TEN projects. Large capital cities such as Berlin, Paris, London and Madrid are separated from their surrounding areas, because the economic activities conducted there can be very different from their hinterlands, and also because their access to certain transport modes, such as the high speed train, is quite different from the areas outside.

There are 62 internal zones and 13 external zones in total; these numbers are kept small for a fast turn-round in model application, yet the zoning design at an appropriate level of detail is maintained to provide sufficient information on the impact of strategic transport networks.

The factors of the regional economic module consist of three types. They are population-based final demand, productive industrial branches as included in the Eurostat Input-Output Tables, and passenger trips. A list of the factors is presented in Table 4.2. Other final demands such as collective consumption of general government and of private non-profit-making institutions serving households, are input as part of the productive factors.

Three types of personal passenger trips are modelled directly as factors that are demanded by the population. They are long-distance inclusive tourist trips, long-distance independent tours and other personal trips, and interurban day trips. Independent personal trips are modelled by two sub-trip types, the high time-value group and the low time-value group. Short-distance passenger travel within the same conurbation area is not included within the model, though the congestion caused by local traffic on road networks is included within the transport model.

Table 4.1.   Zoning scheme used in the model

Country	No	Zone name	Regions included	NUTS 1995 code	Internal External	Centroid
Germany	10	Schleswig-Holstein, Hamburg	Schleswig-Holstein Hamburg	DEF DE6	Internal	Hamburg
	11	Niedersachsen, Bremen	Niedersachsen Bremen	DE9 DE5	Internal	Bremen
	12	Nordrhein-Westfalen	Nordrhein-Westfalen	DEA	Internal	Köln
	13	Hessen	Hessen	DE7	Internal	Frankfurt
	14	Rheinland-Pfalz, Saarland	Rheinland-Pfalz Saarland	DEB DEC	Internal	Koblenz
	15	Baden-Württemberg	Baden-Württemberg	DE1	Internal	Stuttgart
	16	Bayern	Bayern	DE2	Internal	München
	17	Berlin		DE3	Internal	Berlin
	18	South of former E.Germany		DED-DEG	Internal	Leipzig
	19	North of former E.Germany		DE4, DE8	Internal	Rostock
France	21	Ile de France	Ile de France	FR1	Internal	Paris
	22	Bassin Parisien	Bassin Parisien	FR2	Internal	Orleans
	23	Nord-Pas-de-Calais	Nord-Pas-de-Calais	FR3	Internal	Lille
	24	Est	Est	FR4	Internal	Strasbourg
	25	Ouest	Ouest	FR5	Internal	Nantes
	26	Sud-Ouest	Sud-Ouest	FR6	Internal	Bordeaux
	27	Centre-Est	Centre-Est	FR7	Internal	Lyon
	28	Méditerranée	Méditerranée	FR8	Internal	Marseille
Italy	31	Nord-Ovest, Lombardia	Nord-Ovest Lombardia	IT1 IT2	Internal	Milano
	32	Nord-Est	Nord-Est	IT3	Internal	Venezia
	33	Emilia-Romagna, Centro	Emilia-Romagna Centro	IT4 IT5	Internal	Firenze
	34	Lazio, Abruzzi-Molise	Lazio Abruzzi-Molise	IT6 IT7	Internal	Roma
	35	Campania, Sud	Campania Sud	IT8 IT9	Internal	Napoli
	36	Sicilia, Sardegna	Sicilia Sardegna	ITA ITB	Internal	Palermo
Netherlands	41	Noord-Oost-Nederland	Noord-Nederland Oost-Nederland	NL1 NL2	Internal	Groningen
	42	West-Nederland	West-Nederland	NL3	Internal	Amsterdam
	43	Zuid-Nederland	Zuid-Nederland	NL4	Internal	Utrecht
Sweden	44	Stockholm and North	Stockholm Ostra Mellanserige Norra Mellansverige Mellersta Norrland Ovre Norrland	SE01 SE02 SE06 SE07 SE08	Internal	Stockholm
	45	Goteborg	Vastsverige	SE05	Internal	Goteborg
	46	Malmo	Smaland med oarna Sydsverige	SE03 SE04	Internal	Malmo
Finland	48	Uusimaa	Uusimaa	FL11	Internal	Helsinki
	49	Rest of Finland	Rest of Finland	FL12-15, FL2	Internal	Tampere
Belgium-Luxembourg	51	Brussels	Brussels	BE1	Internal	Brussels
	52	Vlaams Gewest	Vlaams Gewest	BE2	Internal	Antwerpen
	53	Région Wallonne-Luxembourg	Region Wallonne Luxembourg	BE3 LU	Internal	Luxembourg
Austria	55	Westösterreich	Westösterreich	AT1	Internal	Wien
	56	Ostösterrreich	Ostösterrreich	AT2	Internal	Graz
	57	Sudösterreich	Sudösterreich	AT3	Internal	Salzburg
Portugal	59	Norte & Centro	Norte Centro	PT11 PT12	Internal	Porto
	60	Lisboa e Vale do Tejo	Lisboa e Vale do Tejo	PT13	Internal	Lisboa
	61	Sul	Alentejo Algarve	PT14 PT15	Internal	Faro

Table 4.1.   Zoning scheme used in the model (continued)

Country	No	Zone name	Regions included	NUTS 1995 code	Internal External	Centroid
Spain	63	Noroeste	Noroeste	ES1	Internal	Santiago de Compostela
	64	Noreste	Noreste	ES2	Internal	Bilbao
	65	Madrid	Madrid	ES3	Internal	Madrid
	66	Centro	Centro	ES4	Internal	Valladolid
	67	Este	Este	ES5	Internal	Barcelona
	68	Sur	Sur	ES6	Internal	Sevilla
UK	71	North, Yorkshire, North West	North	UK1	Internal	Manchester
			Yorkshire and Humberside	UK2		
			North West	UK8		
	72	Midlands, East Anglia	East Midlands	UK3	Internal	Birmingham
			East Anglia	UK4		
			West Midlands	UK7		
	73	South West, Wales	South West	UK6	Internal	Cardiff
			Wales	UK9		
	74	South East	South East	UK5 (-UK55)	Internal	Reading
	75	London	South East	UK55	Internal	London
	76	Scotland	Scotland	UKA	Internal	Glasgow
	77	Northern Ireland	Northern Ireland	UKB	Internal	Belfast
Ireland	81	Dublin and Mid East	Dublin	IE002	Internal	Dublin
			Mid East	IE003		
	82	Rest of Ireland	Rest of Ireland	IE001,IE004-8	Internal	Cork
Greece	83	Voreia Ellada	Voreia Ellada	GR1	Internal	Thessaloniki
	84	Kentriki Ellada	Kentriki Ellada	GR2	Internal	Patrai
	85	Attiki	Attiki	GR3	Internal	Athinai
	86	Nisia	Nisia	GR4	Internal	Iraklion
Denmark	91	Vest for Storebaelt	Vest for Storebaelt	DK001-6	Internal	København
	92	Rest of Denmark	Hovedstadsregionen Ost for Storebaelt	DK007-F	Internal	Arhus
Norway-Iceland	101	Norway, Iceland	n.a.		External	Oslo
Switzerland	103	Switzerland	n.a.		External	Zurich
Czech & Slovak Rep.	105	Czech	n.a.		External	Praha
Hungary	108	Hungary	n.a.		External	Budapest
Poland	110	Poland	n.a.		External	Warszawa
Ex-Yugoslavia	113	Serbia, Macedonia, Albania, Slovenia,Croatia and Bosnia Herzegovina	n.a.		External	Zagreb
Romania and Bulgaria	115	Romania, Bulgaria	n.a.		External	Bucharest
Turkey	116	Turkey	n.a.		External	Istanbul
CIS states	122	Russia, White Russia, Baltic States, Ukraine, Moldavia and other south CIS states	n.a.		External	Moskva
Morocco-Algeria-Tunisia-Libya	124	Morocco, Algeria, Tunisia, Libya	n.a.		External	Alger
Egypt and the Middle East	126	Egypt and the Middle East	n.a.		External	Cairo
East Africa-Asia and Australasia	128	East Africa-Asia and Australasia	n.a.		External	Model node
West Africa and the Americas	130	West Africa and the Americas	n.a.		External	Model node

Note: NUTS FR9, PT2, PT3, and ES7 which are not part of the European continent have been excluded from the above zoning scheme.

Figure 4.2.   The zoning map

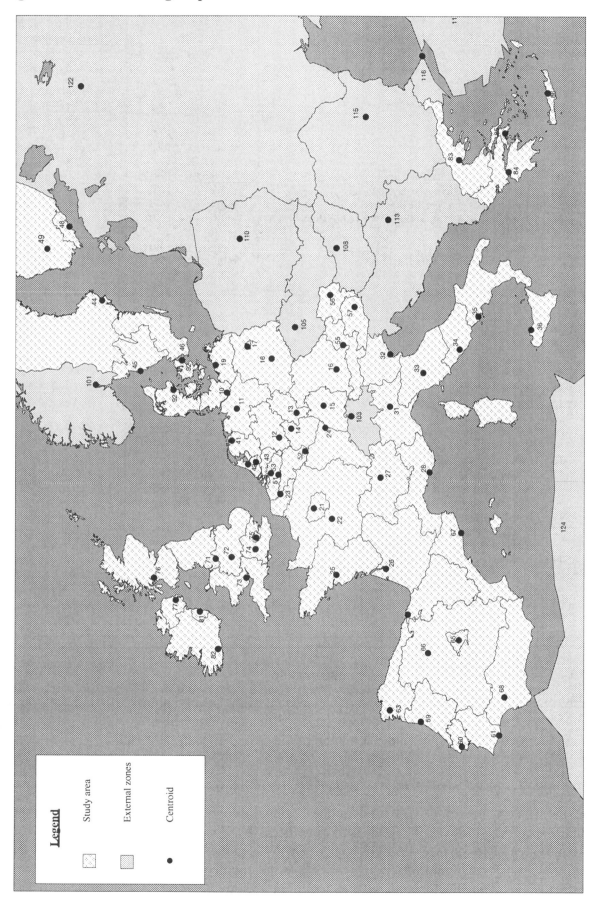

Table 4.2. List of regional economic factors

Factor number	Factor name	Unit	Transportable
1	Population	persons	No
11	Agriculture, forestry and fishery products	million ECU 1991	Yes
12	Coal and coking	million ECU 1991	Yes
13	Crude petroleum	million ECU 1991	Yes
14	Petroleum products	million ECU 1991	Yes
15	Natural gas	million ECU 1991	Yes
16	Other power, water and manufactured gas	million ECU 1991	Yes
17	Ferrous and non-ferrous ores and metals	million ECU 1991	Yes
18	Cement, glass and ceramic products	million ECU 1991	Yes
19	Other non-metallic minerals and derived products	million ECU 1991	Yes
20	Chemical products	million ECU 1991	Yes
21	Metal products	million ECU 1991	Yes
22	Agricultural and industrial machinery	million ECU 1991	Yes
23	Office machines, etc.	million ECU 1991	Yes
24	Electrical goods	million ECU 1991	Yes
25	Transport equipment	million ECU 1991	Yes
26	Food, beverages, tobacco	million ECU 1991	Yes
27	Textile and clothing, leather, footwear	million ECU 1991	Yes
28	Paper and printing products	million ECU 1991	Yes
29	Rubber and plastic products	million ECU 1991	Yes
30	Other manufacturing products	million ECU 1991	Yes
31	Building and civil engineering works	million ECU 1991	Yes
32	Recovery, repair services, wholesale and retail trade	million ECU 1991	Yes
33	Lodging and catering services	million ECU 1991	Yes
34	Railway transport services	million ECU 1991	Yes
35	Road transport services	million ECU 1991	Yes
36	Inland waterways services	million ECU 1991	Yes
37	Maritime transport services	million ECU 1991	Yes
39	Air transport services	million ECU 1991	Yes
40	Auxiliary transport services	million ECU 1991	Yes
41	Communications	million ECU 1991	Yes
42	Credit and insurance	million ECU 1991	Yes
43	Other market services	million ECU 1991	Yes
44	Non-market services	million ECU 1991	Yes
51	Total value added	million ECU 1991	No
61	Long distance inclusive tourist trips	trips	Yes
63	Independent tours: Group A	trips	Yes
64	Independent tours: Group B	trips	Yes

4.2.3. Calibration of the regional economic module

Calibration of the regional economic module consists of the following tasks: first, definition of demand coefficients, including the technical coefficients between sectors of industry and demand for personal trips; second, estimation of the spatial allocation model.

Definition of demand coefficients: use of Leontief input-output tables

The input-output tables (IOTs) used in the regional economic module are the 59-branch country-specific tables for the year 1985, published by Eurostat (Eurostat, 1995). Eurostat have also recently published the 1991 IOT for EUR-12, at the level of 25 branches (*ibid.*). The 1991 table, however, is not officially available at the country level and the industrial sectors are treated in a much more aggregated way. For example, it treats all energy industries, including coal, crude petroleum, refined petroleum products, gas and electricity as one branch. Whilst it may be appropriate to do so from the point of view of input-output analysis, this 25-branch table cannot be readily used in this study where the freight demand of the products is distinct. The 1985 IOTs are processed by Eurostat, thus their values are relatively consistent and can be used without extensive harmonizing work. For this reason, they are widely in use in many policy studies. In other words, the 1985 tables appear to be, to date, the most appropriate source of IOTs for this study.

The 1985 IOTs at 59-branch level are available for seven individual countries; the countries are former West Germany, Denmark, France, Italy, Netherlands, Spain and the UK. These countries represent the major share of the EU economy in value terms. For the purpose of this study, the existing tables are used in some cases to cover a wider geographical area or to represent countries at a similar stage of development, e.g. the Danish table is used for Finland and Sweden, the German table for Austria, and the Spanish table for Portugal and Greece.

In order to keep the number of factors within an appropriate and manageable dimension, some of the branches of the IOTs are amalgamated. Sectors that generate distinctive freight demand are kept separate. Transport services branches are also kept separate as in the original IOTs.

Technical coefficients are then calculated for each of the seven IOTs. The branch totals of final consumer demand, public consumption, investment, import and export volumes of the IOTs are updated to 1991 using harmonized Eurostat National Accounts data for the EUR-12; for the new Member States such data were estimated for 1991 by the study. For each factor and each zone, an existing level of production (i.e. in 1991) is estimated. These 1991 data are then used together with the technical coefficients derived from the 1985 tables. The 1991 model thus reflects the macro-economic conditions of 1991 accurately, though the production structure is modelled using only 1985 coefficients. Updating technical coefficients would have been a major undertaking that demands considerable resources, which may become possible as part of an ongoing FPIV research project.

For the policy year 2005, the forecast totals of final consumer demand, public consumption, investment, import and export volumes are derived from macro-economic projections for each country of the EUR-15 (see Section 3.2.1). These 2005 data are then used together with the technical coefficients derived from the 1985 tables. The 2005 model thus reflects the macro-economic conditions of 2005 as forecast, though the production structure is modelled in a more limited way using 1985 coefficients. However, the policy analysis compares only the differences between scenarios, so some of the limitations due to the use of unchanging technical coefficients will cancel out in the final results.

The costs of transport services as estimated in the input-output table are replaced by costs estimated by the transport module. For details of the procedure, see Appendix C.

Demand coefficients for business and personal travel

The only other demand coefficients used in the regional economic module are those of demand for personal travel. These coefficients are estimated based on the UK National Travel Survey 1989/1991 (UK Department of Transport, 1993b).

The UK National Travel Survey gives the average number of journeys per person per year by trip length and purpose in the country. These are used in conjunction with the overseas passenger trips to derive the travel demand coefficients. The per capita demand for passenger travel derived is assumed to be representative for all zones in the study area. This simplification was made owing to the need to avoid extensive data processing, which would have otherwise been necessary because of the lack of consistent travel demand data amongst the countries of the EU.

Business travel demand is then converted into a demand parameter in terms of trips per million ECU of service trade which generates such journeys. Using total trip-generating service trade volumes originating from the United Kingdom, the travel demand is calculated, which is then applied to all service generating trades in all zones. The total per capita demand for independent travel is split into two categories of trips (Independent A and B), according to the average value of time assumed for personal travellers in each country of the EU.

Definition of the spatial allocation model

Definition of the spatial allocation model primarily involves the estimation of the activity distribution parameters for each transportable factor, so that the trade volumes between each pair of zones are simulated in a way that they reflect the current observed patterns of domestic and inter-country trade.

Due to lack of consistent freight and business passenger matrices no formal estimation procedure was undertaken. Instead an approximate two-step approach was adopted: first, for a number of representative destination zones, the λ value is adjusted so that the average trip length of the trade of supply falls within the expected range for the commodity type that is associated with the trade. Secondly, these starting values of λ are then applied to the regional economic model. Trade matrices are generated, which are then converted into passenger and freight matrices that are used in the transport module. The average trip lengths by flow and mode are compared with observed data, and the modelled passenger- and tonne-kilometres are then compared with the control totals from the DG VII Transport Database. The λ values are then fine-tuned for a group of factors at a time which are related to a given flow, so that the trip lengths and overall volume-km totals compare reasonably with the observed data. The parameters for personal trips were estimated in a similar manner.

4.2.4. Validation of the regional economic module

The regional economic module is built upon the harmonized ESA data of national accounts, taken from the New Cronos database of Eurostat, for its estimation of economic activities. The interrelationship amongst industries and estimation of final demand are consistent with the 1985 Eurostat input-output tables, which is the latest edition available, at a level of detail appropriate for the study.

The estimated distribution of trade in space needs to be checked. In theory, once the interregional and international trade data are processed in categories corresponding to the production factors used in the module, the modelled and observed matrices may be compared to check how close the simulation is. In practice, however, both the inter-regional and international trade matrices and passenger matrices come in a variety of definitions, and demand substantial processing and harmonization before they can be used meaningfully.

For this study a simpler approach is taken, which is to condense the trade matrices into passenger and freight matrices, and some overall comparisons are made with regard to the trip lengths and/or total p-kms and tkms by passenger and freight types. Such comparisons imply an overall degree of accuracy of fit, between the modelled transport demand and the observed one. Such data are presented along with the results of the transport module in the base year 1991. In any case, the aim of this study is to gauge the overall impact of the policies and infrastructure projects; to this end, the aggregate comparisons would seem to meet the requirements.

4.3. The interface module

4.3.1. Theoretical structure

The interface module converts the trade from units used by the regional economic module, to traffic flows in physical units (such as freight tonnes and passenger trips) in the transport module. This module also feeds the generalized costs of transport back into the regional economic module. It makes sure that the conversion in one direction is consistent with that in the opposite direction.

The trade volumes generated by the regional economic module are fed into the interface program which converts trade volumes, which generally are in monetary units, into freight and passenger flows. In the reverse direction, transport costs and disutilities are converted into costs and disutilities to trade. In summary, the main inputs to the interface module are:

(a)   volume to value ratios for all the transportable commodities;
(b)   coefficients to convert from annual (regional economic module) to daily (transport module) time periods.

The output, on the other hand, includes:

(a)   transport demand by flow type between each zone pair in units appropriate for the transport module;
(b)   transport cost and disutility for each transportable factor between each zone pair in units appropriate for the regional economic module;
(c)   also, cost, time and disutility for each factor and flow type combination by destination zone; this information is used when computing travel consumer surplus.

4.3.2. Implementation of the interface module

The implementation of the interface module depends principally on the implementation of the regional economic and transport modules. The key element of the interface module implementation is the correspondence between factors and flows.

These are aggregate passenger and freight flow types which have relatively homogeneous transport and modal split characteristics. For passenger traffic, long-distance business travel is kept separate from personal travel, and inclusive and independent tours are also modelled separately to capture the different characteristics of mode choice. Business and independent personal travel is further differentiated with regard to different values of time and, hence, elasticities with respect to cost and time changes. For freight, the flow types range from cost sensitive long-distance solid/liquid bulk traffic through to high value goods traffic which are very sensitive to journey time, reliability and flexibility.

Table 4.3 lists all transport flow types, and Table 4.4 shows how regional economic factors and flows are related. Note that for each factor, only one flow type is selected which is believed to be the typical traffic being generated by that factor. In reality, each factor may well generate more than one type of transport flow. This simplified approach is due to the time scale of the study.

4.3.3. Calibration of the interface module

The factor-flow relationship having been defined, the tasks of calibration of the interface module are basically the estimation of volume to value ratios and the time period conversion factor. The volume to value ratios for freight in this study are estimated from the total freight tonnes information from the tonnes by mode statistics in the Eurostat New Cronos database, in conjunction with the total trade values estimated in the regional economic module.

For freight, the annual trade volumes output by the regional economic module also need to be scaled down to daily volumes of traffic, after the value-volume conversion. A simple scaling factor is set at 300, which means the typical daily freight traffic on the European transport networks is 1/300 of the annual volume. For passengers, because the demand generated in the regional economic module is defined in terms of trips per year, the same time scaling factor applies.

Correct estimation of the parameters of the interface module is a prerequisite of the validation of the regional economic and transport modules. For this reason, no independent validation is performed on the interface module. In other words, the interface module estimation will be checked indirectly through the two modules that it connects.

Table 4.3.   Transport flows

Flow number	Flow name
	Passengers
1	Business trips A (higher time-value group)
2	Business trips B (lower time-value group)
3	Independent trips A (higher time-value group)
4	Independent trips B (lower time-value group)
5	Inclusive tours
	Freight
6	Liquid bulk
7	Solid bulk
8	Semi-bulk
9	General freight Type A
10	General freight Type B

Table 4.4. Corresponding regional economic factors and transport flows

	Regional economic factors		Transport flows
11	Agriculture, forestry and fishery products	9	General freight A
12	Coal and coking	7	Bulk
13	Crude petroleum	n.a.	
14	Petroleum products	6	Liquid
15	Natural gas	n.a.	
16	Other power, water and manufactured gas	n.a.	
17	Ferrous and non-ferrous ores and metals	7	Bulk
18	Cement, glass and ceramic products	8	Semi-bulk
19	Other non-metallic minerals and derived products	7	Bulk
20	Chemical products	8	Semi-bulk
21	Metal products	8	Semi-bulk
22	Agricultural and industrial machinery	10	General freight B
23	Office machines, etc.	10	General freight B
24	Electrical goods	10	General freight B
25	Transport equipment	10	General freight B
26	Food, beverages, tobacco	9	General freight A
27	Textile and clothing, leather, footwear	10	General freight B
28	Paper and printing products	10	General freight B
29	Rubber and plastic products	10	General freight B
30	Other manufacturing products	10	General freight B
31	Building and civil engineering works	n.a.	
32	Recovery, repair services, wholesale and retail trade	2	Business travel B
33	Lodging and catering services	n.a.	
34	Railway transport services	n.a.	
35	Road transport services	n.a.	
36	Inland waterways services	n.a.	
37	Maritime transport services	n.a.	
39	Air transport services	n.a.	
40	Auxiliary transport services	n.a.	
41	Communications	2	Business travel B
42	Credit and insurance	1	Business travel A
43	Other market services	1	Business travel A
44	Non-market services	1	Business travel A
61	Long distance inclusive tourist trips	5	Inclusive tours
63	Independent tours: Group A	3	Independent personal travel A
64	Independent tours: Group B	4	Independent personal travel B

Notes:

1 Note particularly Factor 13 does not generate freight. The transport of crude petroleum is largely organized separately from the rest of the freight, and is not expected to be affected significantly by the projects and policies included in this study. For this reason, crude petroleum traffic is excluded from the model. Refined petroleum products (Factor 14), however, give rise to the flow of liquid bulk, and are represented separately in the model.

2 Factors 16, 17, 31, and 33 through 40 do not directly generate transport demand either, for obvious reasons. Note that these factors still demand the trade of other factors that generate freight. For example, Factor 31 (Building and civil engineering works) may demand sand and gravel that are represented by Factor 19, which gives rise to bulk freight traffic.

3 For all the factors that do not generate freight, a low, nominal level of transport disutilities is applied, which means that the spatial distribution of these factors is not directly affected by the changes of the strategic transport network. The location of these factors, however, is influenced by the demand from other factors which are directly affected by transport changes.

4.4. The multimodal transport module

4.4.1. Theoretical structure

This module takes the transport demand matrices from the interface module and carries out modal split and network assignment. First, it estimates the probability of a given type of user choosing each available mode of transport between each zone pair. The modal flow volume is then estimated, and assigned to appropriate transport networks in accordance with the generalized cost of competing routes, taking into account congestion effects on the network.

For both passenger and freight movements, there is an increasing body of evidence which demonstrates that the quality of service, in terms of, for example, flexibility, comfort, safety, guaranteed time of arrival, plays a significant role in user choice in addition to the more familiar elements of travel time and cost. The relative importance of the various factors varies by trip purpose. Similarly, the importance of factors such as price is greatest for low value bulk freight movements, while quality factors, such as guaranteed arrival times and safety, play an important role for high value industrial products used, for instance, in just-in-time supply systems. These factors are represented directly within the transport module.

The modal split model takes as input the characteristics of the transport supply and the matrices of trips by type. It then produces as output the number of passengers and freight units by type moving between each pair of zones on each mode of transport.

The Meplan model uses a flexible, user-defined structure of network modes (i.e. travel stages) and user modes (a number of connected travel stages, often dominated by one network mode). In path building through the multi-modal network, a trip between a given pair of zones is allowed to use different network modes at different stages of the journey. For example, a tonne of freight may start by lorry, then transfer to shipping and then continue on rail in the course of a journey, and the user mode is identified by a dominant network mode. This feature allows great flexibility in the treatment of inter-modal trips and allows explicit modelling of multi-stage trips, which is not uncommon in the European scene. A feature of the design of the TENs is the provision of facilities for intermodal centres to allow for the most effective use of the entire TEN system. By modelling inter-modal flows, the model may be used in a natural way to represent interoperability and network integration.

The structure of the transport module is illustrated in Figure 4.3. The actual structure of the transport module involves a number of steps which are executed using an iterative procedure. The model is based on discrete choice theory as opposed to strict transport cost minimization. The modal split model is used to estimate the pattern of flows of passengers and freight in the study area at a particular time. It predicts, using a logit model, how users of transport will choose amongst the modal options, when faced with the different tariffs, travel times and constraints on capacity. In a majority of cases, it is not used to predict how they ought to behave, yet by setting parameters to certain extreme values the model may also be used as an optimization procedure.

Figure 4.3.   The sequence of steps in the transport module

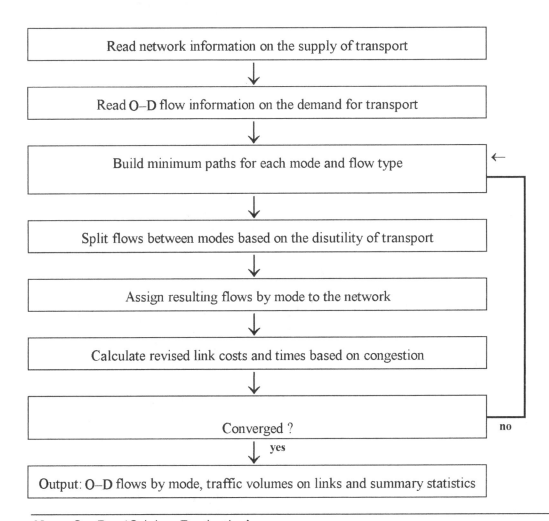

Note: O – D = 'Origin – Destination'

Network modes and user modes

The module uses a two-level description for transport modes. At the individual link level, the movement of a passenger or unit of freight is represented by a *network mode* related to the link type. Network modes correspond generally to the vehicles and vessels on the line haul, and the handling operations at transfer and transhipment sites. At the level of a complete trip door-to-door, movements of passengers and freight are represented by a *user mode*. Each user mode is built up as a collection of network modes, in accordance with the actual stages of travel. The user modes are usually named after the main line haul mode but often include a number of auxiliary network modes. For example, flows fed by lorry into coastal shipping have coastal shipping as their main network mode, lorry being a feeder mode. In the transport module, a passenger or freight movement is qualified to be of a specific user mode provided that it uses the designated main network mode for more than a minimum proportion of the journey. Intermodal transport linkages may be readily simulated in the module.

Modal choice

The modal split procedure estimates the proportion of a flow from zone i to zone j that uses each of the user modes k available to that flow type. The choice between modes is determined by the relative disutilities of the competing modes. The starting point of the discrete choice model for modal split is the hypothesis that each individual, faced with a set of choices, will choose the mode which gives him the greatest utility, or the least disutility. It is generally assumed that journeys have to be made and that travellers will prefer to do so in the way that causes them least cost, time, or discomfort. The modeller therefore has to analyse the components of a disutility function, which will typically include the time and cost of the journey, and then estimate the relative importance of these components.

Network assignment

Network assignment is carried out using a stochastic user equilibrium procedure on a strategic interurban network. In particular, the strategic road network is built with the aim to provide in every transport corridor an accurate measure of the total capacity that is available there to satisfy the demand for transport. This implies that the model is capable of handling reasonably accurately the congestion effects that may arise under a given volume to capacity ratio.

Major motorways and other primary roads are each represented individually and are coded with the actual capacity that each link has. They have a highly non-linear speed flow curve that allows substantial traffic to be carried on the links before there is any significant slowing down of speeds, as is appropriate to represent traffic behaviour on high quality roads. Other important roads are in some cases coded with capacities which represent the sum of the capacities of the roads that pass along the transport corridor in which they lie. In this way the corridor link that is coded may represent more than one road. The speed-flow curve that is used is dependent on the characteristics of these roads, so that if three parallel single lane roads are aggregated, then the speed flow curve will be closer to the quasi-linear shape of single carriageway urban roads, rather than the non-linear shape that would arise with, say, a motorway with a similar total capacity.

Strategic networks are constructed for the other modes in a similar manner. Capacities for these networks are estimated, largely for link load verification, and no capacity restraint is applied. As these networks are sparse relative to road, the aggregation of network links has only been necessary in a limited number of cases.

A stochastic user equilibrium assignment procedure calculates the pattern of flows on the network that minimizes the perceived generalized costs for each user, while ensuring that no capacity restrictions on demand are exceeded (i.e. demand is in equilibrium with supply). At equilibrium, no individual traveller can further reduce his perceived travel costs by changing routes, since all such adjustments have already been made by users in the creation of the user equilibrium solution.

Interaction of national and local road networks

On road the *interurban* traffic is usually a small proportion of the total traffic – the *local* traffic is dominant. The volume of local traffic is estimated as follows:

(a)   The observed total traffic load based on the 'Census of Motor Traffic on Main International Traffic Arteries 1990' (United Nations Economic Commission for Europe, 1993), is coded on each link. Capacity restraint functions are then applied and the resulting link speeds derived.

(b)   The modelled interurban traffic is then assigned on the roads, using the link speed already derived.

(c)   The assigned interurban traffic is subtracted from the total observed traffic, to give estimates of local traffic.

(d)   This local traffic is then pre-loaded by the transport module in the base year before modelled traffic is assigned: this gives the correct overall volume of traffic, and hence the correct network time.

(e)   For 2005 the local traffic is increased by 20%. The links in the vicinity of large metropolitan areas will experience more rapidly increasing congestion due to the higher proportions of local traffic. The assumed rate of growth, on first sight, might seem to be a low estimate; nevertheless, it would seem reasonable to assume that local bottlenecks will be resolved through local network adaptations, and overall the interurban road network would not see local traffic increase as rapidly as inter-regional traffic.

4.4.2. The implementation of the multimodal transport module

The transport module has been implemented on the basis of the following steps:

(a)   definition of the zoning system;
(b)   setting up the multimodal network;
(c)   definition of user modes and network modes;
(d)   description of the characteristics of each mode (cost functions).

The zoning scheme is the same as that applied to the regional economic module which includes 62 internal zones and 13 external zones (Table 4.1 and Figure 4.2). The centroid of each zone represents the origin or the destination of passenger travel or a goods movement and therefore a set of links has been provided to connect the centroid with the multimodal network. Some centroids are connected to more than one node where appropriate.

For passenger movements, five user modes have been defined: car, coach, high speed train (HST), conventional intercity train and air. Freight user modes are: road (lorry), rail, bulk shipping, container shipping and inland waterways. Each user mode has been designed as a combination of network modes, or travel stages.

The strategic multimodal transport network consists of a set of nodes and links. It allows for the representation of movements by land vehicles (such as cars, coaches, lorries and trains), sea vessels (short sea shipping and inland waterways) and air. This allows great flexibility in the treatment of intermodal trips for passengers, when road vehicles transfer to ferries for sea crossings, and freight, when a container is delivered by truck to a port to be loaded onto a ship. The use of an integrated network also has another important advantage: the congestion on a road link affects all transport modes which are present on that link (cars, coaches and lorries).

The pipeline mode of transport for crude petroleum and derivatives is the only mode which has not been implemented in the module. The reason is that this mode does not seem to be relevant for the context of the study: its use is strictly defined by the geographical location of countries, it is not in competition with other modes of transport and it mainly uses private infrastructures.

The link types are defined in Table 4.6.

Table 4.5.   Relationship between flows and user modes

	Type of flow		User modes available				
Passengers	Business travel A	persons	Car		HspeedTrain	Train	Air
	Business travel B	persons	Car		HspeedTrain	Train	Air
	Independent A	persons	Car	Coach	HspeedTrain	Train	Air
	Independent B	persons	Car	Coach	HspeedTrain	Train	Air
	Inclusive tours	persons		Coach			Air
Freight	Liquid bulk	tonnes	Truck	Rail	Bulkship		Waterway
	Solid bulk	tonnes	Truck	Rail	Bulkship		Waterway
	Semi-bulk	tonnes	Truck	Rail	Bulkship		Waterway
	General freight A	feu	Truck	Rail		Container ship	Waterway
	General freight B	feu	Truck	Rail		Container ship	

Table 4.6.   Link type definitions

Class	Link type name	Notes
Road	Toll motorways	Toll motorways[l]
	Non-toll motorways	Free motorways[l]
	Two-carriageway roads	Each carriageway has at least two lanes[l]
	One-carriageway roads	Each carriageway has only one lane[l]
	Road access from centroid	Access from the centroid to the road network
	Car border	Road link for cars only across the border
	Truck border	Road link for trucks only across the border
Rail	Rail access from centroid	Rail access from the centroid
	Rail border	Allows modelling of the time delay at the borders
	Rail tracks	Rail tracks for IC trains and freight trains[l]
	High speed rail tracks	Rail tracks for high speed trains[l]
Ports and shipping	Coastal shipping	Ship moving along short sea shipping network
	Coastal ship in port	Ship in port for loading/unloading
	Deep sea shipping	Ship moving along ocean shipping routes network
	Deep sea ship in port	Ship in port for loading/unloading
	Road connection to port	Transfer from road to port
	Rail connection to port	Transfer from rail to port
	Waterway connection to port	Transfer from waterway to port
	Sea port – liquid bulk	Port activities for liquid bulk
	Sea port – solid bulk	Port activities for solid bulk and semibulk
	Sea port – general freight	Port activities for general freight and high value freight
Inland waterway	Waterway access from centroid	Access from the centroid to the waterway network
	Waterway port – all freight	Port activities for bulk, semibulk and general freight
	Small waterway	1,000 t < barge weight < 3,000 t
	Large waterway	Barge weight > 3,000 t
Ferries	Ferry for passengers	Ferry for cars, coaches, trucks and passenger trains
	Ferry for passengers and freight	Ferry for cars, coaches, trucks, passenger and freight trains
	Road connection to ferry	Road access to ferry lines
	Rail connection to ferry	Rail access to ferry lines
Air	Air connection	Departure and arrival (check-in and check-out)
	Airway	Airway[l]
	Airport access from centroid	Access from centroid to the airport
	Road access to airport	Road access to airport
	Rail access to airport	High speed rail access to airport
Intrazonal	Intrazonal road	Intrazonal roads
	Intrazonal rail	Intrazonal rail lines
	Intrazonal waterway	Intrazonal waterway lines

[l] Link categories are differentiated by country.

Figure 4.4.   The road network in the base year (1991)

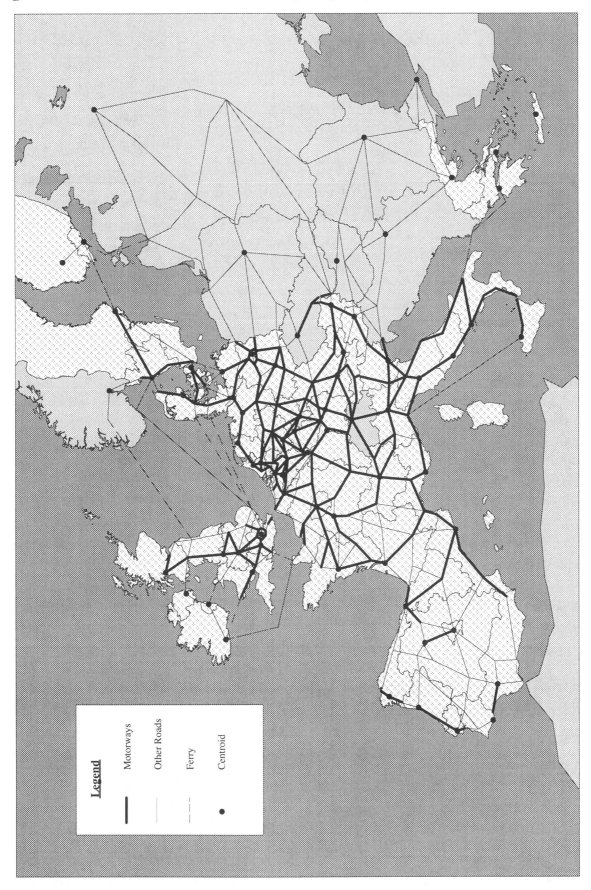

Legend

Motorways ———

Other Roads ———

Ferry - - -

Centroid •

Figure 4.5.   The rail network in the base year (1991)

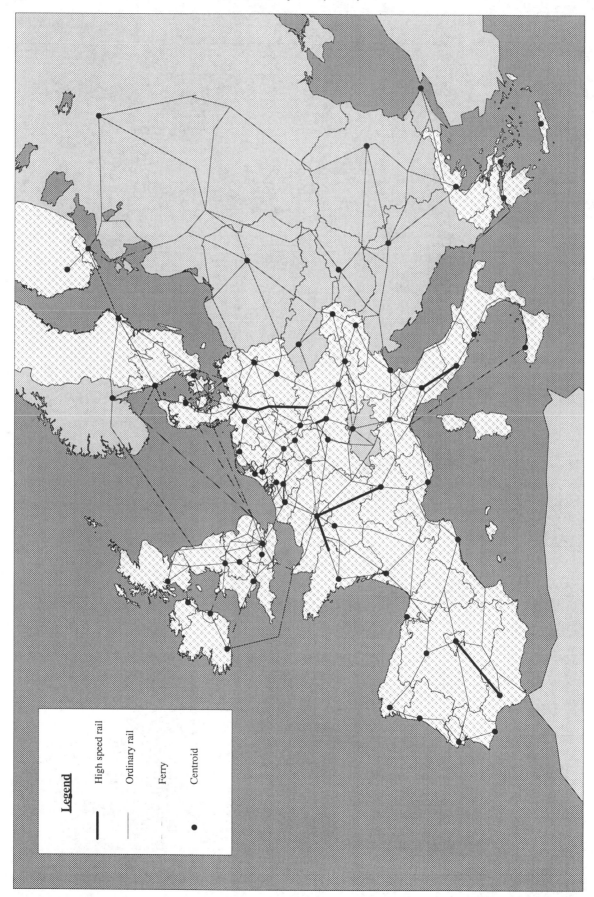

Figure 4.6.   The short sea shipping network in the base year (1991)

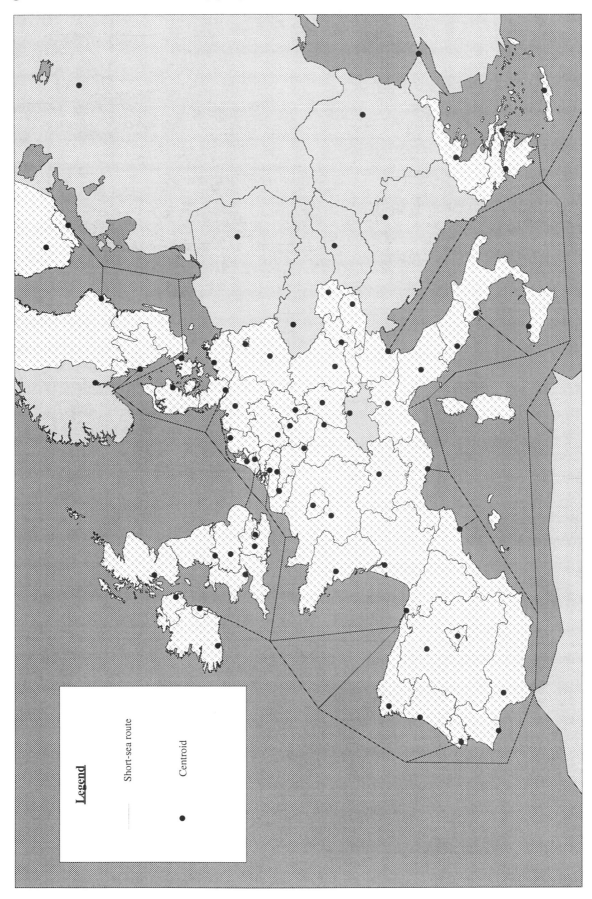

Legend

Short-sea route

Centroid

•

Figure 4.7.   The inland waterway network in the base year (1991)

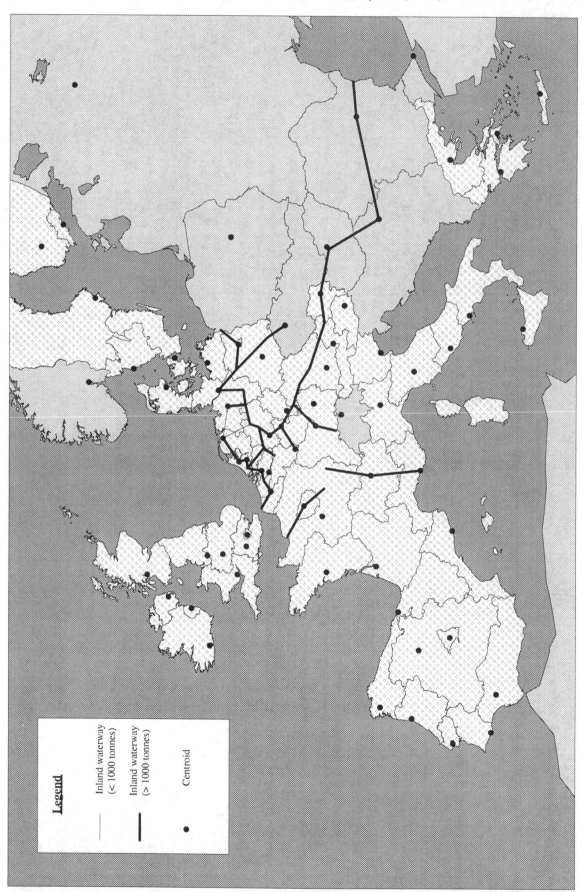

Figure 4.8.   The location of modelled airports in the base year (1991)

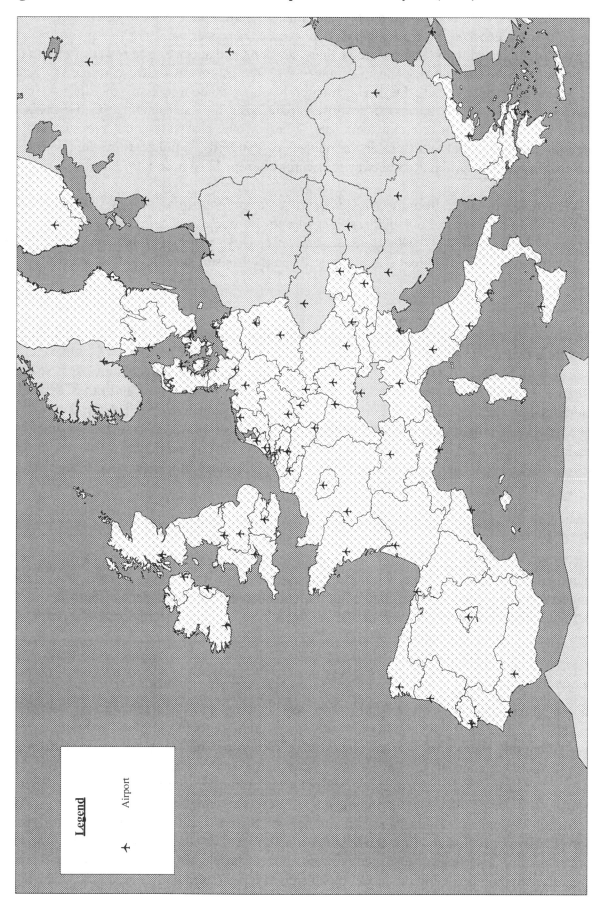

Road network

The strategic network includes all the E-roads plus other important trunk roads (Figure 4.4). It is used by cars, coaches and trucks, which may operate as proper modes or feeder modes. The network is connected to rail stations, ferry lines, sea ports and airports. The road links included in the module are distinguished in toll motorways, free motorways, dual-carriageway roads and single-carriageway roads. Further distinction has been made to classify the links for each EC country. This allows the model to differentiate costs for each country on the basis of different toll rates and of different fuel costs. Where a road crosses a country border proper links for cars and trucks have been introduced to explicitly simulate time delays due to customs formalities. Different motorway tolls across Europe have been introduced.

Link lengths were scaled from the *Michelin Atlante Stradale Europa, 1995* (1:1,000,000 scale for Western Europe and 1:3,000,000 scale for Eastern Europe). Capacities of the E-roads were extracted from UNECE 1990 Census data. Capacity restraint functions have been implemented assigning different free flow speeds on the basis of specific country speed limits.

Rail network

The network represents the international connections among the EU states (Figure 4.5). Links are differentiated into two classes: IC train and high speed train. The first set of links can be used by both passengers and freight, while the second set is for passengers only. The network is connected with roads, ferry lines, sea ports and airports. Link lengths and times were also determined by the *Thomas Cook European Timetable* (November 1995). The structure of the rail network is similar to the road one: border links have been provided in such a way that it is possible to model delays for customs formalities (and this is particularly true for freight movement) and links are differentiated by country to introduce proper national fares for both passengers and freight.

Ferry network

Ferry lines connect Great Britain and Ireland with Europe, Denmark and Germany with Scandinavian countries, Spain with Morocco and Italy with Greece. Ferries are directly connected by road and rail and they could be considered as a component of both networks. Journey times and characteristics of the services have been extracted from *Thomas Cook European Timetable* (November 1995).

Shipping network

The shipping network is divided into short sea shipping and deep sea shipping networks (Figure 4.6). The short sea shipping network connects the ports in the Member States as well as neighbouring states along the mainland coasts in Europe and North Africa. The deep sea shipping network connects the EU Member States to the southern half of Africa, the Americas and the Far East. Sea ports are connected with road, rail and waterway networks in order to simulate the use of all the other freight modes as feeders for the ship mode and to model proper loading/unloading times and costs in the port. Specific port links have been introduced to explicitly model cost and time related to port activities. For coastal shipping (bulk ship and container ship), a herring-bone shaped network connects a selected number of European ports. Short sea shipping is used in the model by all freight types (solid bulk, liquid bulk, semi-bulk, and both types of general freight). Inland waterway is defined as one of the feeders to short sea shipping; thus the option of river-sea shipping is represented in the model.

Note the ferry links for freight are treated simply as a stage in the journey of the road and rail main modes. Passenger travel on sea is limited to main ferry lines where frequent services exist; other uses such as cruise are not considered.

Inland waterway network

The core of the inland waterway network is in Central Europe (Figure 4.7). The links considered are divided in two categories on the basis of barge limits. The canals are directly connected to sea ports in order to simulate the use of inland waterways as a feeder mode for ships. The network has been designed on the basis of documents from the European Commission.

Air network

The air network connects the main European airports (Figure 4.8). The links considered are only those which connect two cities between which there are at least two direct flights per day, and at least four times a week. Airports are directly connected with the road network (to allow for the use of cars as a feeder of air mode) and, when present, with the high speed train network. External zones (Eastern Europe and the rest of the world) have been linked with only 16 European main airports, chosen on the basis of annual traffic data. The representation guarantees a correct simulation of the hub-and-spoke system: minor airports are connected to major ones and in each airport proper departure and arrival links simulate the actual time spent at each interchange before arriving at the final destination. Journey times and distances have been calculated on the basis of the *ABC World Airways Guide* (November 1995).

Transport costs and functions

The perceived cost functions may represent either a cost faced by an operator or a tariff charged to a user. The model requires user cost/tariff information and uses this information in the modal split algorithm. The tables, with all detailed cost functions used in the model and briefly described in this section, are reported in Appendix C. Apart from car, the perceived cost functions for passengers have been derived from fares using linear regression analysis.

(a) *Cars.* The perceived cost function is based on network operating costs. It is related to distance and distinguishes different fuel prices and different tolls currently applied in each country across Europe.

(b) *Coaches.* The perceived cost function is based on tariffs for both national and international long distance trips in different European countries. An average value for all Europe has been used and the fare is linear with distance.

(c) *Train.* Actual fares for each European country were implemented on the basis of a survey study conducted by the Italian Railways. The function is distance-based and allows for distinction among different flows (business and personal trips) on the basis of a different mix of first- and second-class tickets.

(d) *High Speed Train.* As for train mode, actual fares for each European country where a high speed train service is in operation were implemented. The distance-based function allows for distinction among different flows (business and personal trips) on the basis of a different mix of first- and second-class tickets.

(e)   *Air.* On the basis of a study conducted for the European Commission by the Cranfield Institute on Air Transport (the *1996 Review of the impacts and assessment of Internal Market Legislation* published as 'Air Transport', Vol. II. 2, *The Single Market Review*, Impact on services, Office for Official Publications of the European Communities and Kogan Page Publishers, 1997) different cost functions were used to differentiate domestic and international flights. All functions have a fixed component and a component related to distance. Specific domestic functions were implemented for France, Germany, Italy, Spain and the UK.

The perceived cost functions for freight were derived by using different criteria for different modes; in some cases they were calculated on the basis of operating costs, in other cases official fares have been implemented using linear regression analysis. When published fares appear not to be realistic (such as for freight or rail) they were adjusted on the basis of the average revenues per tonne.

(a)   *Road.* Tariffs for lorry transport were derived from the operating costs of the vehicles plus an additional quota which allows for the profit. The cost terms were divided into a number of separate components: distance specific costs: lubricants and oils, tyres, repair/maintenance, variable depreciation, fuel (differentiated by country) and other variable costs; time specific costs: vehicle tax (differentiated by country), interest, fixed depreciation, insurance and drivers' cost (differentiated by country); fixed costs, which are the annual non-trip-dependent costs of administering the transport firm. The costs implemented are the same all over Europe and were calculated as a weighted average of different European values. They are related to distance and time and distinguish different tolls currently applied in each country across Europe. On the basis of the distinction among the operating costs of different specialized trucks, separate values for each flow were derived.

(b)   *Rail.* For bulk flows (liquid, solid and semi-bulk) data collected from different European rail operators was readjusted using average revenues per tonne-km of the major European operators (FS, BR, DB, SNCF, RENFE) from the Strategic Studies Department of the Italian Railways. Specific cost functions (fixed term plus a distance term) were implemented for five groups of countries. Further to the cost function applied to the journey from origin to destination, other costs were included for terminal operations. For containerized flows (general cargo and high value freight) data from national companies offering international services for intermodal swap bodies and containers were found to be reliable and thus were used to estimate a unique function across Europe. The cost function is distance based and in its fixed term also includes terminal traction costs.

(c)   *Bulk and container ships.* As for other freight modes, operating cost based tariffs were applied for bulk and container ships for both short sea and deep sea shipping. The ships' consignment costs were distinguished as ship costs and port costs: the first group includes the costs related to the ship in movement and to the ship in port, the second group makes reference to port activities, such as movement of goods, loading and unloading of the ships. Data sources vary from specialized consultancy (Ocean Shipping Consultants Ltd) to commercial brokers of import-export companies. Three different functions were implemented: one for port activities (fixed coefficient), one for the ship in port (time related term) and one for the ship in navigation (a fixed term plus a time related term).

(d)   *Inland waterways.* The estimation of cost function was based on the brief report *Inland waterway tariffs and cost structure* commissioned by the Netherlands Economic Institute (1996). The function implemented has two terms, one related to distance and one to time.

4.4.3. Calibration of the multimodal transport module

The transport operating costs and tariffs having been determined, the tasks of transport module calibration are basically estimation of the network capacities, capacity restraint functions for certain link types, definition of path choice parameters, and modal choice parameters.

Network capacities and capacity restraint functions

In principle network capacities and capacity restraint functions may be defined for all links included in the multi modal transport network. In practice, time and resource constraints mean that link capacities and capacity restraint function are likely to be implemented only for a selection of link types. Road links are obvious candidates. There exist certain bottlenecks on the rail and inland waterway networks and at some ports, yet in the general European context it would appear that the capacity problem is not as critical as on road. There is evidence of congestion of air space and traffic throughput at certain airports, yet the complex nature of the issues is perhaps beyond the scope of the current study. In particular, according to Eurocontrol (1996), some EATCHIP initiatives have shown remarkable results in capacity improvements amidst rapid traffic growth in the study area. For road links, link capacities are estimated, and capacity restraint functions are developed based on previous experience in interurban road traffic modelling.   For all other links, no specific capacity restraint is applied.

Path choice

At present, path choice is implemented in a detailed way only on road, for car, coach and lorry. For modes which are not used door-to-door, the path choice parameters are adjusted such that the journey length of the auxiliary mode is kept to a minimum. In other words, the main mode is used at the earliest opportunity as the flow originates from the centroid.

For car and lorry the operating cost is used in conjunction with value of time of travel in determining the minimum path. For all other modes, a time-based function is used, which determines the minimum path according to journey time. Path choice parameters are estimated such that most of the traffic from an origin zone to a destination zone uses the minimum path on the strategic network, whilst a small proportion (typically around 10-15%) is spread amongst the alternative paths. The actual spread, however, depends on the specific connectivity in the part of the network.

Modal choice

The modal choice hierarchy for passenger travel is set in the form of a two-tiered structure for business and independent personal travel: HST and train forms a lower hierarchy, whilst the car, coach (where applicable), air and train Group forms the higher hierarchy. This is to represent the relative higher degree of similarity between HST and conventional train, amongst the modal choices. For inclusive personal travel, only one hierarchy is necessary between two available choices: coach and air.

Modal choice calibration was carried out for each of the transport flows. This involves the estimation of value of time and the modal constant in the disutility function, and the modal choice parameter. As there are no systematic origin-destination data available, a two-tiered approximation approach is adopted in place of a direct formal calibration procedure (such as the maximum likelihood method): first, for each flow, a value of time is assumed based on existing knowledge of the flow type. The modal choice parameter and the modal constants are then estimated. For passenger flows, an initial maximum likelihood estimation was carried out on a small dataset obtained from an interurban transport study in Italy. The modal choice parameters and the constants are then readjusted for each individual flow type, based on known relativities of the parameters. For freight, modal choice parameters are estimated against the overall modal shares, and then fine-tuned through readjustments of modal constants. The estimated functions are then examined in a series of sensitivity tests on elasticity with respect to cost and time changes.

4.4.4. Validation of the transport module

The transport module was validated in terms of its representation of the base year situation and its sensitivity to potential policy changes. The former verification was done through comparing the average distances and overall modal split where available. The Eurostat passenger matrices from the tourism data and the freight matrices from the *Carriage of goods* data has served this purpose.

The elasticity tests were done by running the model under modified inputs or parameters, and comparing the changes between model runs to see if the model sensitivities to change fall within the known ranges of values that exist in the transport studies, especially those commissioned by the European Commission.

For details of the comparisons, see Appendix C.

5. Assessment of scenarios

The integrated Meplan regional economic and transport model is run for the following scenarios:

(a)   partial integration (PI);
(b)   full integration (FI);
(c)   full integration with further congestion charging on selected non-motorways (CC) (i.e. in addition to congestion charging on selected motorways that is already applied in FI).

A further sensitivity test is implemented based on CC to test the potential extent of changes that would occur to railways:

(d)   through improvement of service quality on the line haul as well as in terminal freight handling (RQI), including a 10% reduction of freight handling costs and times at the terminals and a reduction in modal constants which is equivalent to about a 10% reduction in cost terms.

At the beginning of each of the scenarios a summary is given of the main assumptions. However, for details of scenario and sensitivity test design please refer to Chapter 3, where the policy basis is discussed in detail. The following text concentrates on the description and analysis of the model results. Appraisal in a wider context is presented in Chapter 6.

5.1. Results from the transport model

5.1.1. Base scenario: evolution 1991-2005

Based on the macro-economic and demographic projections, the model provides an estimate of transport demand in 2005. The purpose of the projection is not so much to provide a precise forecast of the transport demand, as to provide a realistic and consistent future scenario from which the various policy developments can be explored.

The main assumptions made in terms of transport policy and infrastructure in the base scenario can be summarized as follows:

(a)   A collection of committed infrastructure projects and network improvement programmes that are expected to be operational by 2005 are included. (See Chapter 3 for details.)
(b)   On the road, car operating costs are kept at the 1991 level in real terms; no change of coach fares; lorry operating costs within the EU are assumed to reduce because of both higher rates of backloading and lower personnel costs. Outside the EU, lorry operating costs are kept constant. Road tolls and border delays are kept at the 1991 level. (Border costs and delays to/from CEECs are kept at the 1995 level.)
(c)   For rail, fares on conventional passenger trains are assumed to approach the mid-point between the 1991 average level in the EU and that in the home country. In some countries this represents an increase of fares, whilst in others it represents a reduction – the overall level experiencing no significant change. HST fares are kept 25% higher than those for conventional trains. HST terminal times are assumed to reduce by 20%

anticipating a provision of higher service frequencies and better user information. Rail freight rates for 2005 are calculated in a similar manner to the passenger fares. Rail terminal costs and times are kept at the 1991 level.

(d)   Air passenger tariffs are assumed to reduce by 20% owing to increased market competition.

(e)   Port handling costs and times are assumed to decrease by 20% for short sea shipping, and by 10% for ocean shipping.

In addition, some assumptions are made about user behaviour, particularly:

(a)   The demand for medium- to long-distance personal travel is assumed to increase; for independent trips, the growth rate is assumed at 35%, and for inclusive tours, at 50%. Demand for freight transport and business travel is assumed to grow in line with the production of each sector.

(b)   The value of time for passenger travel is assumed to increase by 50% (i.e. roughly in line with the growth of the gross domestic product). As independent passenger travel is modelled in two user groups (i.e. users with high and low value of time, see Chapter 4), the increase in the value of time is implemented in two steps: first, the value of time for each group is assumed to increase by 25%, and then the size of the high-time-value user group is increased and that of the low-time-value group reduced, so much so that the overall effect is a 50% increase in the time value. For inclusive tours and business travel, a 50% time value increase is implemented directly.

A brief review of the main changes expected by 2005 is presented here. Overall, the increase in economic activities and personal mobility as assumed in the projections imply a substantial growth of transport volume and volume-km.

Within the EU, car usage grows by 48% (or 2.8% p.a.) in p-km terms. The car usage may be compared with the historic trends in the DG VII Transport Database, which recorded a growth of 3.3% p.a. for p-km for car during 1980–93. On air, since at present the issues of possible congestion have not been clarified, a somewhat conservative growth rate (3.3% p.a.) was assumed in p-km terms for the base case.[6]

Under these assumptions, conventional rail and high speed train (HST) lose out to road for the shorter distance trips and air for the longer distance travel, due to an assumed 20% reduction of air tariff.

Total freight demand has risen as well, predominantly in general freight. Within the EU the total tonnage is expected to grow by 39%, and by 72% in tonne-km. A large share of the growth goes to the lorry, which is estimated to grow at an average rate of 3.5% per year in tkm. This growth in road freight is largely attributable to inter-country movements, and increased trade between the EU and the CEECs. Short sea shipping is expected to grow as well, due to an assumed reduction of port costs and times. Rail and inland waterways remain relatively static over the period.

Over the period 1991-2005, the total passenger volume is expected to grow by 34%, and the total p-km by 42%. In terms of trip distribution the growth is characterized by a strong

---

[6]   Note that the DG VII database includes all trips, whilst the model output given here includes only trips within the EU.

increase in long distance trips. Within the EU, the intra-country p-km is expected to increase by 39%, whilst the inter-country p-km is expected to increase by 49%; freight transport exhibits the same tendency: domestic freight is expected to grow by 43%, whilst inter-country freight is expected to increase by 77% in t/km. Passenger and freight travel for the rest of the world, particularly for the Central and Eastern European countries, is expected to grow a little more strongly.

Tables 5.1, 5.2a and 5.2b give a summary of the expected growth of transport demand within the EU in volume-km. Data refer to intra-EUR-15 travel demand.

Over the period, energy consumption and emissions increase faster than p-km, which results from increased air travel. For freight, those indicators increase roughly in line with the growth of tkms. It should be noted, however, that in calculating these indicators, no account is taken of technological developments that may improve energy efficiency and lessen emissions per p-km/tkm in individual modes. In other words, constant rates are applied to each passenger-km/tonne-km. (This also applies to similar statements made in the rest of this chapter.)

Table 5.1.   Growth of passenger- and tonne-km over time by mode: 2005 base

		Growth 1980–93 % per year	Model growth 1991–2005 % per year
Passenger	Car	3.1	2.8
	Coach	0.6	2.5
	HST	-	0.5
	Train	0	-1.0
	Air	7 (4.5 for 1990-93)	3.3
	All	2.8	2.5
Freight	Lorry	2.9	3.5
	Rail	-2.5	0.2
	Bulk shipping		5.8
	Other shipping		4.3
	Inland waterways	-0.5	0.6
	All		3.9

Notes:

1 The 1980–93 historic trend is taken from the DG VII Transport Database (data obtained directly from DG VII). The DG VII passenger data include all movements, whilst the modelled trend reflects medium- to long-distance travel only. Note the DG VII passenger data include trips made in the EU as well as those made outside the EU (e.g. the air data include inter-continental travel), whilst the model data include only trips within the EU.

2 The 2005 base run does not include the major HST projects which have been put forward as part of the TENs; those HST projects are included in the policy scenarios. Also the low growth rate of HST above is attributable to the assumed 20% reduction of air fares over the period.

**Table 5.2a.   Expected growth by area and mode: volumes and volume-km for
                 1991 and 2005 base**

		Mode	1991		2005		Growth	
			Volume (million t)	Tonne-km (billion)	Volume (million t)	Tonne-km (billion)	Volume %	t-km %
Freight	Inter-country	Road	795	486	1, 310	844	65	74
		Rail	204	198	227	195	11	-2
		Shipping	792	2, 241	1, 491	4, 198	88	87
		Inland water	99	73	105	78	6	7
		Subtotal	1, 889	2, 997	3, 132	5, 316	66	77
	Domestic	Road	682	419	10, 191	620	33	48
		Rail	343	76	445	86	30	13
		Shipping	23	43	40	74	74	72
		Inland water	97	39	111	44	14	14
		Subtotal	8, 145	577	10, 787	824	32	43
	All freight		10, 034	3, 574	13, 919	6, 140	39	72
		Mode	Trips (million)	Passenger-km (billion)	Trips (million)	Passenger-km (billion)	Trips %	p-km %
Passenger	Inter-country	Car	740	203	1, 117	328	51	61
		Coach	35	10	46	14	34	42
		HST	14	10	17	8	19	-15
		Train	134	70	120	46	-11	-34
		Air	299	257	483	423	62	65
		Subtotal	1, 222	550	1, 783	819	46	49
	Domestic	Car	11, 103	869	15, 072	1, 262	36	45
		Coach	391	35	516	50	32	42
		HST	48	17	45	14	-7	-21
		Train	1, 378	135	1, 448	133	5	-2
		Air	273	122	393	176	44	44
		Subtotal	13, 193	1, 179	17, 473	1, 634	32	39
	All passenger		14, 415	1, 729	19, 256	2, 453	34	42

Notes:

1   All statistics are for movements within the EU.

2   All values are annual totals unless otherwise noted.

Table 5.2b. Expected changes in average distances, costs, travel times and operator revenue: 1991 and 2005 base

Year	Flow	Mode	Av. distance (km)	Av. cost (1991 ECU)	Av. time (hour)	Operator revenue (million ECU/year)	Toll revenue (million ECU/year)
1991	Passenger	Car	91	3	2	-	5,685
		Coach	107	13	5	4,404	1,228
		HST	434	56	6	3,511	-
		Train	136	18	4	27,705	-
		Air	663	158	7	89,864	-
		All	121	11	3	125,484	6,913
	Bulk	Road	69	3	2	18,235	-
		Rail	428	17	17	6,902	-
		Shipping	2,288	58	218	10,224	-
		Water	581	3	61	483	-
		All	164	6	10	35,847	-
	General freight	Road	187	10	4	26,352	1,780
		Rail	700	45	26	6,626	-
		Shipping	2,947	59	156	37,587	-
		Water	519	3	57	102	-
		All	708	20	33	70,667	1,780
2005	Passenger	Car	98	3	2	-	11,850
		Coach	113	13	5	4,809	2,494
		HST	360	48	6	4,546	-
		Train	114	16	3	24,766	-
		Air	684	147	7	128,623	-
		All	127	11	3	162,744	14,344
	Bulk	Road	69	3	2	24,392	-
		Rail	302	17	12	8,009	-
		Shipping	2,375	52	205	19,481	-
		Water	578	3	61	583	-
		All	190	6	12	52,444	-
	General freight	Road	253	14	5	45,053	4,189
		Rail	706	45	26	8,810	-
		Shipping	2,923	56	148	64,947	-
		Water	404	3	50	53	-
		All	887	25	39	118,863	4,189

Notes:

1 All statistics are for movements within the EU.

2 All values are annual totals unless otherwise noted.

3 For simplicity of model results extraction, all toll revenue for lorry is tabulated under general freight transport, though a small proportion of the toll revenue is derived from the small amount of medium- to long-distance bulk and semi-bulk traffic.

Figure 5.1.   Road network improvements in 2005

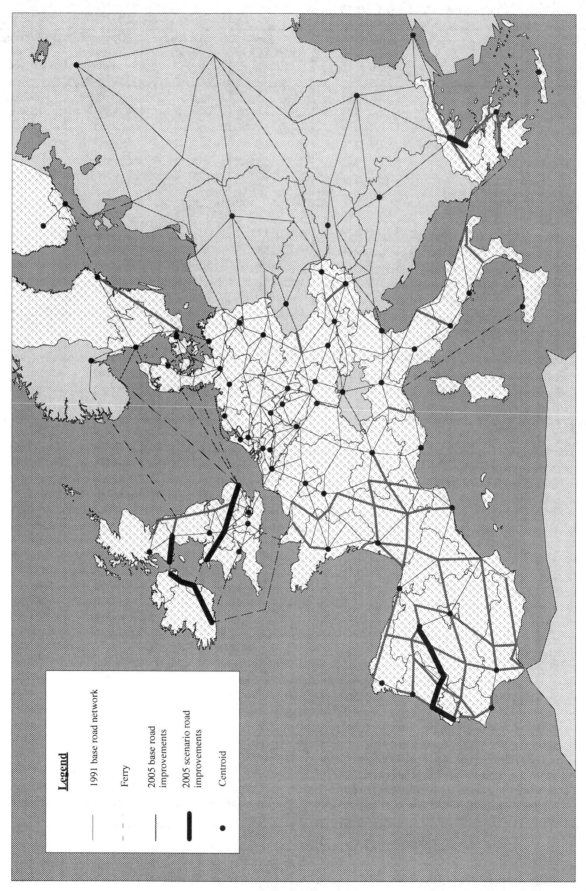

Figure 5.2.   Rail network improvements in 2005

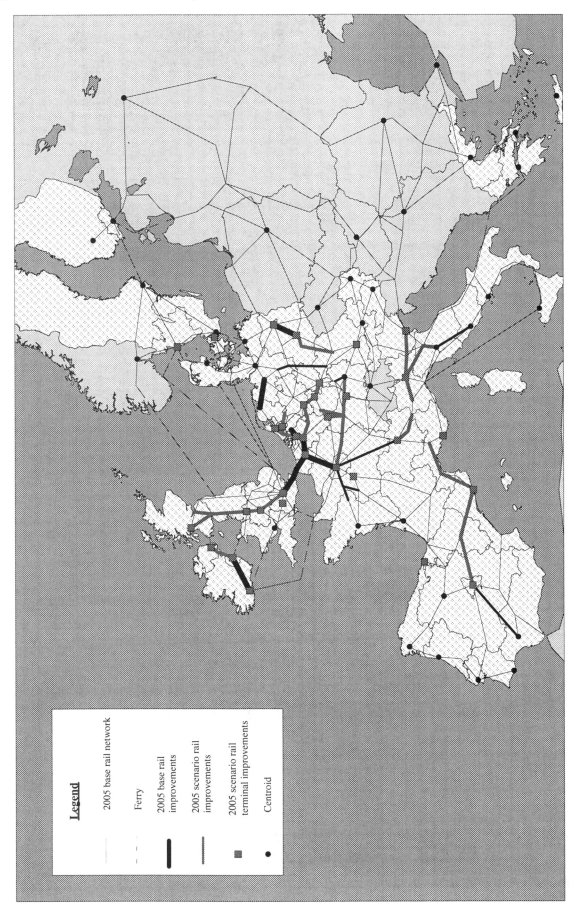

Figure 5.3.   Port improvements in 2005

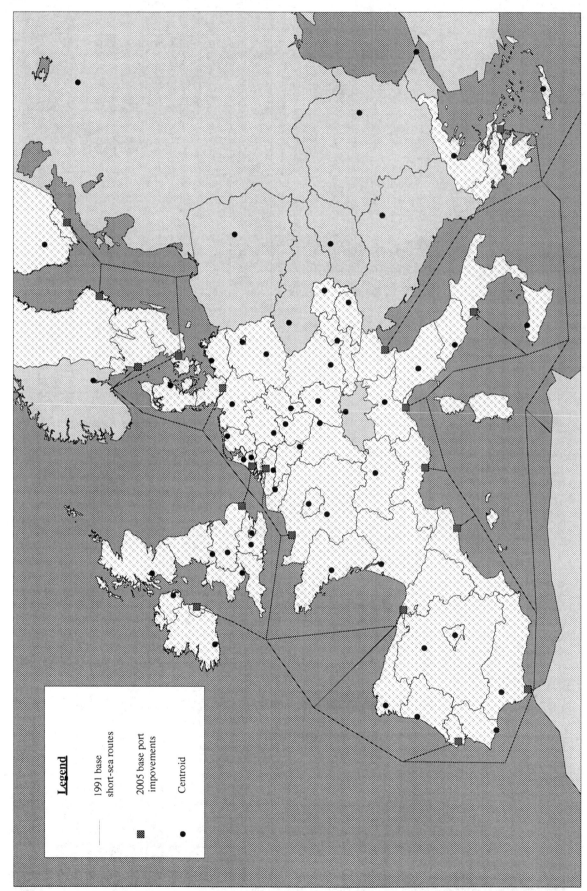

5.1.2. Partial integration scenario

The assumptions made in this scenario are mainly:

(a)   inclusion of major TENs projects (see Chapter 3, Table 3.1);

(b)   on road, the assumptions are the same as in the 2005 base case, except that the border delays within the EU are eliminated;

(c)   on rail, the assumptions are the same as in the 2005 base case, except that the terminal times are reduced by 10% where rail TEN projects are implemented, and that terminal costs for container handling are reduced by 10%;

(d)   air and sea modes maintain their assumptions as in the 2005 base case.

As an essentially infrastructure improvement scenario, the policy inputs of partial integration (PI) appear to stimulate the overall demand for transport. This results from an expansion of capacity as well as an improvement in service quality. Both p-km and tkm grow in comparison with the 2005 base run. Elimination of border delays for cars, coaches and lorries, as well as reduction in rail terminal costs and times, also contribute to the improvement of accessibility, and hence the demand growth.

Passenger travel is characterized by a marked increase in the use of HST, in response to the major projects included in the TENs. In addition to diverting trips from conventional train, HST attracts passengers both from car (for the medium-distance trips) and air (for longer distance trips).

Freight sees small gains in rail and coastal shipping relative to the 2005 base run. This results from an overall increase in freight demand as well as an improvement in intermodal operations/terminal handling. Overall, however, the changes are small and the modal share differs little from the 2005 base run.

Travel consumer surplus calculations indicate that all passenger and freight movements gain in terms of direct and indirect costs, reflecting the improvements of infrastructure.

There is a small decrease in energy use and emissions.

Table 5.3.   Summary transport statistics: partial integration compared with 2005 base

Policy	PI	Volume		Passenger-km		Change in revenue	Energy use	CO$_2$	CO
Passenger	Mode	Million trips	% base	Billion p-km	% base	Million ECU	% base	% base	% base
	Car	16,079	100	1,595	101	-	101	101	101
	Coach	573	102	69	109	236	109	-	-
	HST	184	195	70	205	5,191	205	205	205
	Train	1,572	99	174	96	-761	96	96	96
	Air	847	97	596	100	-1,907	100	100	100
	All	19,256	100	2,504	102	2,759	101	101	101
	PI	Volume		Tonne-km		Change in revenue	Energy use	CO$_2$	CO
Freight	Mode	Million trips	% base	Billion tkm	% base	Million ECU	% base	% base	% base
	Road	11,412	99	1,433	98	-2,567	98	98	98
	Rail	691	103	287	102	473	102	102	102
	Ship	1,604	104	4,390	103	711	103	-	-
	Water	215	99	122	100	0	100	-	-
	All	13,922	100	6,233	101	-1,383	99	98	98
Change in toll operator revenue	-	-	-	-	-	57	-	-	-
Change in total revenue	-	-	-	-	-	1,434	-	-	-

Notes:

1   All statistics are for movements within the EU.

2   All values are annual totals unless otherwise noted.

3   There are many competing estimates of unit p-km/tkm energy use and emission statistics. A set of simple unit multipliers are used here. The energy multipliers are respectively 2,890, 1,445, 6,77, and 7,176 KJ/p-km for car, coach, rail and air, and 2,890, 677, 423 KJ/tkm for lorry, rail, and shipping/inland waterways. The parameters are adapted from John Whitelegg (1993), *Transport for a Sustainable Future: The Case for Europe* (p. 5), except for air passenger travel, which was taken from SC Davis, *US Department of Energy Transport Energy Data Book*, edition 15, p. 2–22, Oak Ridge National Laboratory. The emission multipliers were taken from European Commission (1995b), *Towards Fair and Efficient Pricing in Transport*, COM (95) 691, p. 26. The CO$_2$ multipliers are respectively 180, 78, 160 g/p-km and 207, and 41 g/tkm for car, train, air, lorry and rail freight; the CO multipliers are respectively 11, 0.13, 0.28 g/p-km and 2.4, and 0.05 g/tkm for car, train, air, lorry and rail freight.

4   Modal operator revenue is defined as the receipt of payment by transport users for services of each mode, net of the tolls which users pay via the modal operator; the toll revenue is calculated separately and includes payments made by cars, coaches and lorries whilst using toll roads.

5.1.3.   Full integration scenario

The main assumptions of the full integration (FI) scenario are:

(a)   The same new infrastructure as input in partial integration.

(b)   On the roads, car operating costs are increased, owing to an assumed high level of fuel tax (currently in use in Italy). Lorry operating costs are affected by an improvement of lorry usage through increased backloading (i.e. a reduction in average cost, as in the 2005 base), an assumed high fuel tax/vehicle tax (currently in use in the UK), and an increase in personnel costs. The combined effect is an increase in lorry operating costs.

Congested motorways are charged with a toll, which is set at the average level for the EU for trucks and at the Austrian level for cars. Border delays within the EU are eliminated for cars and lorries (as in partial integration), and, in addition, there is a 50% reduction of the border delays and an abolition of border charges between the EU and CEECs.

(c)   On the railways, conventional trains adopt EU average passenger tariffs of 1991; HST fares are 35% higher than those for conventional trains. Similarly rail freight is charged at an EU-average tariff. Same reduction of terminal costs and times applies as in partial integration.

(d)   Passenger air tariffs are assumed to reduce further, by a total of 35%.

(e)   The same assumptions are maintained for shipping and inland waterways as in partial integration.

The overall pattern is similar to the partial integration scenario. The differences between PI and FI appear to be: passenger travel sees a reduction in road travel as a result of motorway tolling; air captures some of the medium-distance travel from road modes, and a limited amount of the HST market, owing to a further reduction in air tariffs, and a small increase in the HST fares overall. It is interesting to observe that there is a relatively small reduction in HST trips compared with the passenger-km. On the other hand, passenger trains gain in the short to medium distance where air cannot compete effectively. On the whole, there is a slight decrease in passenger travel demand within the EU.

Freight transport sees a small yet significant increase in total tkm. This is achieved, however, mainly through increases in the use of rail, shipping and inland waterway modes. Lorry use reduces slightly in volume yet significantly in tkm, shedding some of the medium- and long-distance movements to the other modes.

Travel consumer surplus calculations show that there is a significant gain in business travel, both in terms of cost, time and disutility. This benefit results mainly from a reduction in air fares. Personal travel loses in cost terms due to motorway tolls, yet achieves an overall gain in disutility terms through benefits derived from increased use of air travel, and to a lesser extent, a small but not inconsiderable saving of travel time on road.

For freight, increases in road freighting costs result in a disbenefit in cost terms. The travel consumer surplus calculations also suggest a loss of time and overall utility, as a result of some freight being diverted to non-road modes which generally involve more transfer and terminal handling, and, hence, a longer door-to-door time. The losses need to be considered with care, however, because in most instances where a decision is made to switch from road to other modes, there are a series of changes to be made in logistics and production planning. The end result very much depends on the balance between the cost involved in logistics changes and adaptation, and on the operational benefit derived from making use of rail, shipping and inland waterway modes, especially for large volume and regular deliveries.

A marked difference of this run in comparison with the partial integration is the application of tolls. The overall benefit needs to be viewed with the toll operator revenue and its use taken into account.

There is a 5% increase in energy consumption for passengers, while freight sees a reduction of energy use. With emissions the changes are similar in direction.

Table 5.4.   Summary transport statistics: full integration compared with 2005 base

Policy	FI	Volume		Passenger-km		Revenue	Energy use	CO_2	CO
Passenger	Mode	Million trips	% base	Billion	% base	Million ECU	% base	% base	% base
	Car	15,914	98	1,500	95	-	95	95	95
	Coach	532	94	62	97	-312	97	-	-
	HST	184	195	61	178	3,745	178	178	178
	Train	1,633	103	183	101	-1,246	101	101	101
	Air	993	113	692	115	-4,900	115	115	115
	All	19,256	100	2,498	101	-2,714	105	100	95
	FI	Volume		Tonne-km		Revenue	Energy use	CO_2	CO
Freight	Mode	Million tonnes	% base	Billion tkm	% base	Million ECU	% base	% base	% base
	Road	11,153	97	1,134	77	-11,394	77	77	77
	Rail	820	122	369	131	5,206	131	131	131
	Ship	1,722	112	4,697	110	7,464	110	-	-
	Water	225	104	126	104	25	104	-	-
	All	13,920	100	6,326	103	1,301	89	79	78
Toll operator revenue	-	-	-		17,539	-	-	-
Total revenue	-	-	-		16,126	-	-	-

Note: See Table 5.3.

5.1.4. Impact of congestion charging

This is a sensitivity test based on the full integration scenario. The main difference is a wider application of congestion charging, which includes all road categories (rather than only motorways) where on average the volume to capacity ratio is over 50%.

As one would expect there is a further decrease of car use, reflected mainly through shorter car journeys, rather than the number of journeys made.

Since the car is the principal mode for medium-distance independent personal travel, congestion charging has affected personal travel more than any other type of traffic in consumer surplus terms. This cost needs to be assessed in conjunction with the gains in tolling revenue. On the freight side there is a decrease in tkm for trucks in favour of the other modes. Tolling revenues increase more than three times in comparison with the FI scenario.

There is a small reduction in energy use, and a significant reduction in emissions for freight transport.

Table 5.5. **Summary transport statistics: full integration with congestion charging compared with 2005 base**

Policy	CC	Volume		Passenger-km		Revenue	Energy use	CO_2	CO
Passenger	Mode	Million trips	% base	Billion	% base	Million ECU	% base	% base	% base
	Car	15,817	98	1,398	88	-	88	88	88
	Coach	563	100	70	110	216	110	-	-
	HST	192	203	65	191	4,565	191	191	191
	Train	1,689	106	195	107	74	107	107	107
	Air	994	113	696	116	-1,891	116	116	116
	All	19,256	100	2,424	98	2,963	102	96	89
	CC	Volume		Tonne-km		Revenue	Energy use	CO_2	CO
Freight	Mode	Million tonnes	% base	Billion	% base	Million ECU	% base	% base	% base
	Road	11,010	96%	1,005	69	-22,629	69	69	69
	Rail	910	135%	417	148	7,900	148	148	148
	Ship	1,775	116%	4,812	112	10,331	112	-	-
	Water	241	112%	135	111	74	111	-	-
	All	13,936	100%	6,370	104	-4,325	84	72	69
Toll operator revenue	-	-	-	-	-	74,374	-	-	-
Total revenue	-	-	-	-	-	73,012	-	-	-

Note: See Table 5.3.

5.1.5. Impact of rail service quality improvements

This is the second of the two rail sensitivity tests, which explores the potential for rail service quality improvements. The rail service quality improvements are represented in the model through modifications of terminal costs and times (owing to improved service frequencies, better information, and increased handling volume which tends to reduce average costs) and modal constants for rail (a proxy, in the model, for the service quality not represented by cost and time). The passenger access/freight handling time is reduced by 10% for this test, so is freight handling cost at the terminals. In monetary cost terms modifications of modal constants also represent approximately a 10% reduction in indirect transport costs for general freight handling. Considerable impact is shown both for passenger and freight.

For passengers there is a considerable volume of medium-distance trips switching from road to rail/HST, and coaches meanwhile benefit from lessened congestion on road and increased volume. For freight there is a considerable increase in tkm by rail diverted from road and, to a lesser extent, inland waterways.

There is considerable benefit to business travel and bulk freight in consumer surplus terms. There is moderate decrease of energy use and emissions.

Table 5.6.   Summary transport statistics: rail service quality improvement test compared with 2005 base

Policy	RQI	Volume		Passenger-km		Revenue	Energy use	CO_2	CO
Passenger	Mode	Million trips	% base	Billion	% base	Million ECU	% base	% base	% base
	Car	14,842	92	1,283	81	-	81%	81	81
	Coach	588	104	73	114	603	114%	-	-
	HST	283	299	92	269	7,942	269%	269	269
	Train	2,565	161	291	160	11,206	160%	160	160
	Air	979	111	677	113	-7,674	113%	113	113
	All	19,255	100	2,415	98	12,077	98%	82	93
	RQI	Volume		Tonne-km		Revenue	Energy use	CO_2	CO
Freight	Mode	Million tonne	% base	Billion	% base	Million ECU	% base	% base	% base
	Road	10,621	92	953	65	-25,332	65	65	65
	Rail	1,338	199	542	192	15,111	192	192	192
	Ship	1,732	113	4,697	110	8,050	110	-	-
	Water	218	101	122	100	5	100	-	-
	All	13,909	100	6,315	103	-2,165	82	70	66
Toll operator revenue	-	-	-	-	69,203	-	-	-
Total revenue	-	-	-	-	79,115	-	-	-

Note: See Table 5.3.

5.1.6.   Changes of transport demand in response to transport projects and policies

In the integrated regional economic and transport model, transport demand is affected by:

(a)   reassignment of traffic *routes* in a modal network due to network improvements, which change the traffic volumes on links and to re-routing of trips over longer routes to avoid congested parts of the network;

(b)   *modal shift* from one mode to another because of changes in relative modal disutilities (costs, times) which change the modal demand between a given zone pair;

(c)   *trip length* changes where the ratio of trips to neighbouring zones relative to trips to distant zones is modified in response to travel disutility changes;

(d)   changes of trip origins and destinations owing to *relocation* of production and consumption, which alter the overall demand between a given zone pair.

The so-called 'generated traffic' is caused by a combination of these four effects.

In particular, there is a large reservoir of short-distance *intrazonal* movements (i.e. from a zone to itself) for each zone and these are not assigned to the interregional network.

When transport conditions improve more of these switch to become *interzonal* movements, thus 'generating' traffic on the appropriate mode in the interregional network.

5.1.7.   Overall economic appraisal

Table 5.7 gives a summary of the user benefits (calculated using the classic travel consumer surplus formulation) and the operators' revenues. The sum of these gains is commonly regarded as a good estimate of the economic benefit, without any double counting, of each policy package as implemented in the scenario. Since the entire process of locational choice, modal choice and route choice is represented in the model, the benefits calculated here include savings derived from redistribution of economic activities as well as shifts in modes and routes.

As stated in Chapter 4, cost savings in the context of the model output imply benefits from direct transport costs; savings on disutility, on the other hand, give an indication of benefits when both direct and indirect transport costs are taken into account.

The small overall gains of the partial integration scenario confirm the consensus that infrastructure alone is unlikely to bring about significant benefits to the user. Nevertheless, the savings are not inconsiderable, both in cost and disutility terms. Passenger travel loses on cost, mainly because of its increased use of HST, but some time savings are made, and in disutility terms passenger travel has gained. Freight benefits from improvements in intermodal operations at a number of rail terminals, which leads to both cost and disutility savings. The loss of time in freight transport results from mainly a lengthened door-to-door journey time, owing to increased use of non-road modes. On the roads, users have certainly saved time to some extent, as more freight is diverted away from it. Nevertheless, it is useful to know that on the whole the freight journey time is likely to increase under the set of policy measures, which indicates the effort that needs to be made in logistics planning in order to make the best of the benefits using non-road modes.

The rest of the scenarios have a level of benefit that is of a similar magnitude. Compared with partial integration the principal difference is the inclusion of the various policy measures. With full integration, passengers are clearly expected to benefit from the tariff regimes, particularly savings made on air travel. The time savings are derived from less traffic on the roads, further elimination of border delays, and increased use of air travel on long hauls. The service quality improved in addition to cost and time savings, which are shown through a higher saving in disutility. Freight users have made a loss on the whole, due mainly to rising operating costs for lorries. Such losses in cost are, however, offset by increasing operator revenues, largely of motorway tolling. The operator revenue accounts for 32% of the total benefits in cost terms, and 19% in disutility terms.

Table 5.7.   Annual savings against 2005 base (million 1991 ECU)

	Transport cost savings	Journey time savings	Total cost & time savings	Total savings (including other indirect costs)
Partial integration (PI)				
Passenger savings	-3,914	3,195	-719	2,854
Freight savings	4,569	-1,649	2,920	5,980
Operator revenue	1,434		1,434	1,434
Total	**2,089**	**1,546**	**3,635**	**10,268**
Full integration (FI)				
Passenger savings	44,280	23,377	67,657	77,708
Freight savings	-6,999	-10,259	-17,258	-1,367
Operator revenue	16,126		16,126	16,126
Total	**53,407**	**13,118**	**66,525**	**92,467**
Congestion charging (CC) (based on FI)				
Passenger savings	102	37,953	38,055	51,330
Freight savings	-12,302	-13,215	-25,517	-5,021
Operator revenue	73,012		73,012	73,012
Total	**60,812**	**24,738**	**85,550**	**119,321**
Rail service quality (RQI) (based on CC)				
Passenger savings	439	39,903	40,342	53,262
Freight savings	-12,661	-12,229	-24,890	-3,412
Operator revenue	79,115		79,115	79,115
Total	**66,893**	**27,674**	**94,567**	**128,965**

Notes:

1   The user benefits are calculated by the 'rule of the half' approximation method (i.e. based on the assumption of a downward slope of the demand curve, the transport users' benefit for each zone pair is measured through $0.5*(V_1+V_2)(C_1-C_2)$, where V_1 and V_2 are the trip volumes of the base and policy scenarios respectively, and C_1 and C_2 are the costs experienced by the users in the base and policy scenarios respectively. Similar calculations may be done for time and total costs savings. Only sums over all zone pairs starting from within the EU are presented here. A positive figure indicates a benefit, and vice versa. Note last column is a composite sum of cost savings, time savings (i.e. hours converted into monetary units using the values of time) and savings on modal constants.

2   For passengers, all times are included in the calculations; for freight, only the times involved in general freight are included. For bulk freight, time and disutility savings are excluded, since for planned, regular bulk transport transit time would not seem to be a main consideration, so long as reasonable punctuality is maintained. Note the times include access, transfer and waiting at the terminal. Thus for some policies where passenger and freight are shifted from road to other modes, the actual door-to-door time may lengthen: this is then shown as a disbenefit. Such losses of time, however, should be taken with caution.

3   The operators' revenues are taken from Tables 5.3 to 5.6 above.

The proportion of tolls revenue increases quite dramatically with the congestion charging scenario, where in cost terms the revenue is greater than overall savings, and in disutility it accounts for 64%. In practice, how much the users stand to gain will depend on how the toll revenues are recycled. A small proportion (about 10%) of the revenue increase comes from increased use of non-road modes such as rail, which is significant in its own right (see Table 5.5).

The sensitivity test on rail service quality improvements indicates that a considerable gain can be achieved through measures to reduce terminal costs and inconvenience. This appears to be effective for both passenger and freight transport. For a mode like rail where fixed costs have a large share in the total operating cost, increase of demand may well imply productivity gains and better utilization of infrastructure, in addition to direct benefits in increased operating revenue.

Overall, the total saving is around 1-1.5% of the expected GDP of the European Union in 2005 in real terms for the full integration scenario and its variants. Nevertheless, these are from model runs in which the macro-economic setting is held constant, and the calculations here do not take into account the multiplier effect of the benefits over time. Also the input-output structure of the economy in 2005 is assumed to be the same as in the base year. These are the issues to bear in the mind when interpreting the results.

5.2. Results from the regional economic model

The results from the regional economic model are essentially levels of production and consumption in each zone, and changes in production cost, production disutility, consumption cost and consumption disutility. These costs and disutilities are defined in some detail in Section 4.1.2, but it is useful to review them briefly here:

(a) *Production cost* is the sum of the cost of all inputs incurred by a producer to produce one unit of the product, in the zone where the producer locates.

(b) *Production disutility* is the sum of all disutilities associated with the inputs a producer uses to produce one unit of the product.

(c) *Consumption cost* is the cost of a product facing a consumer in the zone of consumption. It is a weighted average of the costs of producers in different zones. Transport costs for moving the product from the production zone to the consumption zone are included.

(d) *Consumption disutility* is the disutility associated with a product facing a consumer in the zone of consumption. It is a log sum of the disutilities associated with the same product in different zones that supply the zone of consumption. The log sum formulation takes into account a consumer's range of choice amongst the zones and is consistent with the random utility model used in the regional economic model.

To a certain extent, production cost may be compared with the 'factory gate' price of goods, whereas consumption cost may be thought akin to the average selling price of a product in the consumption zone. Production and consumption disutilities take into account not only the direct monetary cost of a product, but also its quality dimension as represented in the model. There is, however, a clear limit to such comparisons. The regional economic model represents, for all practical purposes, the goods and services in terms of industrial branches (pre-defined in the input-output structure that it adapts). For this reason, the model only represents the heterogeneity of products of different branches and/or from different zones, but not products of the same branch from the same zone. For a strategic model, this is unlikely to be a major shortcoming, yet it is worth bearing in mind when analysing the results.

In the regional economic model, all production, consumption and the costs and disutilities associated with them are accounted for separately. Thus, it is possible to output such information for policy analysis purposes. The model output, however, needs to be read with care. Whilst within the EU, the model has a fairly good representation of production structure, its ability to represent trade with the rest of the world is kept at a bare minimum (as it is not so much the focus of the study). The relative strength of the EU economy to that in the rest of the world depends just as much on what is to happen there as within the EU, e.g. the extent to which working conditions and environmental standards are enforced. Also trade growth with the rest of the world depends on changes in exchange rates and tariff barriers to a much higher degree than within the EU. Even within the EU there are still a myriad of local factors that would affect the growth or decline of the regions in practice. For these reasons, the discussion on the regional economic model results will focus on the relative strength of the regions in terms of production and cost within the EU, rather than the absolute activity levels. Those who are interested in activity levels should refer to the model output annex.

The discussion below follows the same sequence as for the transport results.

5.2.1. Evolution 1991–2005

By 2005, the EU economy is expected to grow by 44% (or an average of 2.6% per annum 1991-2005) in terms of total production. This growth is largely determined by the macro-economic projection of private and public consumption, investment, and demand of export to outside the EU, which is made externally to the model (see Section 3.2.1). The technical coefficients of the input-output table also play their part in this forecast. Limitations are clearly understood of the fixed technical coefficients which are not updated through time, and, for this reason, some parts of the forecast, e.g. sector growth in particular, need to be interpreted with caution. Nevertheless, the overall growth is broadly in line with the EU medium-term forecast (1995-2000), which expects an average GDP growth of 2.5% per year up to 2000, and a slightly higher rate beyond.

The cohesion countries and the new Member States grow significantly faster, at a rate of 48%, or 2.8% per year. This is largely driven by the more rapid increase of private consumption and investment in these areas, and, in some cases, in growth of intra- and extra-EU trade. The differentials in growth rates are reflected in all main sectors of production, though some minor variations may still be found. As a result, production and consumption in peripheral countries and regions are expected to increase their importance in the EU economy, leading to changes in the patterns of trade and, hence, the demand for freight and passenger movements. As already seen in Section 5.1.1, the overall impact is a rapid growth particularly in freight tkms, over and above the freight volume growth (Table 5.2).

Table 5.8.   Projected economic growth by sector by region

		1991 million ECU	2005 base million ECU	Net growth million ECU	Total growth %	Average p.a. %
Agriculture	Cohesion countries	49,822	72,120	22,298	45	2.7
	New Member States	31,534	47,185	15,651	50	2.9
	Rest of EUR-15	247,333	341,109	93,776	38	2.3
	All EUR-15	328,689	460,414	131,725	40	2.4
Heavy industries	Cohesion countries	118,276	156,795	38,519	33	2.0
	New Member States	62,645	83,725	21,080	34	2.1
	Rest of EUR-15	857,414	1,102,193	244,779	29	1.8
	All EUR-15	1,038,335	1,342,713	304,378	29	1.9
Other manufacturing	Cohesion countries	270,684	414,759	144,075	53	3.1
	New Member States	241,191	394,196	153,005	63	3.6
	Rest of EUR-15	2,601,322	3,905,479	1,304,157	50	2.9
	All EUR-15	3,113,197	4,714,434	1,601,237	51	3.0
Services	Cohesion countries	515,831	767,221	251,390	49	2.9
	New Member States	444,829	642,129	197,300	44	2.7
	Rest of EUR-15	4,635,845	6,561,344	1,925,499	42	2.5
	All EUR-15	5,596,505	7,970,694	2,374,189	42	2.6
Total production	Cohesion countries	954,612	1,410,897	456,285	48	2.8
	New Member States	780,197	1,167,232	387,035	50	2.9
	Rest of EUR-15	8,341,913	11,910,125	3,568,212	43	2.6
	All EUR-15	10,076,722	14,488,254	4,411,532	44	2.6

Figure 5.4.   Total production in all scenarios

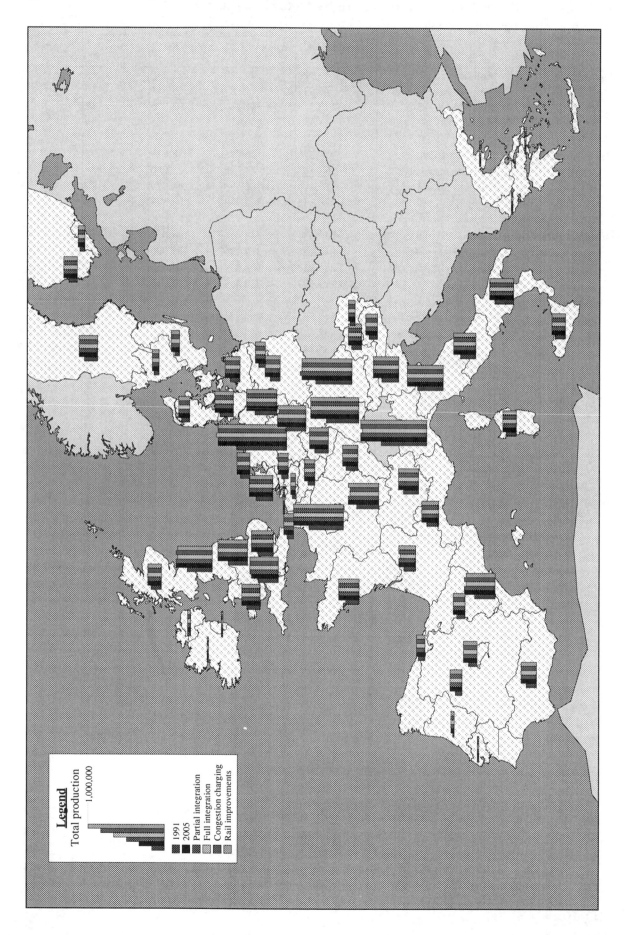

Figure 5.5.   Agricultural production in all scenarios

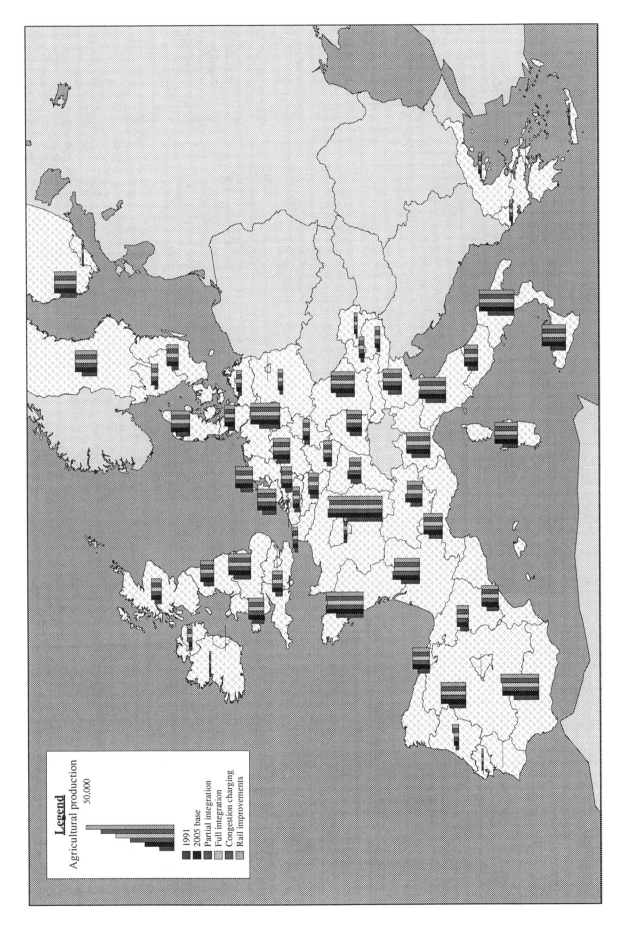

Figure 5.6.   Heavy industrial production in all scenarios

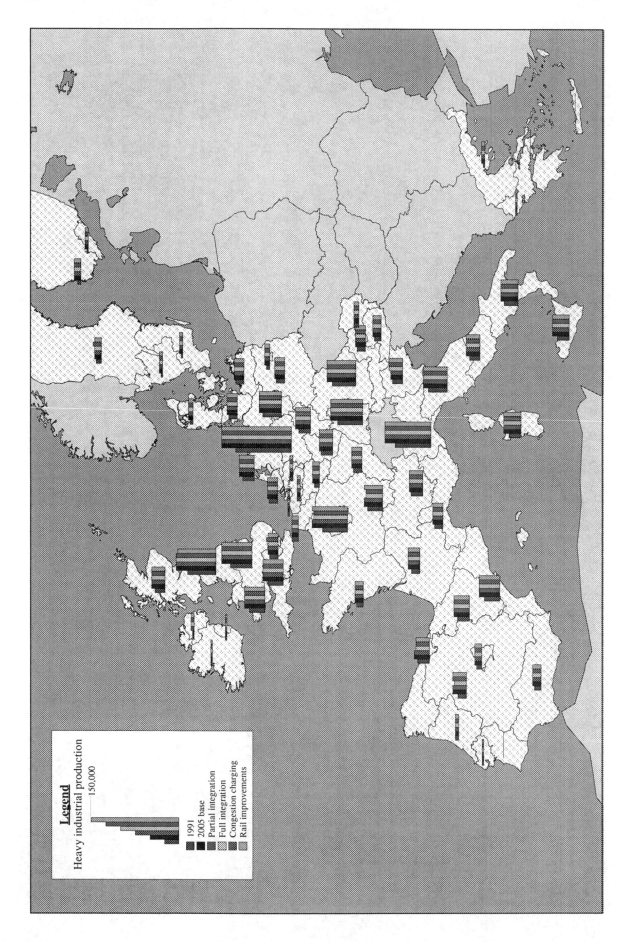

Figure 5.7.   Other manufacturing production in all scenarios

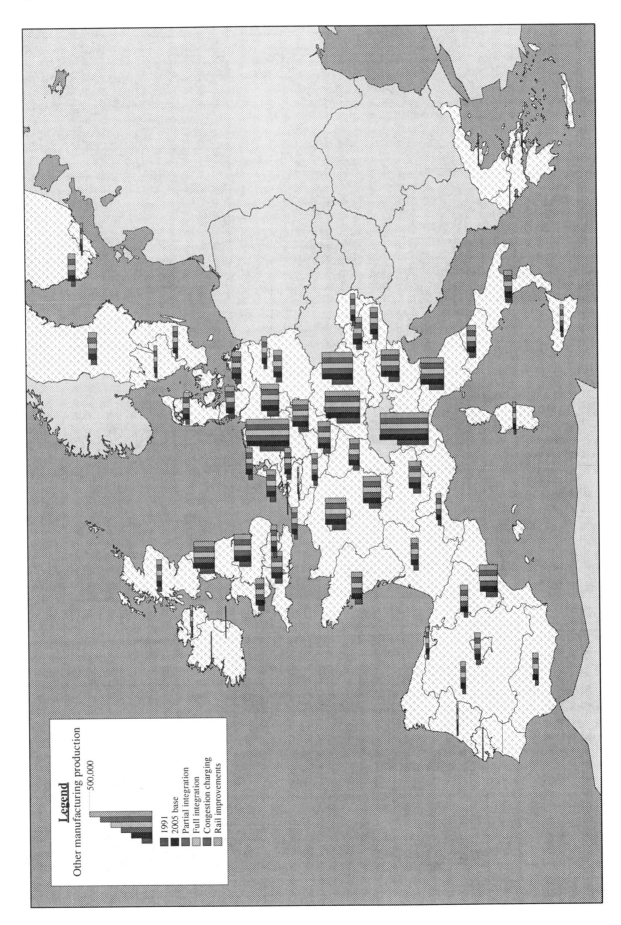

Figure 5.8.   Services production in all scenarios

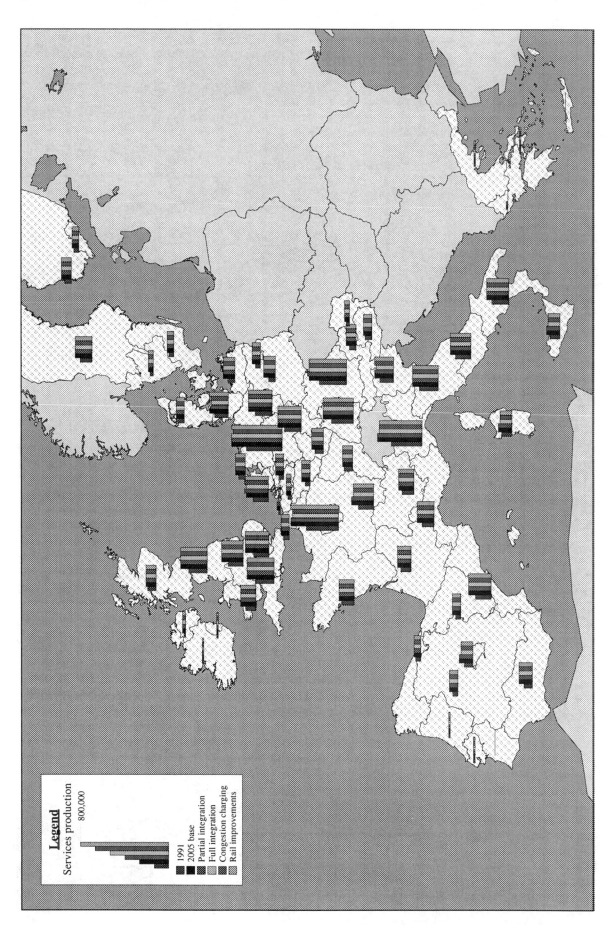

5.2.2. The partial integration scenario

Compared with the 2005 base, under the partial integration scenario there is a small relative reduction in the peripheral countries in total production, due to improved access of other countries to the local markets in the peripheral regions. Table 5.10 represents this tendency in terms of relative strength for growth. The pattern of relative strength is, however, somewhat uneven across the sectors. It seems that in agriculture and heavy industries the peripheral countries and regions are more likely to grow under infrastructure improvements, whereas light manufacturing and services tend to concentrate on the centrally located regions, by a small margin.

There is virtually no impact on production and consumption costs of goods and services, whilst in disutility terms both production and consumption are likely to benefit from the improvement of infrastructure and intermodal operations. This is consistent with what is shown in the transport evaluation. Not surprisingly, at an aggregate level, the overall benefit is small.

5.2.3. The full integration scenario

There seems to be a certain degree of advantage under the full integration scenario for the better developed centrally located countries and the new Member States (Table 5.10). The peripheral cohesion countries appear to lose out somewhat. It has to be remembered, however, that this slight reduction in growth strength is shown comparing with a base case, where the cohesion countries are expected to grow by more than 4% over and above the centrally located countries. Across the sectors, agriculture and light manufacturing are expected to grow more strongly in the cohesion countries than in the base case. Services in particular tend to lose out. This seems to result from the fact that air tariffs are assumed to fall substantially more than in the case of partial integration, which tends to exert an impact on long-distance business travel, which looms larger in the services sector of those outlying regions.

Higher input costs due to higher road and rail transport costs (through tolls and reduced rail subsidies) drive the model to predict a net reduction of total production within the EU. In reality, if the rest of the world would implement the same environmental charging for road, then the reduction would not occur in quite the same way; also, the overall benefit/disbenefit would depend on how road tolls are treated in taxation. The increase in transport costs is shown in the increases in production and consumption costs, and even with production disutility, with indirect cost savings taken into account (Tables 5.11-5.14). This is again consistent with the results shown in transport economic evaluation. Of course, the cost and disutility changes presented here do not take any account of the gains in toll revenue and reduced rail subsidies.

5.2.4. Impact of congestion charging

The locational impact in general seems to be similar to that of full integration. One noticeable change appears to be a tendency for the centrally-located countries and the new Member States to reduce their overall level of production in all primary and secondary industries. From the transport economic evaluation, it is understood that there is substantial loss of user benefits on cost, and it seems that this is what is behind the loss of relative strength in growth. Tolling on long-distance traffic, which tends to be fairly inflexible with respect to transport cost, results in a rise in production costs.

This increase is shown in both cost and disutility terms. However, in disutility terms (i.e. when indirect transport costs are taken into account), the cost rise does not seem to be as severe. Again, none of the cost and disutility signals include the redistribution of the toll revenue, as well as the benefit of increased revenue for the non-road modes, where fixed costs are high and marginal operating cost is low.

5.2.5. Impact of rail quality improvements

Again, there seems to be little difference in activity distribution from the congestion charging run. A major difference that can be identified is the reduction of production and consumption disutilities, which demonstrates the potential of rail service quality improvement to the economy as a whole. This has affected practically all sectors of economy, through a better use of rail in freight as well as in business travel. In terms of production disutility, heavy industries and services see the largest fall, indicating the areas where rail has a natural advantage over other modes, i.e. bulk and semi-bulk freight and business travel.

5.2.6. Appraisal from the regional economic perspective

In summary, the insight obtained from the regional economic model is important for us to understand the potential impact of the transport policy scenarios. In fact the output from the regional economic and transport models offers parallel and consistent stories of what is going on in the interaction of regional economic activities and transport. It is particularly interesting to observe the capability of the regional economic model in representing the direct and indirect cost impacts. On the other hand, it is useful to point out that the model structure is simple and crude, and the direction of changes predicted by the regional economic model is only indicative.

Tables 5.9a and 5.9b compare the regional growth and its relative strength by sector and region. The model does output the actual levels of regional production for each industrial branch in each zone; yet since in reality national and regional growth are affected by so many factors that are not covered by the model, it is felt that the model estimations are best used as relative indicators. These indicators demonstrate the potential impact of the transport policies upon regional growth; the seemingly small variations of 0.1%-0.5% are in fact quite substantial, given the magnitude of the GDP. Nevertheless, the extent to which such impacts are felt in the actual policy process would very much depend on a wide variety of factors operating in the local context. Similarly, Table 5.10 compares the relative strength in trade growth between regions. The tendency of faster trade growth between regions is clearly indicated by the figures. The transport policy scenarios exert some influence on the distribution of trade. Although such influence, when compared with the overall growth 1991-2005, is one magnitude smaller, the impact is quite considerable in absolute value.

Tables 5.11 to 5.14 give the production and consumption costs and disutilities by sector by region. Here the costs are affected by the direct user costs incurred through using transport, while the disutilities reflect the possible trade-offs between direct costs, time savings and service quality. It is interesting to observe that the tables demonstrate higher direct cost impacts (particularly in those scenarios where congestion charging is in force), yet the changes in disutility are often less pronounced, and often indicate an overall benefit. It is important to note that the cost increases indicated in the tables are caused directly by application of the road tolls (compare scenario PI with the rest), and they should not be taken out of the context of the model: the model design has not considered the ways in which the toll revenues may be recycled in the financial systems throughout the EU (e.g. the increase of toll revenue may lead to possible reductions of other taxes). Furthermore, the costs incurred by the road users should be weighed against the potential benefits to the environment, and the potential improvement of efficiency in transport operations.

Table 5.9a.   Regional growth by sector by region: all scenarios

		PI	FI	CC	RQI
Agriculture	Cohesion countries	72,280	72,613	73,049	72,967
	New Member States	47,324	47,825	47,855	47,799
	Rest of EUR-15	340,810	339,976	339,510	339,648
	All EUR-15	460,414	460,414	460,414	460,414
Heavy industries	Cohesion countries	156,950	155,906	156,596	156,183
	New Member States	83,750	84,061	84,032	83,566
	Rest of EUR-15	1,102,013	1,102,746	1,102,085	1,102,964
	All EUR-15	1,342,713	1,342,713	1,342,713	1,342,713
Other manufacturing	Cohesion countries	413,392	414,445	417,953	417,199
	New Member States	394,391	395,770	394,682	393,627
	Rest of EUR-15	3,906,652	3,904,219	3,901,799	3,903,608
	All EUR-15	4,714,435	4,714,434	4,714,434	4,714,434
Other services	Cohesion countries	765,885	745,607	746,916	747,430
	New Member States	641,927	644,948	642,506	640,494
	Rest of EUR-15	6,562,881	6,580,139	6,581,272	6,582,770
	All EUR-15	7,970,693	7,970,694	7,970,694	7,970,694
Total production	Cohesion countries	1,408,507	1,388,572	1,394,514	1,393,779
	New Member States	1,167,392	1,172,603	1,169,075	1,165,486
	Rest of EUR-15	11,912,356	11,927,080	11,924,666	11,928,990
	All EUR-15	14,488,255	14,488,255	14,488,255	14,488,255

Note: In the above presentation, the model estimated regional production and sectoral production totals under the policy scenarios are scaled to those of the 2005 base for ease of comparison.

Table 5.9b.   Relative strength in regional growth by sector by region: all scenarios

		Base	PI	FI	CC	RQI
Agriculture	Cohesion countries	100.00	100.22	100.70	101.30	101.19
	New Member States	100.00	100.30	101.34	101.39	101.26
	Rest of the EU	100.00	99.91	99.68	99.55	99.59
	All EUR-15	100.00	100.00	100.00	100.00	100.00
Heavy industries	Cohesion countries	100.00	100.10	99.44	99.88	99.62
	New Member States	100.00	100.03	100.33	100.27	99.57
	Rest of the EU	100.00	99.98	100.06	100.00	100.08
	All EUR-15	100.00	100.00	100.00	100.00	100.00
Other manufacturing	Cohesion countries	100.00	99.67	99.93	100.77	100.59
	New Member States	100.00	100.01	100.35	100.10	99.84
	Rest of the EU	100.00	100.03	99.97	99.91	99.95
	All EUR-15	100.00	100.00	100.00	100.00	100.00
Services	Cohesion countries	100.00	99.83	97.19	97.36	97.42
	New Member States	100.00	99.97	100.40	100.01	99.71
	Rest of the EU	100.00	100.02	100.29	100.31	100.33
	All EUR-15	100.00	100.00	100.00	100.00	100.00
Total production	Cohesion countries	100.00	99.83	98.44	98.86	98.80
	New Member States	100.00	100.00	100.41	100.10	99.80
	Rest of the EU	100.00	100.02	100.15	100.13	100.16
	All EUR-15	100.00	100.00	100.00	100.00	100.00

Note: In the above presentation, the model estimated regional production and sectoral production totals under the policy
          scenarios are scaled relative to those of the 2005 base, which are set as a base line of 100.00.

Table 5.10. Relative strength in trade growth by sector by region: all scenarios

Sector	From region	To region	Growth 1991-2005	Relative growth: 2005 base and policy scenarios				
				2005 base	PI	FI	CC	RQI
Agriculture	Cohesion countries	Cohesion countries	24%	1.000	.991	.989	.992	.991
		New Member States	68%	1.000	1.008	1.025	1.034	1.032
		Rest of EU	61%	1.000	1.009	1.017	1.025	1.024
	New Member States	Cohesion countries	65%	1.000	1.003	1.021	1.025	1.023
		New Member States	22%	1.000	.996	1.009	1.013	1.012
		Rest of EU	61%	1.000	1.006	1.013	1.012	1.011
	Rest of EU	Cohesion countries	62%	1.000	1.004	1.008	1.011	1.010
		New Member States	62%	1.000	1.007	1.012	1.010	1.009
		Rest of EU	34%	1.000	.998	.994	.992	.993
	Total		40%	1.000	1.000	1.000	1.000	1.000
Heavy industries	Cohesion countries	Cohesion countries	32%	1.000	.998	1.001	1.004	1.003
		New Member States	45%	1.000	.996	.980	.984	.964
		Rest of EU	40%	1.000	1.010	.990	.995	.993
	New Member States	Cohesion countries	46%	1.000	.997	.990	.993	.990
		New Member States	32%	1.000	.997	1.007	1.011	.993
		Rest of EU	40%	1.000	1.006	.996	.989	.992
	Rest of EU	Cohesion countries	45%	1.000	1.005	.989	.992	.992
		New Member States	39%	1.000	1.007	.994	.986	.984
		Rest of EU	29%	1.000	.999	1.001	1.001	1.002
	Total		31%	1.000	1.000	1.000	1.000	1.000
Other manufacturing	Cohesion countries	Cohesion countries	30%	1.000	.985	.993	.995	.997
		New Member States	89%	1.000	1.013	1.025	1.039	1.033
		Rest of EU	94%	1.000	1.031	1.030	1.046	1.037
	New Member States	Cohesion countries	108%	1.000	1.007	1.021	1.023	1.019
		New Member States	25%	1.000	.987	1.002	1.015	1.014
		Rest of EU	100%	1.000	1.021	1.002	.981	.976
	Rest of EU	Cohesion countries	101%	1.000	1.022	1.011	1.013	1.007
		New Member States	85%	1.000	1.021	.997	.976	.974
		Rest of EU	39%	1.000	.998	.999	.999	1.000
	Total		43%	1.000	1.000	1.000	1.000	1.000
Services	Cohesion countries	Cohesion countries	43%	1.000	.994	.949	.950	.953
		New Member States	53%	1.000	.998	1.020	1.022	1.017
		Rest of EU	47%	1.000	1.009	1.023	1.026	1.021
	New Member States	Cohesion countries	77%	1.000	.995	1.020	1.021	1.015
		New Member States	30%	1.000	.996	.995	1.000	.998
		Rest of EU	48%	1.000	1.009	1.019	.996	.989
	Rest of EU	Cohesion countries	65%	1.000	1.009	1.022	1.023	1.020
		New Member States	45%	1.000	1.008	1.019	1.001	1.000
		Rest of EU	35%	1.000	.999	1.001	1.002	1.002
	Total		37%	1.000	1.000	1.000	1.000	1.000

Note: In the presentation above, the model estimated sectoral trade volume totals under the policy scenarios are scaled to those of the 2005 base, which are set as a base line of 1.000.

Table 5.11. Indicative changes in production cost: all scenarios

Production cost		Base	PI	FI	CC	RQI
Agriculture	Cohesion countries	1.000	1.000	1.003	1.003	1.003
	New Member States	1.000	1.000	1.002	1.003	1.002
	Rest of the EU	1.000	1.000	1.003	1.003	1.003
	All EUR-15	1.000	1.000	1.003	1.003	1.003
Heavy industries	Cohesion countries	1.000	1.000	1.002	1.003	1.002
	New Member States	1.000	1.000	1.001	1.001	1.001
	Rest of the EU	1.000	1.000	1.001	1.001	1.001
	All EUR-15	1.000	1.000	1.001	1.001	1.001
Other manufacturing	Cohesion countries	1.000	1.000	1.005	1.005	1.004
	New Member States	1.000	1.000	1.003	1.004	1.003
	Rest of the EU	1.000	1.000	1.004	1.004	1.004
	All EUR-15	1.000	1.000	1.004	1.004	1.004
Services	Cohesion countries	1.000	0.999	1.004	1.005	1.004
	New Member States	1.000	1.000	1.005	1.006	1.005
	Rest of the EU	1.000	1.000	1.007	1.008	1.007
	All EUR-15	1.000	1.000	1.006	1.007	1.006
Total production	Cohesion countries	1.000	0.999	1.005	1.006	1.005
	New Member States	1.000	1.000	1.005	1.005	1.005
	Rest of the EU	1.000	1.000	1.005	1.006	1.005
	All EUR-15	1.000	1.000	1.005	1.006	1.005

Note: In the presentation above, the model estimated costs under the policy scenarios are scaled relative to those of the 2005 base, which are set as a base line of 1.000.

Figure 5.9.   Indicative changes in production cost

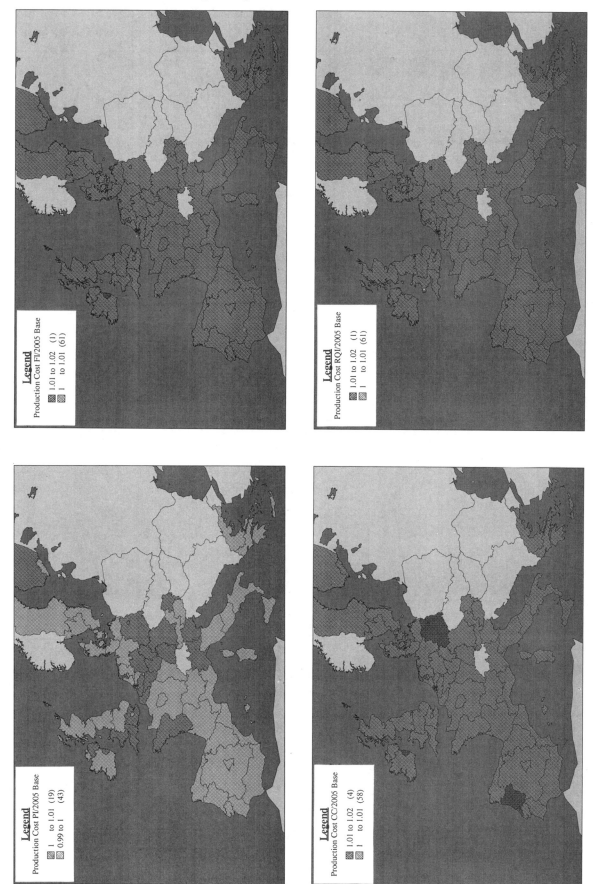

Table 5.12.   Indicative changes in production disutility: all scenarios

Production disutility		Base	PI	FI	CC	RQI
Agriculture	Cohesion countries	1.000	0.998	1.001	1.002	0.999
	New Member States	1.000	0.999	1.000	1.002	0.999
	Rest of the EU	1.000	0.999	1.002	1.004	1.000
	All EUR-15	1.000	0.999	1.002	1.004	1.000
Heavy industries	Cohesion countries	1.000	0.997	1.001	1.002	0.995
	New Member States	1.000	0.998	1.002	1.004	1.006
	Rest of the EU	1.000	0.999	1.005	1.007	1.001
	All EUR-15	1.000	0.999	1.004	1.006	1.000
Other manufacturing	Cohesion countries	1.000	0.998	1.001	1.002	0.999
	New Member States	1.000	0.999	1.000	1.002	0.999
	Rest of the EU	1.000	0.999	1.002	1.004	1.000
	All EUR-15	1.000	0.999	1.002	1.004	1.000
Services	Cohesion countries	1.000	0.999	0.996	0.998	0.995
	New Member States	1.000	0.999	0.996	0.997	0.993
	Rest of the EU	1.000	0.999	0.999	1.002	0.997
	All EUR-15	1.000	0.999	0.999	1.001	0.996
Total production	Cohesion countries	1.000	0.998	1.002	1.003	1.000
	New Member States	1.000	0.999	0.999	1.000	0.997
	Rest of the EU	1.000	0.999	1.002	1.004	0.999
	All EUR-15	1.000	0.999	1.001	1.003	0.999

Note: In the presentation above, the model estimated disutilities under the policy scenarios are scaled relative to those of the 2005 base, which are set as a base line of 1.000.

Figure 5.10. Indicative changes in production disutility

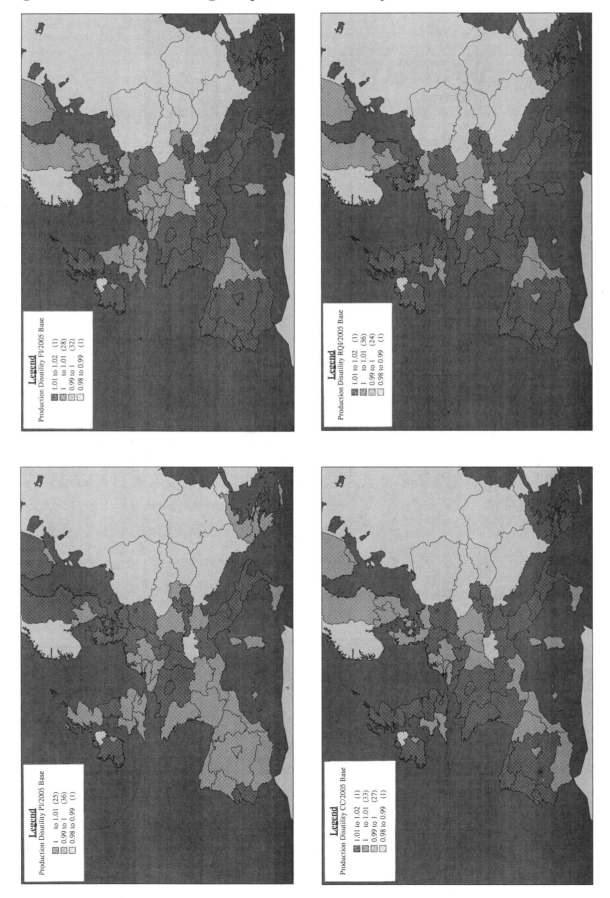

Table 5.13.   Indicative changes in consumption cost: all scenarios

Consumption cost		Base	PI	FI	CC	RQI
Agriculture	Cohesion countries	1.000	0.999	1.002	1.003	1.003
	New Member States	1.000	0.999	1.002	1.003	1.003
	Rest of the EU	1.000	0.999	1.003	1.005	1.004
	All EUR-15	1.000	0.999	1.003	1.004	1.004
Heavy industries	Cohesion countries	1.000	1.000	1.000	1.000	1.000
	New Member States	1.000	1.000	1.000	1.000	1.000
	Rest of the EU	1.000	1.000	0.999	0.999	1.000
	All EUR-15	1.000	1.000	1.000	1.000	1.000
Other manufacturing	Cohesion countries	1.000	0.999	1.002	1.002	1.002
	New Member States	1.000	1.000	1.003	1.004	1.003
	Rest of the EU	1.000	1.000	1.003	1.004	1.004
	All EUR-15	1.000	1.000	1.003	1.004	1.003
Services	Cohesion countries	1.000	0.998	1.037	1.038	1.034
	New Member States	1.000	1.000	1.020	1.023	1.021
	Rest of the EU	1.000	1.000	1.022	1.026	1.022
	All EUR-15	1.000	1.000	1.024	1.027	1.024
Total production	Cohesion countries	1.000	0.999	1.020	1.021	1.019
	New Member States	1.000	1.000	1.011	1.013	1.012
	Rest of the EU	1.000	1.000	1.012	1.015	1.013
	All EUR-15	1.000	1.000	1.013	1.015	1.014

Note: In the presentation above, the model estimated costs under the policy scenarios are scaled relative to those of the 2005 base, which are set as a base line of 1.000.

Figure 5.11.   Indicative changes in consumption cost

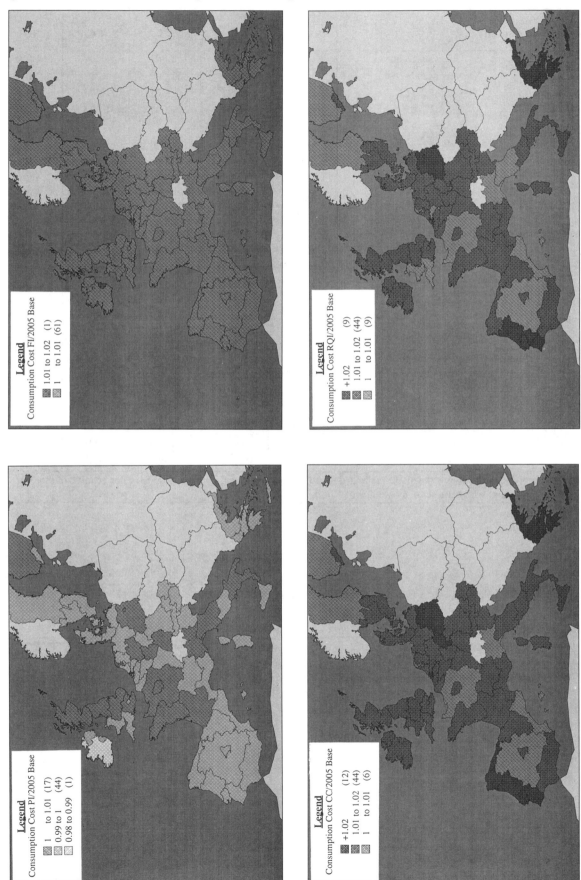

Table 5.14.   Indicative changes in consumption disutility: all scenarios

Consumption disutility		Base	PI	FI	CC	RQI
Agriculture	Cohesion countries	1.000	0.997	1.001	1.002	1.001
	New Member States	1.000	0.996	1.000	1.002	1.002
	Rest of the EU	1.000	0.997	1.003	1.005	1.005
	All EUR-15	1.000	0.997	1.002	1.004	1.004
Heavy industries	Cohesion countries	1.000	1.000	1.000	1.000	1.000
	New Member States	1.000	1.000	1.000	1.000	0.990
	Rest of the EU	1.000	1.000	1.002	1.002	1.000
	All EUR-15	1.000	1.000	1.001	1.001	0.999
Other manufacturing	Cohesion countries	1.000	0.996	1.000	1.001	0.999
	New Member States	1.000	0.997	1.001	1.003	1.001
	Rest of the EU	1.000	0.998	1.003	1.005	1.002
	All EUR-15	1.000	0.997	1.002	1.005	1.002
Services	Cohesion countries	1.000	0.999	0.995	0.995	0.993
	New Member States	1.000	0.999	0.999	1.001	0.997
	Rest of the EU	1.000	0.998	0.999	1.001	0.995
	All EUR-15	1.000	0.999	0.998	1.000	0.995
Total production	Cohesion countries	1.000	0.999	0.998	0.999	0.996
	New Member States	1.000	0.999	0.999	1.002	0.997
	Rest of the EU	1.000	0.998	1.000	1.003	0.997
	All EUR-15	1.000	0.998	1.000	1.002	0.997

Note: In the presentation above, the model estimated disutilities under the policy scenarios are scaled relative to those of the 2005 base, which are set as a base line of 1.000.

Figure 5.12.   Indicative changes in consumption disutility

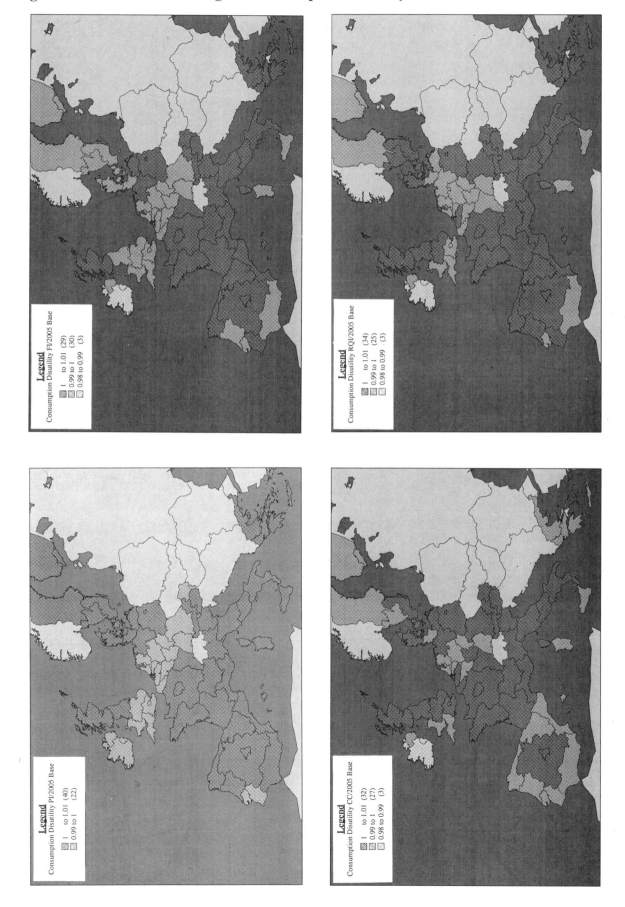

6. The impacts on the functioning of the single market

6.1. The main impacts

The main impacts commented on here are a selection of a wide range of possible implications of the CTP, and the ones more significant and probably more meaningful for the decision-makers in terms of possible actions.

An important finding from the results presented in Chapter 5 is the varied impact of the modelled variations in transport conditions on the European economy in different sectors as well as in different regions. This requires some interpretation.

There are certain general trends in the use of transport. First of all the relative importance of the monetary costs of transportation to firms as well as to the population is declining. This is clearly shown by:

(a)   the direct survey made on a sample of firms;[7]
(b)   the historical decline of low-cost low-performance transport modes (traditional rail and waterway services);
(c)   the increasing transport demand of low-weight high-value goods, or zero-weight goods like information and services.

User demand for high quality transport services has been growing. For passenger and freight transport alike, there are more and more strong demands of speed, reliability, flexibility and safety. In many instances the quality dimension has become the dominant consideration in the choice of transport modes. In return, transport services have been adapting themselves to the new market conditions. Against this general trend, different sectors of industries gain accessibility to a wider market area while at the same time finding themselves open to increased competition. The extent to which an industry in an area is able to benefit depends on its backward and forward linkages, the economies of scale and future growth of local final demand. The model results show clearly that the impact is different for different sectors of the economy and in different areas. Yet given its crude structure the results should be treated as suggestive indicators.

The impact on the overall European economy is shown to be limited because of the averaging of winners and losers; this does not imply that changes in the provision of transport infrastructure or in transport costs will not have a significant impact at the regional and local level. Also, the impact on particular industrial sectors and firms can be large. These results are also a consequence of the modelled options which were tailored for a study aimed at measuring impacts at Europe-wide level at the expense of detailed changes to be demonstrated at a local level.

A second significant result is that transport investments generate less impact than the cost and pricing policies. Again this result is plausible, because the TENs, while large engineering works in themselves, are limited in their geographical coverage and are mainly dedicated to improvement in passenger services (high speed trains). In contrast, the policy measures

---

[7]   See Chapter 2 and Appendix A.

included in the full integration scenario generally impact across all trips and modes across the whole of the EU.

Thirdly, the model shows that high congestion charges on road transport generate large social benefits, that nevertheless materialize mainly in the hands of those who impose the tolls, i.e. the State (on the assumption that all the revenues above the operating costs of the roads will be captured by the public sector). The State may then choose to use them in part to cover the construction costs of new transport infrastructure or to offset existing or future taxes, giving back the revenues to the users who have paid the charges. This result is consistent with the theory of efficient congestion charging, but opens up a major distributive and fiscal issue.

If congestion is relevant only for the efficiency of road users (it is a 'club' externality), any charge levied has to be given back to road users, either directly, which is impractical, or through more road investments. (In theory, road investment and congestion charges must balance out in the long run, since no 'externality' to third parties is involved.)

It should also be noted that since the model deals mainly with medium- to long-distance trips, differences in environment-related externalities are 'internalized' by the taxes (on fuel mainly) to a substantial extent. In any case, the environment-related costs are far larger in densely populated and urban areas than on medium- to long-distance routes. (The difference of environment-related costs between urban and non-urban areas is estimated to be tenfold.)[8]

Finally, there is the important result that changes in transport costs and infrastructure provision tend to favour the more centrally located regions. This is consistent with recent theoretical work in this area, but is contrary to the common attitude that better infrastructure links necessarily benefit peripheral regions. Of course, this finding could be misleading, if changes in accessibility are only a component of a package of measures to assist peripheral regions. Transport changes by themselves would not be sufficient to help peripheral regions; the real issue is the overall impact of a set of measures. These wider packages and a full analysis of economies of scale in different economic sectors were beyond the scope of this study, but it is clear that transport improvements internal to peripheral regions will be beneficial for their economies.

The main observation resulting from the thrust of the European policies (which can be summarized as more rail infrastructure, more road charges and free competition for the services) is that they generate a modal shift from road to rail and air transport. This in turn raises the total costs for freight, due mainly to the higher direct and indirect costs of the rail mode (especially total journey time[9] but also terminal costs and reliability) in comparison with the door-to-door service provided by trucks, and lowers the generalized costs for passengers, due to the high 'utility' of high speed trains and air transport, that more than compensate for their higher monetary costs. In fact, high-income medium- to long-distance travellers (as the future Europeans will be) have a high willingness to pay for fast modes. Air transport is a strong case: the expected decline of tariffs (still assumed to remain higher than in the

---

[8]   cf. European Commission (1995b) *Towards Fair and Efficient Pricing in Transport – Policy options for internalizing the external costs of transport in the European Union.*

[9]   The effect on time of modal shift is such that total time savings are negative in all the scenarios for freight. Nevertheless, further analysis is needed to determine the extent to which the loss of time impacts on the industries because in many industries the length of journey time is not as important as punctuality.

American or Asian context), connected with the income growth, will generate an extremely high demand pressure on this mode.

As already underlined, the major impacts will materialize in terms of modal split, and only in minor variations in total flows of freight and passengers, as compared with the base scenario. Therefore, the impacts on trade will mainly concern industries and the passengers more strictly linked with a specific transport mode.

This means that industries with a higher proportion of traffic moving by truck will be more affected by congestion charging, while industries that are more 'vocational' for rail transport (i.e. either dealing with basic, heavy commodities, or with fully containerized inputs/outputs) will take advantage from policy incentives for rail. A different phenomenon occurs for passenger transport: since the more favoured modes are high speed rail and air transport, the sectors that generate important flows with these modes will profit, i.e. the high-skill, service and export-oriented industries.

The model results, in terms of economic savings, are summarized in Table 6.1.

Table 6.1.   Ranking of overall benefits of each scenario compared with the 2005 base (annual savings against 2005 base – million 1991 ECU)

	Cost savings	Time savings	Total cost & time savings	Total savings[1]
Partial integration (PI)				
Passenger savings	-3,914	3,195	-719	2,854
Freight savings	4,569	-1,649	2,920	5,980
Operator revenue	1,434		1,434	1,434
Total	**2,089**	**1,546**	**3,635**	**10,268**
Full integration (FI)				
Passenger savings	44,280	23,377	67,657	77,708
Freight savings	-6,999	-10,259	-17,258	-1,367
Operator revenue	16,126		16,126	16,126
Total	**53,407**	**13,118**	**66,525**	**92,467**
Congestion charging (CC) (based on FI)				
Passenger savings	102	37,953	38,055	51,330
Freight savings	-12,302	-13,215	-25,517	-5,021
Operator revenue	73,012		73,012	73,012
Total	**60,812**	**24,738**	**85,550**	**119,321**
Rail service quality improvement (RQI) (based on CC)				
Passenger savings	439	39,903	40,342	53,262
Freight savings	-12,661	-12,229	-24,890	-3,412
Operator revenue	79,115		79,115	79,115
Total	**66,893**	**27,674**	**94,567**	**128,965**

Notes: See Table 5.7.
[1]   including other indirect costs

6.2. Critical points outside the level of detail of the models

The scenarios tested were chosen to highlight the broad differences between the main types of options. Implementing the scenarios would involve major practical and political issues. There are also some dimensions in the scenarios which the study was not supposed to take into account, for example the capital costs of projects and their financing. Nor have we in any scenario taken into account the shadow costs of public funds that reduce net public expenditure or raise public revenue. The order of magnitude of this shadow value is expected to be high, given the fact that the reduction of state debts is one of the main objectives of the Treaty on European Union.[10] For example, a reduction of needed state subsidies to railways and an increase of toll revenues can generate resources for new infrastructures, and/or reduce the general fiscal burden.

As mentioned above, modelling at a European level means that some of the local effects are blurred, and hence the overall impacts maybe somewhat under- or over-estimated. This may be particularly true for road congestion because:

(a)   congestion is linked mostly with local traffic, and medium- to long-distance movements are only a minor percentage of total traffic;

(b)   acute congestion phenomena tend to present themselves in a very discontinuous form, both in space and in time (weekends, peak holiday time, bad weather, etc.), while the model deals only with average situations and costs;

(c)   demand raises with congestion. Night hours will be used more, as will longer routes. But also empty return will be reduced, the average load of vehicles can increase, and the improvement of traffic management and information (RTI) is also helpful.

A special case of congestion concerns air transport. Air traffic control (ATC) constraints are the main problem as well as terminals and access to airports, while airstrips *per se* seem not to be a major bottleneck.

The air traffic increase forecast in all the scenarios is substantial, and as a consequence a capacity threshold has been assumed in all the scenarios – in the form of a limited growth in the base case. Nevertheless, one has to consider:

(a)   Options to increase ATC efficiency with limited costs, and Eurocontrol intense activity in this direction;

(b)   Options of increasing the average size of aircraft (from 150 to 300 seats), with some time loss in terminal congestion due to longer loading and unloading times;

(c)   the fact that investments in air terminals are quite flexible and profitable (so long as airstrips are not involved).

However, resolving some of these capacity issues obviously depends on a host of economic, financial and political decisions which the model cannot reflect. Also, the consequences of reduced pollution and road accidents will be important, but are not expressed in this study in any economic form. Here too, in theory, shadow values can be derived, based on indications contained in the recent Commission Green Paper *Towards Fair and Efficient Prices in Transport* (1995b).

---

[10]   Empirical simplified valuation made for the Italian context has derived value in the order of 1.4, which means that for every lira saved by the State in rail subsidy, there is a net benefit of LIT 0.4 (see Petretto, 1991).

6.3. Specific impacts on the transport industries

The CTP and the TEN will generate important effects on the transport industries more directly involved. Air transport will grow further, reinforcing its role on medium to long distances. The same can be expected for rail services. Nevertheless, this result is prone to uncertainty, given the problem of its capability, still unproved, of reversing the negative trends of the past. In fact, an issue concerning the 'relative speed' of railways in improving efficiency and market-orientation, compared with the pressures in cutting subsidies, which results in sharp tariff increases. This problem has been fully focused on in the recent Commission White Paper *A Strategy for Revitalizing the Community's Railways* (1996a).

The impact on road transport (both freight and passenger) is by definition negative (though on certain routes it would probably relieve congestion), a major goal of the CTP being to reduce the relative role of road transport. Nevertheless, long- to medium-distance road transport represents a very limited share of total road transport, and therefore the negative consequences on related services and industries (including vehicle manufacturers) will be negligible.

The impact on transport industries will have also implications for economies of scale and for the level of competition within the sector. Economies of scale are a normal feature of major transport infrastructure investments (i.e. investment costs per unit of traffic generally decrease with the traffic served). However, where economies of scale exist in services provision, they may in certain cases reduce market competition and result in monopoly. This provides strong arguments in favour of State intervention/regulation, as is the case for other natural monopolies. There are few doubts about the fact that road haulage, coach and, perhaps, air services present only limited economies of scale, and therefore variations in total demand may be assumed not to generate significant variations in unit production costs.

This assumption is less certain for rail services for a number of reasons: entrance barriers are strong due to investment and organization costs, and there are 'network' and frequency effects, i.e. the quality of the services depends on total demand; for example, a high level of demand on a line implies a more frequent service, even if there are no economies in the cost of providing a unit of service (this last aspect is true for every transport service but is particularly strong for railways because of the large number of persons or tonnes per train). On top of that, the presence of politically influential and subsidized State companies may make the entrance of new operators extremely difficult.

An increase in transport demand can be a very favourable opportunity for fostering the entrance of new operators in railway services, but a very strong and explicit political will is required to 'create' a market for new entrants. The scenario of rail quality improvement appears most likely to take place only in the face of pressure from real competition, of which few signals currently exist, or through strong financial incentives to improve operating practices.

Correspondingly, a (relative) reduction in road freight demand will not generate diseconomies of scale. The problem here is the opposite: if the overall charging on the road haulage industry increases, there is a real risk of 'overcompetition', given very low entrance barriers and of owner and worker (driver) coinciding in most cases. The effect can be that of avoiding any cost increase to the shipper via longer working hours, low-cost labour, insufficient amortization of assets, etc. There is accordingly a danger of increased pollution and accident costs. The extent to which this is a real risk will depend partly on the effectiveness with which qualitative regulations are enforced in the industry.

6.4.   Further policy implications derived from the study

A further point concerns discontinuities in transport performance. Transport networks are characterized by peak demands, and policy decisions have to consider whether capacity should be expanded or prices raised.

For example, creating extra capacity in the road system in order to reduce the frequency of local collapses in traffic has to be considered with great care. In economic terms, it is generally inefficient to expand capacity in order to meet peak demands. There can be a strong argument in favour of pricing off the excess peak demand.

This can also be true for air transport and railway systems. Some attempts to differentiate rail tariffs in order to optimize the use of assets are starting to take place in Europe by the adoption of Directive 91/440/EEC,[11] but the traditional concept of 'protecting' commuters from peak-tariffs remains strong, even if these commuters are no longer blue-collar workers (who often have to travel by car at a higher price). Also for airports, correct price signals, which could reduce peak demand and lower overall new infrastructure needs, would result from efficient slot allocation.

The general point is that decisions to increase capacity have to be considered in conjunction with pricing decisions. From this point of view, the congestion charging scenario, either by itself or in association with rail quality improvements, spreads demand more evenly on the available transport modes, thereby reducing the likelihood of discontinuities in transport performance. In general, widening the range of available transport modes reduces the costs related to unforeseeable crises in one mode (congestion, long strikes, physical interruptions, etc.).

---

[11]   See note 5 p. 33

APPENDIX A

Analysis of inefficiencies

A.1. Logistics excellence

A.1.1. Introduction/summary

Transport effectiveness must be considered as a key objective that companies have to pursue to be competitive. In order to fully appreciate the importance of transport, it is necessary to understand the changes in the business environment and the evolution in the logistics process, where transport still represents the main logistics cost. In fact, as transportation is part of a 'system', it has to be able to evolve as required by other parts of the process, and, at the same time, it can be the factor that promotes more general improvements.

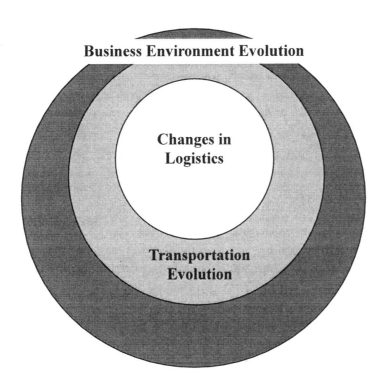

This analysis is based on the A.T. Kearney research on these subjects and particularly on the last run of the 'European Logistics – Quality & Productivity Survey' completed in 1994. The research shows, among several topics regarding the overall logistics process, how transportation proceeds in its trend of performance improvement.

As a summary of this document we can say that performance improved both in cost and service levels, and projections include further significant improvements.

(a)   Service level is vital in order to match market expectation of service improvement with regard to all service dimensions. Transportation is a key element for punctuality and lead time, while for other dimensions, such as invoice accuracy and order fill rate, its contribution is not the most significant.

(b)   Transportation cost remains the biggest part of logistics costs, but it continues to decrease despite the overall longer transportation distances. In fact, both source and distribution markets are becoming geographically wider.
There are several reasons for these improvements, for instance:

(i)   deregulation within the transportation industry;
(ii)   removal of barriers within the European Community;
(iii)   operational improvement within the shipping and carrier areas of responsibility;
(iv)   technical improvement of transportation vehicles and load utilization.

Even if transportation performance is expected to continue to improve, the trend will be weaker than in other logistics areas, like inventory and administration, as it is generally considered that transportation has already shown most of its improvement potential.

A.1.2. A view of the business environment to the year 2000

A company's ability to grow, compete and survive depends on different factors which have a high impact on the logistics process and can raise the standard against which goals and results are measured.

Escalating customer demand

Customers, who represent the main asset of a business, have become more exacting. High quality products and excellent service are required. Customers expect not only a basically flawless delivery, but also cost reduction or higher revenue. In order to be competitive in such a changing environment, companies will be forced to redesign their productivity. The supplier's mandate is therefore the following:

(a)   product design must be right and products have to perform as expected, the first time;
(b)   service must be appropriate and reliable in order to have the right product for the right customer at the right time for the right price.

Logistics issues pervade both areas, but especially the second one. Materials management and physical distribution practices affect product availability and delivery reliability.

Cycle time compression

Companies have reduced their development times, brought new products and services to the market months earlier, assumed major responsibility for production and service quality, enhanced the order integrity and have cut days and weeks from purchasing, production and distribution cycles. The lever for many of these gains remains information technology. This allows a company to adopt new approaches and to improve the use of traditional ones by identifying gaps, selecting options to obtain strategic service advantage and offering the required service.

Figure A.1.   Supplier performance: quality of service is expected to increase

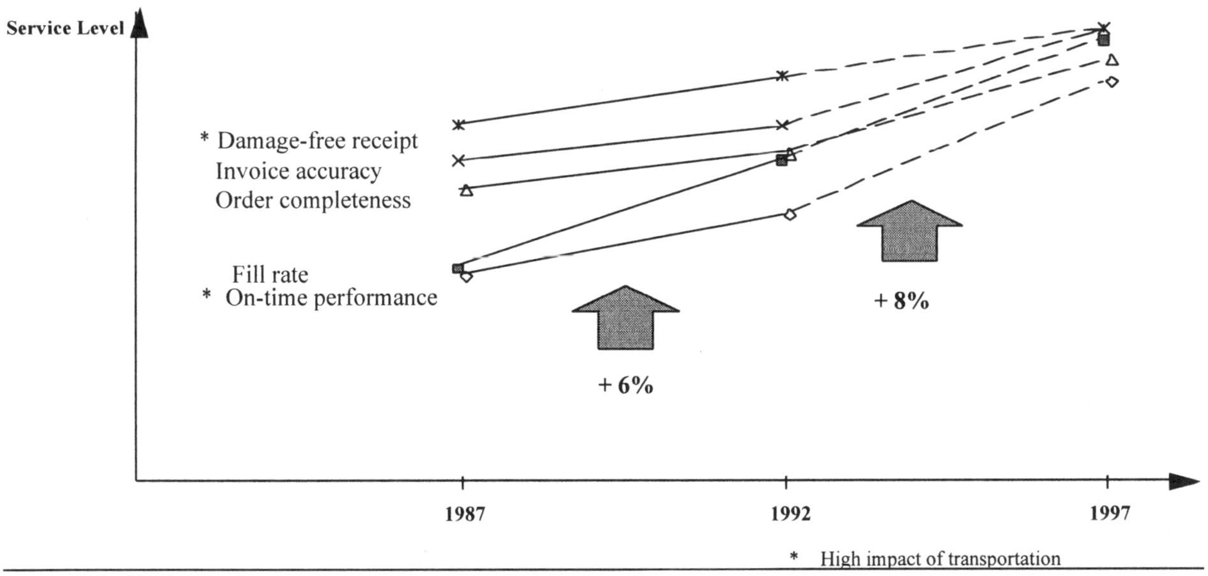

Service Level

* Damage-free receipt
  Invoice accuracy
  Order completeness

  Fill rate
* On-time performance

+ 6%

+ 8%

1987   1992   1997

* High impact of transportation

Sector: Distributive Trade.
Source: European Logistics – Quality & Productivity Survey.

Globalization of markets

One of the forces which is currently reshaping business and certainly has a significant impact on the logistics process is the globalization of markets. International trade offers new opportunities and challenges. Companies search for customers world-wide and, in order to be competitive, they need to understand the specific needs, requirements and customs of hundreds of regional markets.

Figure A.2.   Order cycle time reductions in Europe

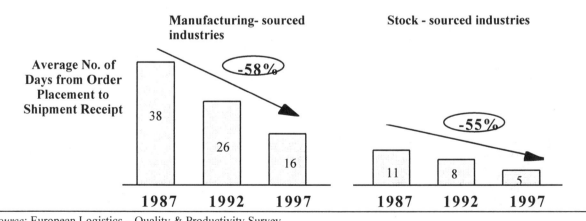

Manufacturing- sourced
industries

Stock - sourced industries

Average No. of
Days from Order
Placement to
Shipment Receipt

-58%

38

26

16

-55%

11

8

5

1987   1992   1997   1987   1992   1997

Source: European Logistics – Quality & Productivity Survey.

Figure A.3.   Reductions in cross-industry logistics cycle times in the United States

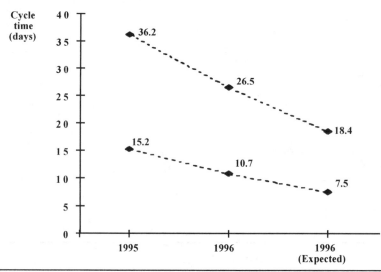

Source: A.T. Kearney research.

Globalization means targeting the best markets world-wide. Transportation, handling, inventory, damage, time, paperwork and formalities increase with distance. Companies look for less expensive sources of materials and components on an international level, and domestic markets are no longer safe. World-wide sourcing is evolving and supply chains are lengthening.

Figure A.4.   The market is becoming European

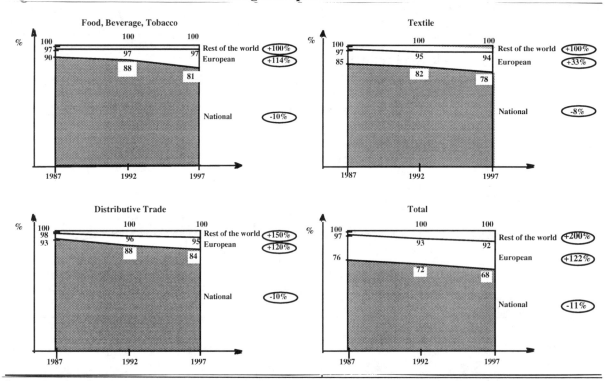

Source: European Logistics – Quality & Productivity Survey.

Figure A.5. Sourcing is becoming global

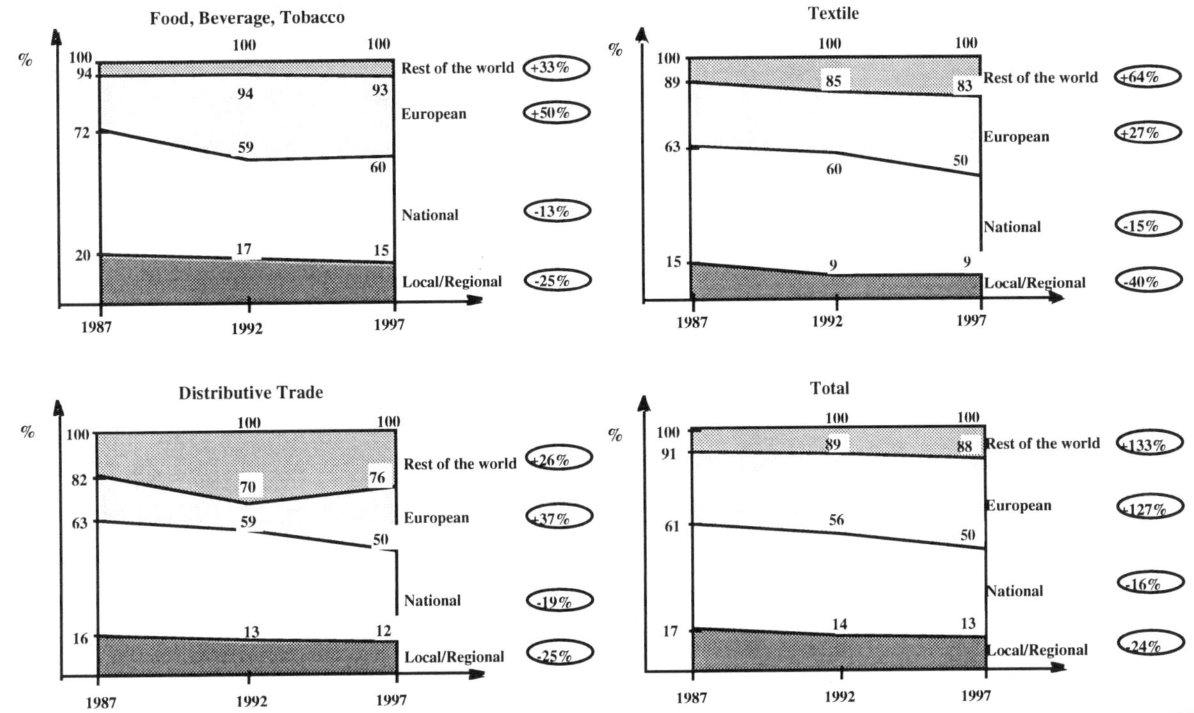

Food, Beverage, Tobacco

Rest of the world (+33%)
European (+50%)
National (-13%)
Local/Regional (-25%)

Textile

Rest of the world (+64%)
European (+27%)
National (-15%)
Local/Regional (-40%)

Distributive Trade

Rest of the world (+26%)
European (+37%)
National (-19%)
Local/Regional (-25%)

Total

Rest of the world (+133%)
European (+127%)
National (-16%)
Local/Regional (-24%)

Note: In Europe, globalization is intensified by rapid economic integration.
Source: European Logistics – Quality & Productivity Survey.

Despite this, Europe in the year 2000 will not be a single unified logistics market; companies must therefore remain sensitive to a country's specific needs in order to respond to different requirements and expectations. Success will heavily depend on how well the logistics process can cope with such complexity and link global operations together.

The first pay-off comes from sourcing and manufacturing, while downstream activities such as marketing and distribution will consolidate more slowly. For logistics the challenge is to manage the complexity of materials and information flows resulting from these mismatches.

In any case the restructuring of the network is proceeding on a significant scale. This process regards both manufacturing and distribution networks. The stage of development and the speed of evolution are different according to the different industries and different geographical areas.

Corporate restructuring

In the European market, many companies are expanding, acquiring or merging with other firms. The focus shifted to increasing shareholder value by bringing together businesses that are naturally partners. This is to achieve economies of scale and, above all, a long-term pay-off. Other companies are repositioning themselves, breaking chains of integration and divesting themselves of non-core businesses and activities

Figure A.6.   Instead of a 'single' logistics market, Europe will more likely consist of 6 to 15 different logistics markets

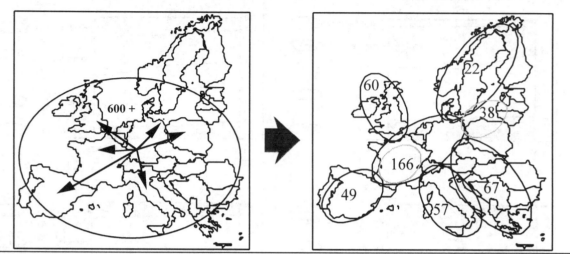

Note: Figures in millions of consumers.
Source: A.T. Kearney.

Figure A.7.   Different networking restructuring tasks depending on the 'status quo' situation

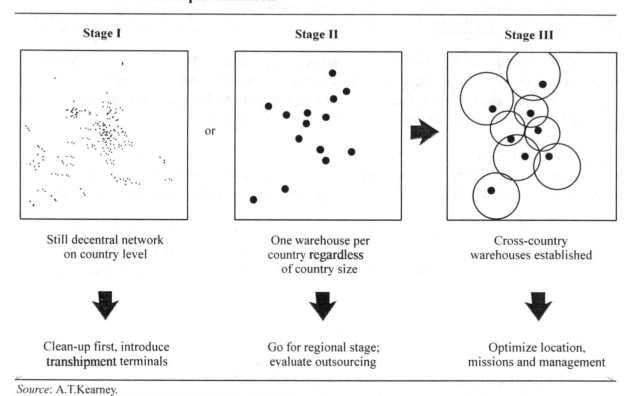

Source: A.T.Kearney.

Supply chain partnership

If globalization becomes the norm, only a few companies will be able to cover the entire logistics supply chain by themselves. To get the right product in the hands of the final consumer and provide an efficient service, many partners are required along the logistics flow.

Trends to reduce complexity mean selecting and working closely with suppliers, creating partnerships between shippers and carriers, promoting common research activities and developing new thinking.

Figure A.8.   Organizational difficulties across borders[1] – Industry data

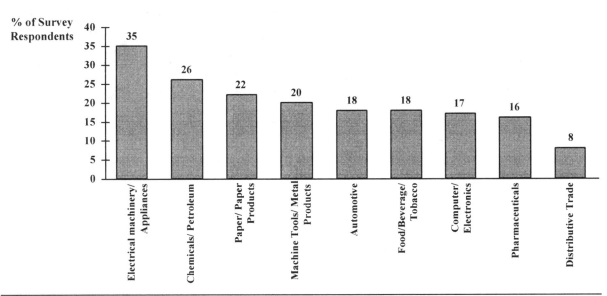

[1] Frequency of difficulties can be considered high depending on intensity of interactions.
Source: European Logistics – Quality & Productivity Survey.

Figure A.9.   Organizational difficulties[1] across borders – Country data

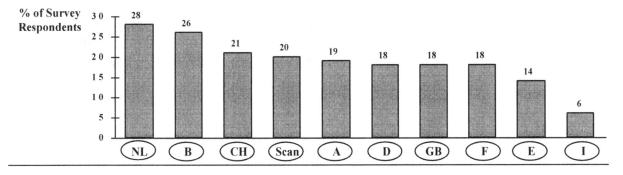

[1] Frequency of difficulties can be considered high depending on intensity of interactions.
Source: European Logistics – Quality & Productivity Survey.

Productivity pressure

Economic integration gives European companies a major opportunity to improve productivity, but in a global market providing high-level service to customers, it is not sufficient to gain or sustain a competitive advantage. To be a major player, a company must be at least as productive as any other in its industry.

Figure A.10. Logistics cost as a percentage of revenue

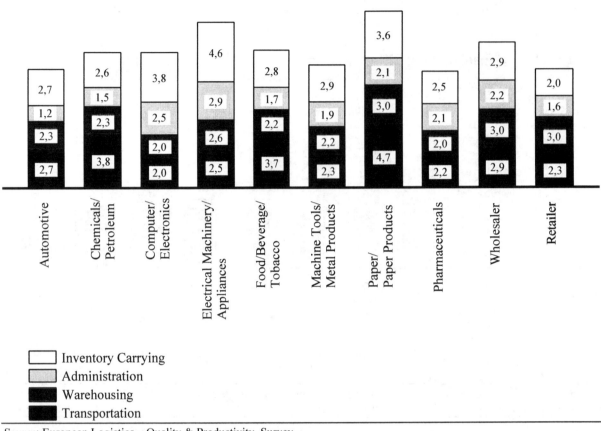

Source: European Logistics – Quality & Productivity Survey.

Environmental awareness

In order to limit the impact on the environment, governments have adapted regulations and many of them affect logistics. Refuse must be recycled or eliminated, and all decisions regarding packaging design, materials, transportation and manufacturing locations have to be considered from an ecological point of view.

A.1.3. The response: logistics excellence

Changes imply a strong evolution in the way companies design and manage their logistics. The new approach has three main components:

(a)   establishing strong connections with customers, suppliers and service providers through strategies that meet customer requirements, synchronizing product and information flows;
(b)   satisfying customer needs, providing a defect-free service by integrating planning and procedures internally across functional areas and locations;
(c)   providing effective management capabilities and achieving a continuous quality improvement process.

Within this framework, we will explore how European companies are preparing themselves to meet the challenge in the improvement of their logistics efficiency in order to achieve logistics excellence.

Where European companies are today

Not many European companies are ready to understand customer service requirements and support a strategy to meet them using a total supply quality approach. The main shortfalls which have been pointed out are:

(a)   insufficient connection between customers and suppliers;
(b)   lack of integration operations and internal planning;
(c)   insufficient externally orientated information system;
(d)   poor implementation of quality improvement initiatives.

Weak links between customers and suppliers

Having strong links between suppliers and customers is a necessary condition to gain the leadership in excellence. This means effectively communicating in order to clearly identify customer requirements and achieve customer satisfaction. Through the survey it was found that only 6% of the companies have leadership characteristics when dealing with customers and just 21% with suppliers.

Limited integration for internal planning

At many companies, the chief executive officer or chief operating officer is responsible for the integration of all elements of the process in order to keep a continuous link between the different functions of the company. Real integration is measured on how well the organizational units, which report to the executives, develop plans that link with, support and complement one another. Among the national organizations in various countries, multinational companies face the additional problem of limited integration. For many firms, integrated internal planning is a strength to build on; for most of them it is an opportunity for improving performance.

Lack of externally orientated information system

Even if a company recognizes the need for closer relationships between suppliers and customers, deficiency in information capabilities may limit success. Systems that link suppliers with customers are still in their early stage and information technology (IT) is often under-utilized as a support to logistics integration. Information technology is used mostly to support order processing; however, about two-thirds of the companies interviewed utilize IT to support purchasing. It is fundamental to underline that the lack of good basic purchasing activities is a concrete barrier to logistics excellence.

Also, on a basic level, there are more advanced applications such as computer-to-computer ordering, electronic ordering systems and electronic point of sales systems. Thanks to this technology, suppliers will no longer predict customer demand based on past orders. It will be possible to get current sales/usage data and use them to plan replenishment shipments.

In the USA, some retailers have given suppliers full responsibility for reordering and inventory management, and a similar trend is also developing in Europe within the ECR (efficient consumer response) philosophy. Integration across the logistics process comes from a commitment to close co-operation and partnerships.

Overlooking the importance of IT can limit the degree of integration and the benefits that companies could achieve.

Poor implementation of quality improvement initiatives

Total supply quality evolves around a series of incremental and/or fundamental changes. In order to achieve total supply quality, companies that have formal processes for driving change and securing improvements are certainly better positioned. Having a formal quality improvement initiative is not enough. Shortfalls in implementing programmes must be avoided. To achieve total supply quality, it is necessary to reach excellence across the eight dimensions of the logistics process.

Figure A.11.   The eight dimensions of logistics excellence

First, it is necessary to determine where a company falls within each dimension and what it should do to strengthen its position; then, action tailored to individual capabilities must be taken in order to obtain a competitive advantage.

Measuring excellence in logistics

To assess the company's status against the eight dimensions, A.T. Kearney has developed a framework called the 'stages of excellence'. This study also helps to point out the way to correct action.

Table A.1.   Characteristics of the stages of logistics excellence

	Stage I	Stage II	Stage III
Customer orientation	• Handle each transaction as a separate situation • Keep 'noise level' down	• All customers are treated the same • Attain internally set goals	• Provide differentiated service • Meet/exceed customer requirements
Integrated long-range planning	• Not formally carried out • Fragmented planning	• Narrow scope (e.g. distribution) • 1- to 3-year horizon	• Full logistics scope, all departments • 3- to 5-year horizon
Supplier partnerships	• Crisis-driven • Unmanaged • Adversarial	• Cost-driven • Multiple sources • Competitive bid orientated	• Result -driven • Partnership • Joint improvement
Cross-functional operations	• Today • Transaction based	• Periodic (e.g. monthly) • Budget-period based	• Rolling periods • Integrate all functions
Continuous improvement process	• Quick-fix 'stop the bleeding'	• Formal process • Cost reduction • Average quality	• CEO commitment • Continuous improvement toward goals • Quality and productivity
Employee empowerment	• Employees versus management	• Limited employee involvement	• Training • Empowerment • Shared goals/rewards
Integrated IT systems	• Process transaction • Little or no data • No analysis capabilities	• Report period's financial results • Fragmented data • Limited analysis capabilities	• Support planning with operational data • Easy-to-use shared data • Flexible analysis capabilities
Measurement, comparison and action	• Cost versus last year • Cost as percent of sales • Service 'noise level'	• Cost versus budget • Productivity versus past levels • Service versus competition	• Cost versus standard • Productivity versus goal • Service versus customer requirement

Source: A.T. Kearney.

The basic approaches used to manage a company define the stages through which companies and functions within companies evolve. If until then, they are not stimulated by a compelling need to change these tend to rest within a stage.

When these needs arise (trigger point), a fast change can be made. Trigger points such as a merger or an acquisition are a significant challenge to a company's usual conduct of business. It is advisable to put traditional rules and assumptions aside, because the risk in not changing may outweigh the risk of changing.

In stage I the emphasis is on informally running today's business; this approach can be successful mainly for a small company, in which the entrepreneur can keep control of the business and make it successful.

Figure A.12. Evolution across stages of excellence

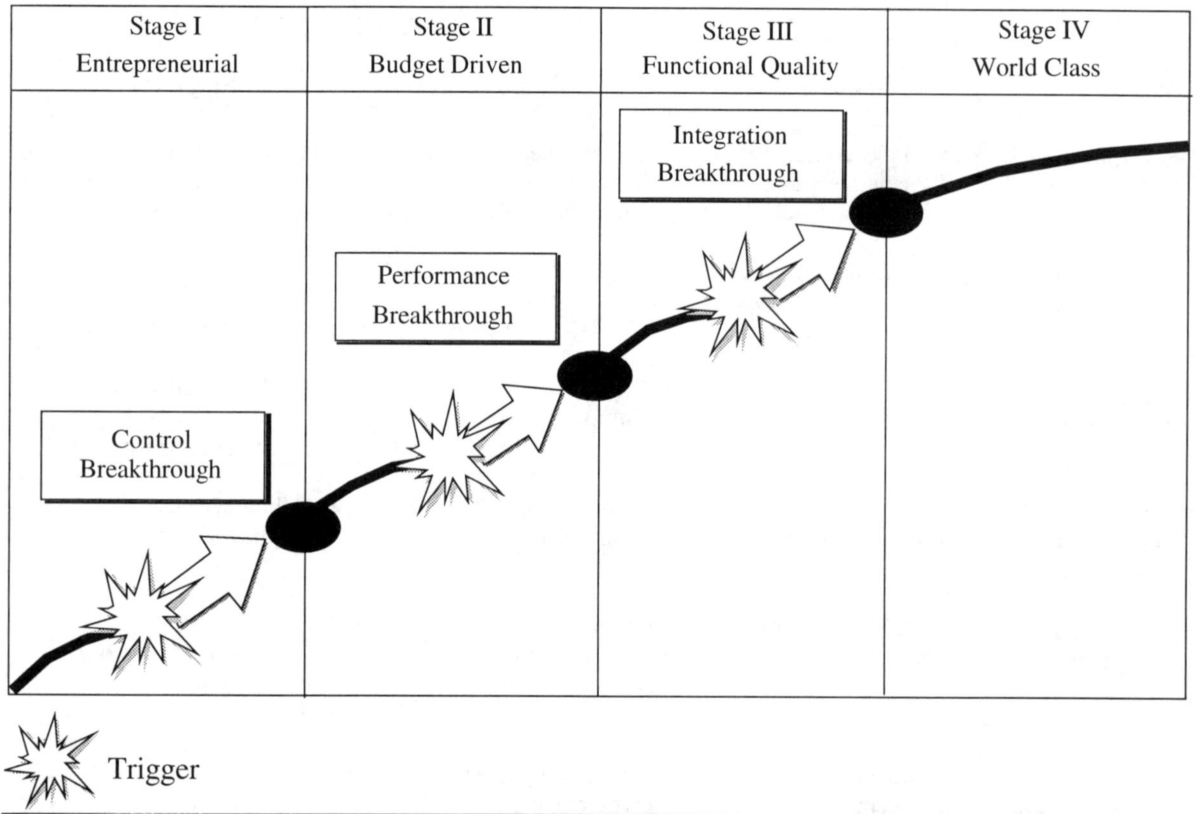

Stage I Entrepreneurial	Stage II Budget Driven	Stage III Functional Quality	Stage IV World Class

Integration
Breakthrough

Performance
Breakthrough

Control
Breakthrough

Trigger

Source: A.T. Kearney.

When a company grows, this approach is no longer feasible. Operations are too difficult to be managed and controlled by one individual, long-range planning for the process is required and the need for information increases.

Further success depends on the product of a company challenging tradition and taking risks. It is this breakthrough which determines a movement into stage II.

In stage II, the emphasis is on long-range planning, on measurement and control. Stage II firms tend to limit employee freedom, responsibilities and decision-making. In fact, these companies supervise employees closely in an effort to control costs. While control is important, too much control leads to bureaucracy. When this happens, improvement efforts are stifled and a breakthrough is needed.

In stage III, the different parts of the logistics process are functionally excellent, and companies apply non-financial performance measures to drive management decisions. Logistics process management establishes service goals to meet or exceed customer requirements. Generally, in this stage companies strive to attain functional excellence throughout each area of the business.

Often, departments and functions are at different stages. Only after all key areas of the business have reached stage III is it possible to make the breakthrough to stage IV which requires a different approach to managing the company.

In order to pursue excellence, companies must manage key business processes. This requires a different degree of integration within each area as well as integration across functions.

For each dimension based on analysis of responses to several key questions, A.T. Kearney survey respondents were classified into one of the three stages. Compared to a similar study made in the USA in 1992, a nearly equal number of respondents are in stage I on both continents. Only 4% of companies surveyed in Europe are in stage III, and 10% in the USA. US firms have stronger external links between customers and suppliers and manage a lower level of internal/international complexity compared to European firms.

The percentage of leading stage III companies in Europe varies widely across the eight dimensions of logistics excellence.

Figure A.13. Leaders in logistics excellence: Europe vs USA

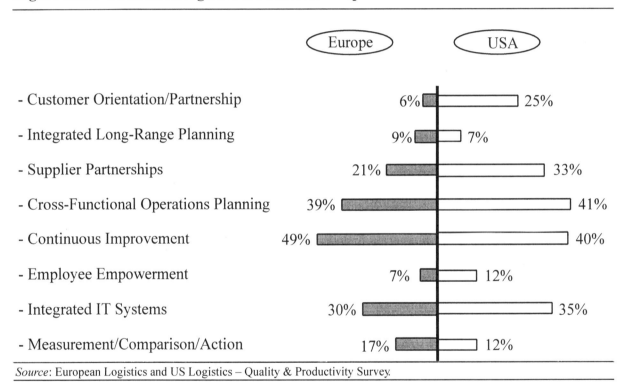

Source: European Logistics and US Logistics – Quality & Productivity Survey.

For certain dimensions, significant differences arose. Of Belgian, French and Dutch companies 11% use leadership approaches for customer orientation. However, only 2% of the Italian companies are in stage III. Where information capabilities are concerned, the leading companies are in France, Sweden and the UK. German companies lag behind because of their failure to use information technology in their relationship with customers and suppliers. By contrast, several German firms have a well integrated long-range planning process.

Is becoming a leader worth the effort?

In considering service performance, cost levels and cycle time reduction, the answers of the leading companies in Europe were compared to those of the others firms surveyed. The conclusion of this comparison was that companies that excel in all eight dimensions of logistics quality obtain better results than others.

Figure A.14. Logistics excellence of European companies: respondents by stage of logistics excellence for each of the eight dimensions

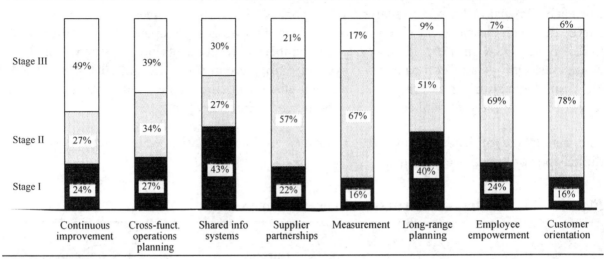

Source: European Logistics – Quality & Productivity Survey.

Service performance

Service performance and goals of leading companies were confirmed by the survey results on the following service dimension:

(a)   on-time delivery,
(b)   order completeness,
(c)   invoice accuracy,
(d)   damage-free delivery.

Firms that are within stage II achieve results that are 18% better and plan to enlarge their service level. In 1997 these companies will have logistics processes that will provide service reliability 44% better than that of their competitors.

Cost levels

By comparing cost levels of stage III companies with the survey average, it appeared that leading companies have cost levels that are 36% lower than those of the average company. Furthermore, stage III companies have inventory carrying costs which are much lower compared to the overall levels reported.

Cycle time reduction

Referring to this dimension, stage III companies obtain an average 40% reduction versus a survey average of 35%. These firms plan, for the ten-year period 1987-97, a 67% reduction versus 57% on average.

By-products of logistics excellence are better service, faster service cycle and lower costs. However, the real benefit is that companies which have reached stage III are able to provide total supply quality. Only at this point is it possible for a company to obtain total customer satisfaction.

Figure A.15. Leading companies have 36% lower logistics costs

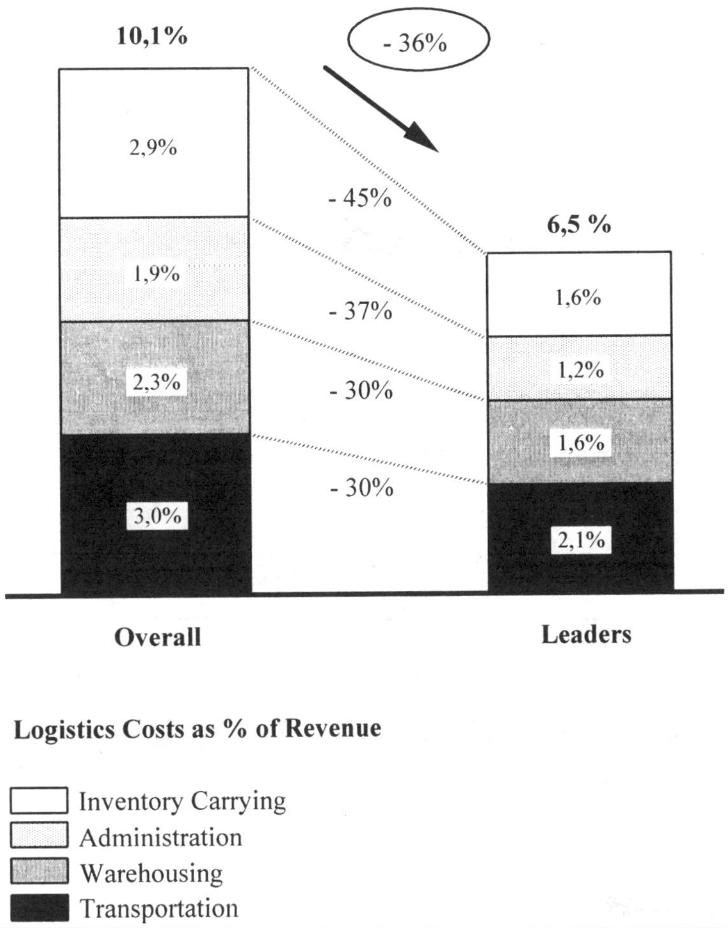

Logistics Costs as % of Revenue

☐ Inventory Carrying
▨ Administration
▨ Warehousing
■ Transportation

Source: European Logistics – Quality & Productivity Survey.

A.1.4. Transportation effectiveness

Companies wanting to expand their quality and productivity improvement process must consider transport as a key element. Companies using external transportation services have, to some extent, a less direct influence on transportation productivity than firms operating their own vehicles. In any case, the users of outside transportation must affect the productivity of the service. Companies engaged in partnerships with carriers measure their business not only on rates, but also on service quality, which plays a fundamental role in customer satisfaction. The majority of firms interviewed require speed, consistency and delivery on schedule.

Transport represents the main element of logistics costs. In the past, transport has contributed significantly to increasing productivity (despite the increased distance of the sourcing and sales markets) and will also do so in the future.

The further reduction in transportation cost is justified on the basis of a highly segmented list of actions in place in most of the companies interviewed. From these actions, service improvements are expected as well.

The increasing transport productivity must be understood through specific changes in liberalization and in the removal of barriers within the single market.

Figure A.16. Supplier interface

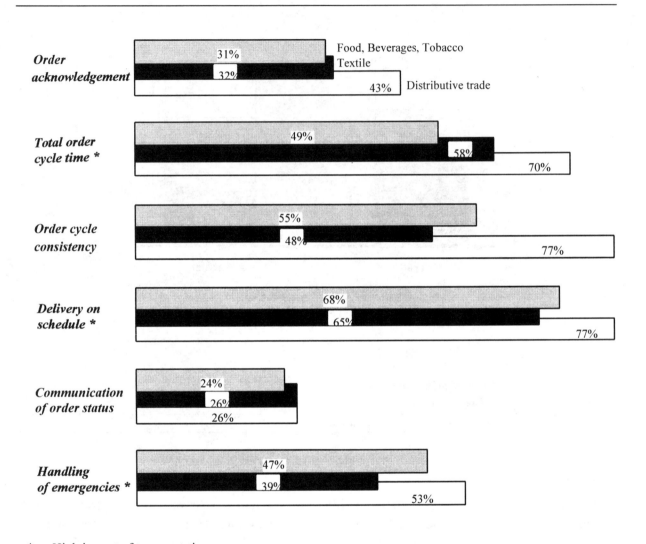

* = High impact of transportation

Note: Percentages represent the interviewed companies which consider that item as a driving factor to evaluate the service offered.

Source: European Logistics – Quality & Productivity Survey.

The changing European marketplace

Two driving forces are changing the market for services, in particular transportation, in a fundamental way.

Firstly, the deregulation of road, air and rail transportation is rapidly changing the marketplace and causing considerable competitive pressure among service providers. It is opening up and liberalizing closed national markets, harmonizing technical standards and social regulations, and eliminating border and customs formalities. Also, in 1994 the largest market in Europe, Germany, abolished its compulsory minimum road transport prices. The last ten years in the USA have made it obvious that the effects of deregulation can be dramatic. Since 1987, half of the top 100 US service providers have disappeared, while on-time deliveries have improved from 80 to 95% and costs of inventories were reduced by US $ 35 billion. These productivity improvements will probably change due to other cost components, such as pollution or congestion.

Secondly, as price levels come down, operating costs for transport companies will increase as a result of road pricing, taxation and environmental costs. Europe, with a population density six times that of the USA, will soon be faced with almost unmanageable road congestion. Driven by European market integration, economic growth and the continuining specialization of industrial processes, transported volumes are expected to double by the year 2010. In the industrial core of Europe (Germany, France, the Benelux, the Alpine countries, northern Italy, and southeast England), governments are planning to use a mixture of policy measures, including structure regulations, road pricing, taxation and the stimulation of other transport modes, such as rail. Environmental costs will shift from the taxpayer to the user, being increasingly internalized into the operating cost, e.g. in the form of excise duty on oil.

Figure A.17. Logistics costs reduction (European average)

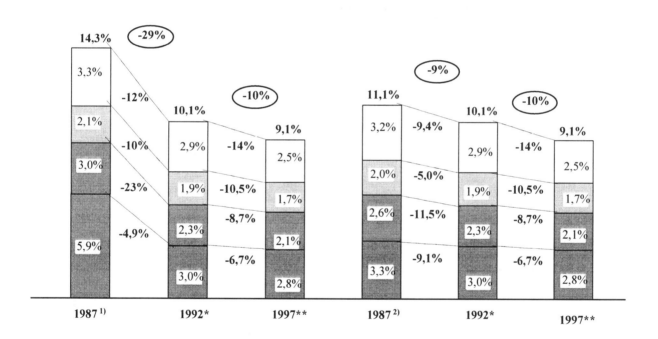

Logistics costs and % of revenues

☐ Inventory carrying
▨ Administration
▨ Warehousing
▨ Transportation

1)   1987 actual values obtained from the European Logistics Survey 1988.
2)   1987 estimated values obtained from the European Logistics Survey 1993.
*   1992 actual values obtained from the European Logistics Survey 1993.
**   1997 forecast values obtained from the European Logistics Survey 1993.
Note: Differences in 1987 data can depend on:
-       different samples in terms of countries, industries, companies;
-       different perceptions of what the real improvement was.

Table A.2.   Transportation – Strategy

Improvement actions	Strategy in progress (%)[1]	Extent of improvement[2]	
		Productivity	Quality
A. Increase leverage in negotiations by reducing number of carriers	70	66	62
B. Capitalize on volume discounts, backhaul rates and other discounts	63	62	46
C. Develop long-term contracts with carriers	61	62	62
D. Establish cost-plus based rates with carriers (open-book)	27	50	41
E. Develop customized price structures	44	67	43
F. Integrate long-distance trucking with deliveries at transit terminals	34	73	54
G. Establish transportation service standards for own fleet and carriers	36	55	65
H. Use more cost-/time-effective transportation mode mix	35	54	47
I. Increase use of non-national carriers	29	36	27
J. Establish electronic data linkages with carriers for capacity planning/workload scheduling	35	68	62
K. Establish formal partnership relations with selected carriers to achieve improved customer service and productivity	62	73	79
L. Develop a transportation-flow database and analysis model	31	62	53
M. Outsource fleet operations to a third-party contractor	40	67	51
N. Outsource transportation management to a third-party contractor	27	53	45

Notes: [1]Percentage of respondents having implemented the strategy in their firms.
        [2]Percentage of respondents evaluating the strategy in terms of productivity/quality.
Source: European Logistics – Quality & Productivity Survey.

Table A.3.   Transportation – Operations

Improvement actions	Operations in progress (%)[1]	Extent of improvement[2]	
		Productivity	Quality
A Consolidate or pool outbound shipments to customers	67	80	58
B. Capitalize on volume discounts, backhaul rates and other discounts	40	60	44
C. Develop long-term contracts with carriers	40	60	39
D. Develop customized price structures	45	69	46
E. Unitize to reduce individual piece handling	51	73	63
F. Pre-schedule deliveries into specific market area with scheduled dispatch dates	58	72	59
G. Use incentive programmes to encourage higher service/productivity	18	37	38
H. Use specialized equipment which complements the type and size of load to be transported	48	63	69
I. Concentrate deliveries into specific market area on selected days to reduce inter-stop distance	37	67	50
J. Reduce drivers' time 'at depot' to maximize time spent en route and delivering	41	60	44
K. Review routes regularly to minimize distance travelled	36	66	45
L. Improve equipment procurement and retirement methods	21	45	45
M. Apply standard times to plan routes better	20	53	42
N. Measure service performance	46	57	66
O. Improve maintenance effectiveness	12	44	46
P. Use computer-based vehicle routing and scheduling	23	61	47

Notes: [1]Percentage of respondents having implemented these operations in their firms.
        [2]Percentage of respondents evaluating the operations in terms of productivity/quality.
Source: European Logistics – Quality & Productivity Survey.

**Figure A.18. Respondents reporting expectation of productivity improvements over
10%**

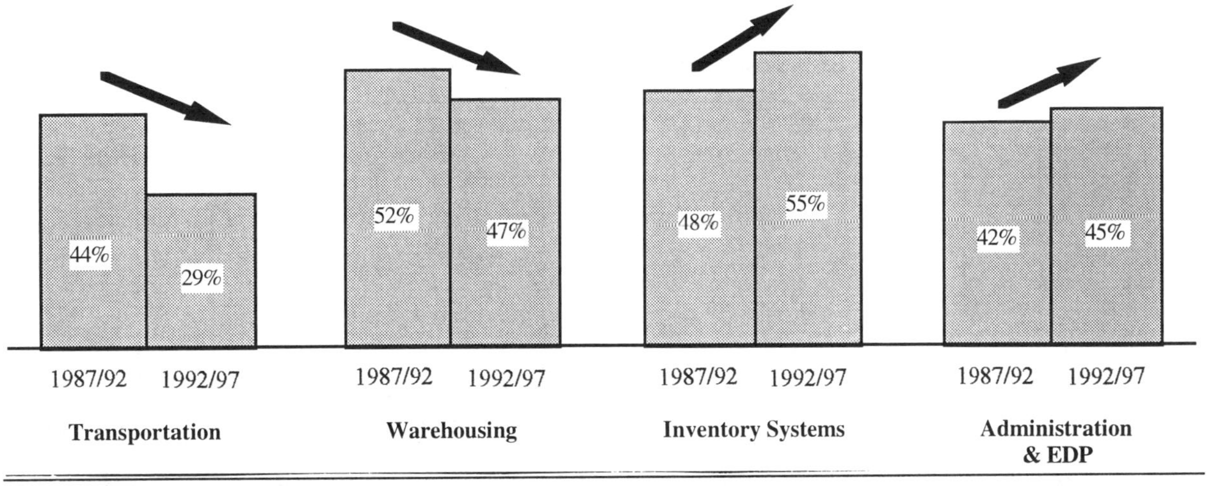

1987/92	1992/97	1987/92	1992/97	1987/92	1992/97	1987/92	1992/97
44%	29%	52%	47%	48%	55%	42%	45%
Transportation		**Warehousing**		**Inventory Systems**		**Administration & EDP**	

Source: European Logistics – Quality & Productivity Survey.

Integration is the road to success

In the past, productivity and quality improvements in transportation and warehousing have
been achieved by traditional, internally orientated actions. These typically include:

(a)   using specialized equipment that complements the loads to be transported,
(b)   co-ordinating and optimizing backhaul and roundtrip scheduling,
(c)   regularly reviewing routes and drops to minimize distance travelled,
(d)   using computerized warehouse operations,
(e)   training personnel in handing methods,
(f)   incorporating engineering analysis of warehousing methods.

These actions are no longer enough to gain improvement in other areas such as inventory
management and systems. Under various names – quick response, efficient consumer response
or supply chain integration – shippers in Europe are increasing their focus on total product
cycle time as the key driving force of logistics quality and productivity.

In order to obtain tangible results, these efforts must include computer assisted ordering,
continuous replenishment systems, automated accounts payable systems, electronic store
receiving system, item price and promotion databases and integrated purchase order
management systems, along with redesigned distribution systems to enable rapid continuous
movement of products.

Specific action required

Similar to the US transport sector in the 1980s, the logistics industry in Europe will go through
a period of deep restructuring in the late 1990s. A dual market will develop; on one side, there
will be a small group of leading providers closely integrated with their customers, while on the
other side, there will be a large group of subcontracted road transport, terminal and
warehousing companies, and air, sea and rail operators. The consequence will be a wave of
consolidations, divestments and new entrances.

In order to be a leading provider, the operator needs to be closely linked with the customer's supply chain and the financial power to make substantial investments in information technology systems, hubs and networks. The trend is to integrate transport in wider logistics services.

Figure A.19. Comparison of European contract logistics markets

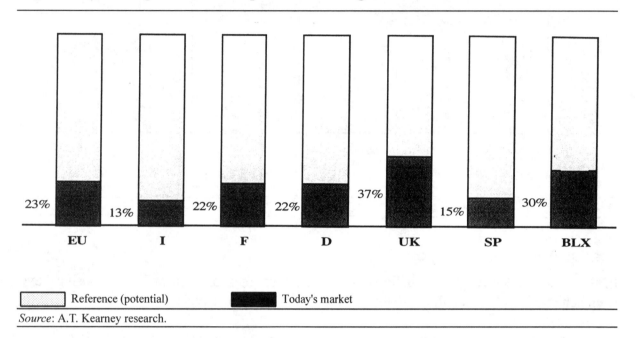

| | Reference (potential) | ■ Today's market |

Source: A.T. Kearney research.

Table A.4.   Logistics operator productivity improvement

Improvement areas	Productivity (%)	
	Actual 1987–92	**Planned 1992–97**
Transportation	14	10
Warehousing and materials handling	13	11
Value added services	13	14
Overall	14	13

Source: European Logistics – Quality & Productivity Survey 1993.

European service providers' performance

Service providers have been pushed by market conditions to make improvements in quality and productivity.

As shown in Table A.4, logistics service companies have succeeded in increasing their productivity from 1987 to 1992 and plan to do so again. However, the productivity improvement focus is shifting towards the area of value added service.

Figure A.20. Evolution in the outsourcing of logistics services

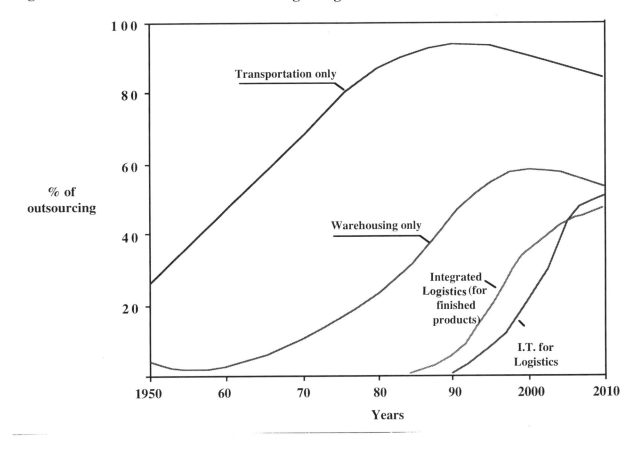

Source: A.T. Kearney estimate.

The expectations of decreasing costs and service performance improvement are due to clearly identified or ongoing actions. It is possible to group these actions according to operations and strategies:

(a)   high achieved professional level in transportation management;
(b)   increased number of long-term partnerships between shippers and carriers (this also means concentration of the business with fewer but larger and more international suppliers).

Table A.5.   Close ties with carriers

Actions linking shippers with carriers (% of respondents)	
Reduce number of regular carriers	70
Establish formal partnerships with carriers	62
Negotiate long-term contracts with carriers	61

Source: European Logistics – Quality & Productivity Survey 1993.

The supplier-customer partnerships offer the greatest promise for the future in the form of close ties with carriers. The majority of the firms will form partnership with their suppliers and customers. In the future, operators will have a more international scope and a larger size.

Figure A.21. Logistics service demand tends to be more selective

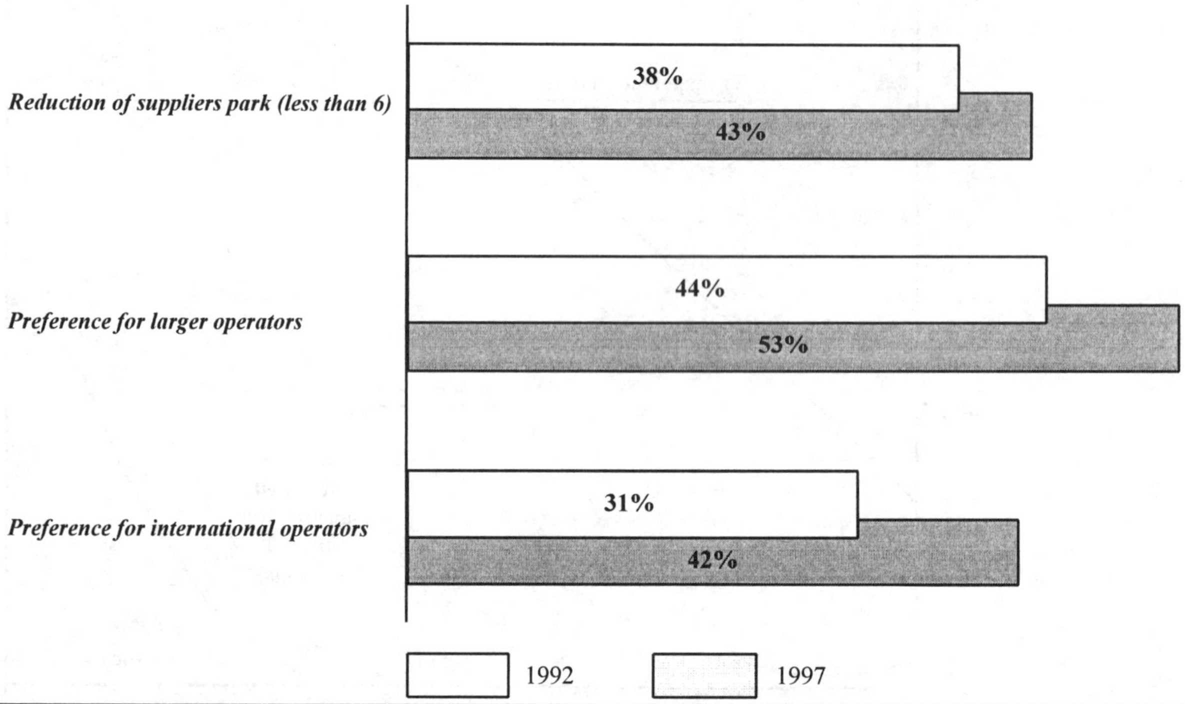

Reduction of suppliers park (less than 6) — 38% (1992), 43% (1997)

Preference for larger operators — 44% (1992), 53% (1997)

Preference for international operators — 31% (1992), 42% (1997)

1992   1997

Source: European Logistics – Quality & Productivity Survey.

A.2. Operational analysis: opinion leaders survey

A.2.1. Objectives

To quantitatively rank the preliminary set of sources of inefficiency identified by the European Commission (DG XV) at the beginning of the project (and identify possible additional items).

To identify the major relationship among the stated sources of inefficiency, productivity and adequacy of transportation infrastructures, structure and/or productivity of carriers, logistics and/or other factors of shippers, logistics and/or other factors of the channel/sector.

To understand major relative differences between European regions, shippers and carriers.

A.2.2. Methodology

The methodology is based on a segmented questionnaire form tested in pilot interviews. The questionnaire was designed to measure the perception of the impact of the identified set of inefficiencies. The companies contacted are very active in terms of international trade and are corporations or subsidiaries of multinational groups. The persons contacted are employed at a high level of responsibility and can be considered opinion leaders; the majority of them are personally known to the A.T. Kearney consultants involved in the present assignment.

Findings are mainly based on the interpretation of data from the survey. Data are provided in the following sections, and, of course, in some cases there may be several interpretations. The statistical meaning, in absolute terms, cannot be guaranteed in view of the size of the sample. Nevertheless, most of the answers received are basically consistent with our expectations, based on our knowledge of the market. When answers were unexpected, telephone checks were made in order to ask for explanations on specific elements, and this has influenced the interpretation.

A.2.3. Major findings

It is interesting to note that all the inefficiency sources considered are perceived to have a similar impact on the functioning of the single market. Similar considerations regard the relationship with productivity and adequacy of transportation infrastructures, structure and productivity of carriers, logistics and/or other factors of shippers, logistics and/or other factors of the channel/sector.

The highest single impact is perceived to be the capacity constraints with regard to productivity and the adequacy of the transportation infrastructure. This might have been emphasized by the high expectations of new investments in transport infrastructure.

The lowest single impact is perceived to be limited accessibility with regard to the logistics and/or other factors of the channel/sector. This may be considered an indicator of the low perception of barriers within the single market.

Shippers and carriers segmentation

Shippers confirm the high impact of capacity constraints with regard to the productivity of the transportation infrastructure and the low weight of barriers on their international trade. They also seem to perceive that relationships between operators and the transportation infrastructure are not yet efficient. Shippers also see a lack of clarity in the pricing policy of carriers and complain that there are a lack of efficient structures.

Carriers consider shippers a constraint to their efficiency improvement. They seem to judge the market sufficiently accessible and transparent, especially in terms of their industry supply and productivity. Another constraint for the carriers' productivity increase is the high fragmentation of supply and demand: suppliers are very fragmented in terms of company structure, especially with regard to certain regions and service supply segments. Different manufacturers have different needs in terms of transportation, warehousing operations, handling equipment, etc. This limits their operating capacity significantly. Trade barriers do not represent a relevant problem for carriers within their industry.

By comparing the opinions of carriers and shippers, it would appear that they do not know each other well enough. In fact, the evaluations of structure and productivity of carriers and logistics or other factors about shippers are significantly differently percieved by the two parties. There is a lack of communication between them.

Geographical segmentation of shippers

In general, sources of inefficiency are perceived to have a higher impact in the south (and in the east) than in the centre and north. The infrastructural problems are perceived to be greater in the south and in the east than in the centre and north. Furthermore, it must be considered that in the south companies are smaller and less organized than in the north. One direct consequence is the disadvantage in terms of economies of scale (DY).

In the north and in the centre of Europe, companies consider the market easily accessible. Unexpected are the high figures related to the unproductive use of assets in the centre; the operators in these regions are probably stricter in their judgements than their colleagues in the south.

The leading problem of the east is that the market is not yet well interconnected with that in the west. The operators are not yet European, the majority of the products are not competitive in terms of quality, image, design, and there is a consistent lack of technological innovation as well as of skilled workers and qualified employees. There is a high perception of monopoly protection, in particular, limiting the carriers' activity and productivity. The pricing policy is not considered as a problem relevant for the intra-European trade increase.

A.2.4. European statistics

All Europe

It is interesting to note that all the inefficiency sources considered are perceived to have a similar impact on the functioning of the single market (column Z range 3,2 – 3,6). Similar considerations regard the relationship with productivity and adequacy of transportation infrastructures, structure and productivity of carriers, logistics and/or other factors of shippers, logistics and/or other factors of the channel/sector (row I range 3,3 – 3,6).

The highest single impact is perceived to be the capacity constraints with regard to the productivity and the adequacy of transportation infrastructures. This may explain the high expectation of new investments in infrastructure (AS).

The lowest single impact is perceived to be the limited accessibility with regard to the logistics and/or other factors of the channel/sector (FY). This may be considered an indicator of the low perception of barriers within the single market.

		S	T	X	Y	Z
		All Europe			**Population 63**	
		Productivity and adequacy of transportation infrastructures	Structure and/or productivity of carriers	Logistics and/or other factors of shippers	Logistics and/other factors of the channel/sector	
A	Capacity constraint	4.0	3.6	3.2	3.4	3.5
B	Unproductive use of assets	3.7	3.8	3.6	3.3	3.6
C	Lack of interoperability and interconnection	3.4	3.6	3.4	3.4	3.5
D	Market fragmentation	3.4	3.6	3.5	2.8	3.5
E	Monopoly protection	3.4	3.6	3.1	2.8	3.4
F	Limited accessibility	3.4	3.3	3.0	2.5	3.2
G	Low quality of international services	3.3	3.5	3.5	2.8	3.4
H	Pricing policy	3.5	3.8	3.3	3.0	3.5
I		3.5	3.6	3.4	3.3	

Shippers

In the table below it is also possible to observe that all the inefficiency sources are perceived to have a similar impact on the functioning of the single market (column Z, row I range 3,2 – 3,7).

Shippers confirm the high impact of capacity constraints with regard to the productivity of transportation infrastructures (AS) and the low weight of barriers on their international trade (FY). They also seem to perceive that relationships between operators and the transportation infrastructure are not yet efficient (BT–BH).

Shippers also see a lack of clarity in the pricing policy of carriers and complain that there is a lack of efficient structures (HS-HT).

		S	T	X	Y	Z
		Shippers			Population 49	
		Productivity and adequacy of transportation infrastructures	Structure and/or productivity of carriers	Logistics and/or other factors of shippers	Logistics and/other factors of the channel/sector	
A	Capacity constraint	4.1	3.5	3.0	3.2	3.5
B	Unproductive use of assets	3.6	3.8	3.6	3.2	3.5
C	Lack of interoperability and interconnection	3.3	3.6	3.4	3.4	3.5
D	Market fragmentation	3.5	3.6	3.4	3.0	3.5
E	Monopoly protection	3.3	3.7	3.1	3.1	3.4
F	Limited accessibility	3.6	3.5	3.1	2.7	3.3
G	Low quality of international services	3.5	3.6	3.6	2.9	3.5
H	Pricing policy	3.7	4.0	3.5	3.2	3.7
I		3.6	3.7	3.4	3.2	

Carriers

By comparing the opinions of carriers and shippers, it appears that they do not know each other well enough. In fact the columns of structure and productivity of carriers (T) and logistics or other factors of shippers (X) are significantly different in the perception of the two parties. There is a lack of communication between them. Carriers consider shippers a constraint to their efficiency increase. They seem to judge the market sufficiently accessible and transparent (row F), especially in terms of their industrial supply and productivity (FY).

Another constraint for carriers' productivity increase is the high fragmentation of offer and demand: suppliers are very fragmented in terms of company structure especially with regard to certain regions and service offer segments. Different manufacturers have different needs in terms of transportation, warehousing operations, handling equipment, etc. This limits their operating capacity (AY) significantly. Trade barriers do not represent a relevant problem for carriers within their industry (FY).

		S	T	X	Y	Z
			Carriers		Population 14	
		Productivity and adequacy of transportation infrastructures	Structure and/or productivity of carriers	Logistics and/or other factors of shippers	Logistics and/other factors of the channel/sector	
A	Capacity constraint	3.7	3.6	3.6	4.0	3.7
B	Unproductive use of assets	3.8	3.8	3.7	4.1	3.8
C	Lack of interoperability and interconnection	3.7	3.8	3.6	3.8	3.7
D	Market fragmentation	3.1	3.6	3.8	2.1	3.5
E	Monopoly protection	3.5	3.2	3.2	2.1	3.3
F	Limited accessibility	2.5	2.6	2.6	2.0	2.7
G	Low quality of international services	2.5	3.1	3.1	2.4	3.0
H	Pricing policy	2.9	3.1	2.8	2.4	3.0
I		3.2	3.3	3.3	3.6	

Southern shippers

In general, sources of inefficiency are perceived to have a higher impact in the south (and in the east) than in the centre and north (column T).

The infrastructural problems are perceived to be higher in the south and in the east than in the centre and north (AS).

The pricing policy also has a relevant influence on the intra-European trade, above all in terms of price transparency and differentiation (HS).

Furthermore, it must be considered that in the south companies are smaller and less organized than in the north. One direct consequence is the disadvantage in terms of economies of scale (DY).

		S	T	X	Y	Z
			Shippers south		Population 11	
		Productivity and adequacy of transportation infrastructures	Structure and/or productivity of carriers	Logistics and/or other factors of shippers	Logistics and/other factors of the channel/sector	
A	Capacity constraint	4.0	3.3	3.2	3.7	3.5
B	Unproductive use of assets	3.6	3.4	3.5	3.1	3.5
C	Lack of interoperability and interconnection	3.6	4.1	3.8	3.5	3.8
D	Market fragmentation	4.0	3.6	3.5	4.3	3.8
E	Monopoly protection	3.6	3.9	3.4	3.8	3.7
F	Limited accessibility	3.8	4.0	3.9	3.5	3.8
G	Low quality of international services	3.4	3.7	4.2	3.0	3.6
H	Pricing policy	4.0	4.2	3.8	3.8	3.9
I		3.9	3.8	3.6	3.6	

Northern and central shippers

In the north and in the centre of Europe companies consider the market easily accessible (FY). Unexpected are the high figures related to the unproductive use of assets in the centre (BS); the operators in these regions are probably stricter in their judgements than colleagues in the south.

In this table, data also show that a problem is percieved regarding relationships between operators and transportation infrastructures (AS). The perception of structural problems seems not to exist in the distribution channel (column Y).

		S	T	X	Y	Z
		Shippers centre			**Population 17**	
		Productivity and adequacy of transportation infrastructures	Structure and/or productivity of carriers	Logistics and/or other factors of shippers	Logistics and/other factors of the channel/sector	
A	Capacity constraint	4.4	3.7	3.3	3.3	3.8
B	Unproductive use of assets	3.9	4.0	3.6	3.4	3.8
C	Lack of interoperability and interconnection	3.5	3.3	3.1	3.2	3.3
D	Market fragmentation	3.8	3.9	3.5	3.3	3.7
E	Monopoly protection	3.3	4.1	3.0	3.2	3.4
F	Limited accessibility	3.8	3.7	3.1	3.0	3.4
G	Low quality of international services	3.5	3.5	3.5	3.2	3.5
H	Pricing policy	3.4	4.2	3.8	3.5	3.8
I		3.8	3.8	3.4	3.3	

		S	T	X	Y	Z
		Shippers north			**Population 8**	
		Productivity and adequacy of transportation infrastructures	Structure and/or productivity of carriers	Logistics and/or other factors of shippers	Logistics and/other factors of the channel/sector	
A	Capacity constraint	4.5	4.0	3.4	3.3	3.9
B	Unproductive use of assets	3.5	3.8	3.8	3.1	3.6
C	Lack of interoperability and interconnection	3.3	3.3	3.3	3.0	3.2
D	Market fragmentation	3.9	3.8	3.4	2.9	3.5
E	Monopoly protection	2.9	3.9	3.5	3.1	3.4
F	Limited accessibility	3.4	3.4	2.9	2.9	3.2
G	Low quality of international services	3.6	4.0	3.8	3.5	3.8
H	Pricing policy	3.5	3.8	3.6	3.4	3.6
I		3.7	3.8	3.4	3.2	

Eastern shippers

The leading problem of the east is that the market is not yet well interconnected with that in the west (row C).

The operators are not yet European, the majority of the products are not competitive in terms of quality, image, design, and there is a consistent lack of technological innovation as well as of skilled workers and qualified employees (GT–GX).

There is a high perception of monopoly protection, in particular, limiting the carriers' activity and productivity (ET).

The pricing policy is not considered as a problem relevant for the intra-European trade increase (row H).

		S	T	X	Y	Z
			Shippers east		Population 2	
		Productivity and adequacy of transportation infrastructures	Structure and/or productivity of carriers	Logistics and/or other factors of shippers	Logistics and/other factors of the channel/sector	
A	Capacity constraint	4.5	2.5	2.0	3.0	3.0
B	Unproductive use of assets	2.5	2.5	4.0	2.5	2.9
C	Lack of interoperability and interconnection	3.5	4.0	4.0	4.0	3.9
D	Market fragmentation	3.5	4.0	3.5	4.0	3.8
E	Monopoly protection	4.0	5.0	4.0	3.0	4.0
F	Limited accessibility	3.5	3.5	3.5	3.0	3.4
G	Low quality of international services	3.5	4.0	4.0	3.5	3.8
H	Pricing policy	4.0	4.0	4.0	3.0	3.8
I		3.6	3.7	3.6	3.3	

APPENDIX B

Transport policies in the European Union and their impacts on transport costs and prices

B.1. Introduction

As far as policy measures are concerned, each scenario should be considered an attempt to combine in a coherent package (a) *horizontal* measures in the agenda for a Common Transport Policy (CPT) with (b) *vertical* ones that are currently being implemented within the European competition and regulatory framework designed to achieve a competitive single market.

The degree of achievement of consumer gains expected from deregulation – in lower prices and better services – as well as the degree of integration that can be achieved at European scale, are expected to be significantly affected by the degree of implementation of harmonization CTP policies aimed at removing distortions and at levelling the field for competition within and between different transport modes.

Based on an intensive review both on EU transport policies objectives and targets and analysis of current trends and perspectives in the evolution of different transport industries – whose results are presented in this Appendix – assumptions made to design policy scenarios are summarized in Table B.1 in which the degree of achievement of objectives set in different policy areas and relationships between horizontal and vertical policies are shown in the year 2005.

Table B.1.   Degree of achievement of European transport policies in different scenarios (year 2005)

	Reference scenario	Partial integration	Full integration
(1) TENs			
Completion of 14 priority TENs	X	XXX	XXX
(2) Common Transport Policy			
Harmonization measures			
(a) environment and safety	XX	XX	XXX
(b) social standards	X	X	XXX
(c) external dimension		X	XX
(d) fair and efficient pricing			XXX
(3) Liberalization and competition			
Road freight	XXX	XXX	XXX
Rail	X	X	XX
Air	XX	XX	XXX
Water	XX	XX	XX
Consolidation of EU regulatory powers	X	X	XXX

Notes: X= low degree of achievement;
XX = medium degree of achievement;
XXX = high degree of achievement.

B.2. Competition and harmonization

Historically the option of State ownership and direct political control is used in most European countries as a substitute for economic regulation in the transport sector. The emergence of a Community regulatory framework in the 1990s can be considered the result of increasing recognition of the fact that national regulations were a threat to the achievement of an 'optimal' level of output at European scale, with higher cost and lower variety and quality of transport services available to European citizens and manufacturers. The need for adopting more effective regulatory frameworks was also recognized by national governments, increasingly dissatisfied with the huge cost of subsidizing monopolistic industries in the public sector.

These concerns have resulted in a variety of options to liberalize transport markets. Of particular importance are those designed to deregulate road haulage and civil aviation and to re-regulate the railways in order to introduce market guidance in their restructuring at both national and European scale.

The option to deregulate and return to free market competition in the road haulage industry was already explored as a component of the 1992 single market programme. After a transitional period, tariff liberalization was introduced in national markets and marked restrictions on frontier crossing road haulage were relaxed. In 1990, concessions were granted for limited regular cabotage. Unrestricted cabotage is scheduled for 1997, leaving time for Member States to implement appropriate measures in harmonizing national markets.

With high fares (especially for business travel) and demand for flights booming in the 1980s, European civil aviation is also being deregulated in stages. Starting in 1988, the tariff system was eased and automatic authorization was given for capacity increase in bilateral scheduled flights. Since 1990, the second liberalization stage has allowed for further tariff liberalization and has further opened access to the market. By 1997, the third stage should be completed to introduce freedom in both setting tariffs and market entrance (freedom of establishment and unrestricted cabotage).

To halt the decline of the railway, Council Directive 91/440/EEC of 29 July 1991 on the development of the Community's railways focuses on competitive access. Each country would have carved out their fixed facility either as a separate entity or as a distinct cost centre. In either case 'the State would have ensured non-discriminatory access to its railway network for international groupings of railway undertakings, and for railway undertakings engaged in the international combined transport of goods'. In other terms, competitive access would have had to be provided for international traffic.

The directive *suggests* that Member States find suitable solutions to restructure railway companies in the following areas: the separation of commercial and non-commercial services and the provision of public service obligation grants by the State or local authorities; the separation of commercial production into companies or cost centres to enhance railway managers' commercial orientation; and the rationalization of the debt structure to strengthen the autonomous management of the railway. As the railways' restructuring becomes more effective in achieving organizational efficiency and larger in scale of operations, it is expected that competitive access will become more feasible, provided that appropriate planning of train operations and protocols for resolving conflicts are agreed and commonly adopted in Europe.

The three main European regulatory frameworks are entering into operation quite a few years after the deregulation of transport markets has proved effective throughout the world (including in a number of European countries, such as the UK and Sweden) by making transport industries able to provide a larger variety of services at a lower cost for users.

The key difference is that, while previous deregulatory efforts have been domestic in nature, the liberalization process started in Europe is one of the first attempts ever made with the explicit purpose of enlarging transport output on a continental scale. Other than differences in the competitive positions of national transport companies – which may slow the liberalization process in the Union as a whole – the main difficulty is in understanding structural conditions that may affect the development of integrated, competitive transport markets on a European scale.

Furthermore, difficulties and delays so far experienced by Member States in the adoption of EU regulatory frameworks designed to liberalize transport markets – including resistance opposed by State-owned companies and transport lobbies – are increasingly recognized as being the result of a number of circumstances for which workable policies are still under exploration at European level. In broad terms these belong to the category of *harmonization measures* and the most critical ones can be categorized as follows:

(a)   The need for regulation is not reduced in the case of reliance on market forces instead of direct regulation, i.e. regulators should focus on appropriate actions to ensure that the conditions for contestability, such as free entry and exit, and slow price response by the incumbent, are met as closely as possible.

(b)   The transport sector is an outstanding example of external effects which do not operate through the market mechanism, with congestion, pollution and safety strictly associated with road transport. With a number of both theoretical and practical attempts to internalize external costs, the objective is also emerging to influence actual transport choices by giving their producers and users direct pricing signals.

Other than to level the field for competition between different transport modes, the latter set of issues is at the core of the Common Transport Policy package, discussed in the next section.

B.2.1. Common Transport Policy

Policies and actions in the action programme 1995–2000 (and beyond) presented by the European Commission (1995c) (COM (95) 302 final) to implement the Common Transport Policy (CPT) have provided the guidelines both to specify common assumptions and to design alternative policy scenarios describing respectively partial and full levels of integration that may be achieved in the European Union by the year 2005.

The action programme consists of policies and initiatives in three fundamental areas:

(a)   improving quality by developing integrated and competitive transport system based on advanced technologies which also contribute to *environmental and safety objectives*;

(b)   improving the functioning of the single market in order to promote choice of user-friendly provision of transport services while safeguarding *social standards*;

(c)   broadening the *external dimension* by improving transport links with non-EU countries and fostering the access of EU operators to other transport markets.

Increasing quality and environmental sustainability of European transport systems is one of the key reasearch issues in the Fourth Research Framework for transport, launched in 1995. At the same time, the adoption of CTP policies in the area of environment and safety has been considered of common interest for local and national governments and European authorities. A higher degree of co-operation has therefore been considered a common assumption, particularly for qualitative measures designed to increase environmental and safety standards. At national and European level these include:

(a)   standards and targets for CO_2 emission levels;
(b)   standards and targets for transport safety;
(c)   standards and requirements for transport infrastructure.

Measures that are associated with planning at local level are also considered, including:

(a)   policy measures to reduce transport demand;
(b)   policy measures aimed at improving current patterns in land use in integration with transport policies.

The assumption that subsidiarity will work in any scenario – in terms of local, national and European governments devoting a good deal of their efforts (in terms of both planning and standard setting) to the upgrading of present standards of transport systems – has been considered consistent with both current perspectives in economic and social growth in the Union and growing environmental and safety concerns.

In the adoption of vertical regulatory frameworks outlined earlier, the most critical horizontal policy issues in order to achieve a truly international, fully integrated transport regime in the single market have been identified in the establishment of a set of 'level playing- field' measures to achieve a context in which:

(a)   all competitors have equivalent financial objectives;
(b)   all operators have equivalent commercial freedom;
(c)   operators are required to cover all the costs they impose on society.

Relevant issues and options in order to harmonize possible distortions indicated in items (a) and (b) above are discussed in Section B.3 below with particular regard to present disparities affecting road freight operations and the railways. Pricing policies are then considered a horizontal issue, whose main requirement implications are discussed in Section 2.2, using as guidelines the principles and options outlined in the Green Paper: *Towards Fair and Efficient Pricing in Transport: policy options for internalizing the external costs of transport in the European Union* (European Commission, 1995b).

As far as the external dimension is concerned, the achievement of the CTP's objectives in area (c) is only considered by means of reducing border delays in both the partial and the full integration scenarios. Also in the full integration scenario, cross-border fees currently levied on Western lorries entering Eastern countries are abolished. In the absence of an EU framework to sustain in financial terms the upgrading and further development of transport infrastructure in neighbouring countries – which may be a particularly acute requirement in Eastern European countries – such options have been considered an acceptable proxy for the establishment of fair patterns in trade.

B.2.2. Towards fair and efficient pricing in transport

A well-established option in the making of the European Union, the principle of 'users and polluters pay', is increasingly becoming a key option in the design of CTP policy targets. The Fair & Efficient Pricing document recognizes that transport policies have, in the past, focused largely on direct regulation and – despite significant improvements in some areas – have still not been able to give citizens and businesses incentives to find solutions to problems. It also recognizes that individuals' decisions – with respect to their choice of transport modes, their location and investments – are to a large extent based on prices and that the Union's objective of ensuring sustainable transport requires that prices reflect underlying scarcities, including energy and capacity.

As an aggregate, the level of transport costs, which are not directly borne by those who caused them, are estimated in the document as being up to 2% of GDP for congestion and 0.6% for pollution. The costs of accidents are also considered only partially paid for, adding up to 1.5% of GDP per year.

The purpose of the policies under consideration at the Commission is not to increase the costs of transport or the level of taxation: on the contrary, a radical change in transport pricing is envisaged to reduce both the real cost of transport (i.e. those paid by individual users plus those paid by other affected categories or society as a whole) and (if it is effective) also the level of taxation.

The paper therefore concentrates on road transport, where 90% of external costs are considered to be generated and where motor-fuel taxes up to an average of 3% to 4% of GDP per year are levied in European countries. The paper recognizes that the degree to which infrastructure costs are covered varies significantly between countries and within and across modes: 'Some transport users pay too much, others too little. This situation is both unfair and inefficient.'

From road taxation to direct charges

As a rule, in the past, average expenditure on inland transport in ECMT countries has been lower than road taxation, declining from 1.5% of GDP in 1975 (ECU 20.4 billion) to 0.9% in 1984, although GDP grew by 22% over the same period and traffic rose by almost a quarter for both passengers and freight. Over the period 1975–84 roads accounted on average for 75% of inland transport investment, the railways for 23% and waterways for 3%.

In most European countries, road taxation is also an outstanding general taxation source as such, often making an increase in its level the easiest/faster way for the Treasury to balance public budget, with poor, if any, consideration given to the impacts of transport on mobility.

With evidence from aggregated figures indicating that an overall balance may be the case, the Green Paper (European Commission, 1995b) envisages a move from conventional road taxation towards more direct, market- and behaviour-related approaches being adopted also to charge for the use of roads. Within the Maastricht option of stricter financial discipline in the public sector, pricing policies are considered a means of reducing pollution and congestion as well as a way to indicate priorities for public investment. Within the TEN framework, direct charges are also considered a condition to make roads and other transport systems profitable for private investors.

Table B.2.   Road taxation as a percentage of GDP in selected countries

Year	France	Germany	UK	Italy	Spain
1986	3.13	1.8	4.0	3.8	2.16
1987	3.09	1.7	5.9	3.7	1.65
1988	3.10	1.6	4.7	4.0	4.70
1989	3.43	1.9	4.8	4.1	
1990	3.31	1.7	3.7	4.3	4.67

Source: International Road Federation, *World Road Statistics 1986–1990*, 1991 edition.

Table B.3.   Road taxation as a percentage of total tax revenue

Year	France	Germany	UK	Italy	Spain
1986	14.4	3.9	9.5	15.9	7.60
1987	15.0	3.7	11.5	16.2	4.16
1988	14.1	3.6		16.7	11.83
1989	17.1	4.1	10.6	16.8	
1990		3.8	9.6	17.3	17.43

Source: International Road Federation, *World Road Statistics 1986–1990*, 1991 edition.

Possible policy instruments to increase transparency and effectiveness of pricing in given appropriate incentives are identified in the Green Paper with temporal priorities also given as summarized in Table B.4.

The harmonization of pricing policy in transport sectors is considered a key option in the full integration scenario. The implementation of strategies currently under discussion in the EU is represented by three indicators:

(a)   increase in HGV taxation rates and their harmonization across Europe to the highest national rates charged in the 1990s, i.e. in the UK, where diesel and vehicle taxation is used to approximate the costs lorries induce also on road infrastructural and maintenance standards;

(b)   increase in car taxation rates and their harmonization across Europe to the highest rates charged in the 1990s – i.e. in Italy – to approximate the adoption of a CO_2 tax for global warming;

(c)   the adoption of a pan-European toll scheme to be levied only on the most congested links of the European motorway network and its harmonization to the level of tolls currently levied on cars and HGVs in Austria.

Table B.4.   Possible policy instruments for efficient and equitable pricing

	Short/medium term		Long term	
	Road	**Other modes**	**Road**	**Other modes**
Infrastructure costs & congestion	– more differentiation according to use and damage in existing charging systems – kilometre tax for HGV (axle based) – tolls	– infrastructure-use related charges	– electronic road pricing for congestion and infrastructure costs	– track charges and other infrastructure-use related charges
Accidents	– progress in gearing insurance systems to the desired long-term structure – labelling		– insurance systems covering full social costs and differentiating according to risk (e.g. bonus/malus)	
Air pollution & noise	– for cars: emission (and possibly mileage) dependent annual taxes – for HGV: surcharges on kilometre tax – differentiated excises according to environmental characteristics of fuel – CO_2 tax for global warming – identical across modes	– introduction of emission based charges, e.g. landing charges in aviation based on noise emissions	– fees based on actual emission/noise with differentiated costs according to geographical conditions (and, possibly, time of day)	

Source: European Commission *Towards fair and efficient pricing in transport*, 1995.

B.3. Costing and pricing of policy scenarios

Assumptions on likely evolution in individual transport sectors/markets are based on assessed trends in the evolution of the relevant markets as well as on the status in the adoption of EU policies and early impacts of liberalization directives that were adopted in the 1990s.

The likely evolution of costs/prices in different scenarios are discussed separately for four modal sectors:

(a)   road freight transport: for which – in a competitive context – production costs are assumed to be close to prices actually charged to users, once a 10% proportion is added to take into account general costs and profit margins;

(b)   civil aviation: prices are expected to fall (especially for business fares) as a result of pan-European liberalization;

(c)   the railways: for which published tariffs across Europe are adjusted in different scenarios for passenger services (both conventional and HST). Unit revenues are used for freight services to take into account that published rates are subject to market negotiation;

(d)   waterborne transport: for which – despite wide fluctuations taking place in both fleet capacity and trade flows in ocean shipping – official rates were considered both competitive and reasonably transparent as far as strict transport operations and handling are concerned.

Table B.5.   Transport policies implemented in the scenarios – Passengers

	Base scenario	Partial integration scenario	Full integration scenario
Car tolls	No change	No change	Unified tolls on TEN road projects and on the most congested EU motorways – more than 50% of the capacity in the base scenario; tolls are currently in use in Austria
Car operating costs	No change	No change	Increase of operating costs (fuel tax) to the highest level in the EU (Italy)
Coach fares	No change	No change	No change
IC train passengers	All countries tend toward EU average increase (or decrease) of 50% of the difference between each country and EU average	All countries tend toward EU average increase (or decrease) of 50% of the difference between each country and EU average	Fares unified in all EU countries to the EU average
High speed train passengers	In each country fares are 25% higher than conventional (IC) trains	In each country fares are 25% higher than conventional (IC) trains	In each country fares are 35% (25% + 10% of infrastructure costs) higher than conventional (IC) trains
Air passengers	20% reduction of fares	20% reduction of fares	35% reduction of fares

Note: Changes are expressed in terms of increases and reductions in comparison with the base year, 1991.

As shown in Tables B.5 and B.6 – in which quantitative estimates of scenario-specific variations in costs, prices and performances are summarized for different transport markets – a *benchmark* approach has been used intensively in order to modify prices and costs or to harmonize them to those in use in different countries in case actual conditions were considered to reflect relevant policies that may be adopted in the Union.

Table B.6.   Transport policies implemented in the scenarios – Freight

	Base scenario	Partial integration scenario	Full integration scenario
Truck operating costs **(1) Distance based**	Change of empty back-flow for general cargo and high value cargo due to cabotage	Change of empty back-flow for general cargo and high value cargo due to cabotage	Change of empty back-flow for general cargo and high value cargo due to cabotage Increase in operating costs (diesel tax and vehicle tax) to the highest in Europe (UK)
(2) Time based	10% reduction of personnel costs due to the use of non-EU drivers	10% reduction of personnel costs due to the use of non-EU drivers	5% increase of personnel costs due to increase qualitative standards
Truck tolls	No change	No change	Unified tolls on TEN road projects and on the most congested EU motorways – more than 50% of the capacity in the base scenario; truck tolls are set at the EU weighted average
Delays at border links	No change	Abolition of delays at EU border links for trucks and cars	Abolition of delays at EU border links for trucks and cars 50% reduction of delays at EU-eastern countries border links
Truck costs at eastern countries border links	Same costs as in 1995	Same costs as in 1995	No costs as in 1991
Rail fares	All countries tend toward EU average increase (or decrease) of 50% of the difference between each country and EU average	All countries tend toward EU average increase (or decrease) of 50% of the difference between each country and UK fares	Fares unified in all EU countries to the EU average level
Rail terminal times	No change	10% reduction in all nodes involved in rail TEN projects	10% reduction in all nodes involved in rail TEN projects
Rail terminal costs for containers	No change	10% reduction in all nodes	10% reduction in all nodes
Inland waterway	No change	No change	No change
Short sea shipping	20% reduction of port costs and times	20% reduction of port costs and times	20% reduction of port costs and times
Ocean shipping	10% reduction of port costs and times	10% reduction of port costs and times	10% reduction of port costs and times

Note: Changes are expressed in terms of increases and reductions in comparison with the base year, 1991.

B.3.1. Road freight transport

Despite the constraints imposed by quantitative regulation, not to say by poor infrastructure, the road haulage sector has been historically able and relatively quick to meet in a flexible way structural changes taking place in demand (different products, different locations and different industrial practices) through a combination of growth and changes in operating practices which have raised quality and improved productivity.

Also in Europe, fleet capacity has risen less than demand, safety and environmental performances have improved and prices have fallen in real terms. In the last three decades, the growth in road border crossing was up to 62% in tonnes, the growth in tonnes-kilometres was up to 44%.

As a whole, the sector has also proved very flexible in taking into account variations in relative prices of production factors by introducing operating changes. In the 1980s, increased fuel prices resulted in companies concentrating their investment on reducing energy costs. Analysts seem to agree on the fact that further growth in relative prices will tend to result in companies concentrating investment on capital costs, depots and storage and better fleet utilization.

The dominance of road freight transport in Europe is particularly marked in domestic markets, where market share is over four-fifths and average length is 50 km. But its importance was growing fast also in international traffic (three-fifths of the market in 1995).

A large number of very small professional hauliers predominate in terms of operator numbers. However, it is a relatively small number of large hauliers that command the major part of total operations both directly, through their own haulage operations, and indirectly, i.e. by controlling forwarding, warehousing and value added services.

International markets are dominated by professional operators and larger firms (nine-tenths in terms of tonnes-km). The trend is for professional operators to capture an even larger share of international markets.

The deregulation of road haulage in the EU

Since the beginning of the 1990s, the impacts of the general economic recession have been combined with adjustment problems following both domestic and international deregulation. The impact of recession has not been uniform. In the long-established liberal markets (such as the UK and Sweden), there has been remarkable stability in the number of operators, with financial performances superior to many other industrial sectors. In newly deregulated transport markets, operator numbers have risen and prices fallen.

In the perspective of freedom of cabotage, most of the benefits of removing quantitative barriers to market entry and price control are materializing in the formation of cross-frontier strategic alliances within a wide range of combinations: haulier/shipper; haulier/haulier; haulier/freight forwarder; freight forwarder/freight forwarder; haulier/vehicle manufacturer.

The existence of extensive sub-contracting has further consolidated larger operators. Different types of sub-contracting are applied: long-term contracts (often involving financial and technical assistance for vehicle purchase and maintenance) or spot contracts for a single load (often owner-drivers over longer distances and smaller quantities). Freight forwarders and prime contractors appear to contribute to unauthorized operations by setting standards that are too high.

Wide divergence in operating practices across the Union are considered to create harmful distortion in the market. The lack of harmonization is considered particularly critical in the following areas:

(a)   access to the profession, with potential benefits from rising qualitative standards in terms of safety and the environment;
(b)   financial standing, to assure equity of treatment for enterprises in different Member States.

In dirigist markets, State aids are still provided both to restructure small companies operating in local markets and to encourage operators to leave the market (over-capacity). But in liberal markets – where the sector has been quicker to restructure – the number of small operators was reduced with a further move from own-account to professional operations and strategic alliances.

Higher qualitative standards than present 'minimum level harmonization' are also envisaged across the Union in the following areas:

(a)   training of drivers and managers;
(b)   enforcement and control of unauthorized operations, ranging from better design of documents against fraud to effective monitoring of vehicles and drivers' hours, the latter requiring a progressive harmonized adoption of IT technologies in the Union (both on-board and road-side).

In dynamic terms, as freedom of cabotage is fully introduced, unauthorized operations may also become even broader in diffusion and consequences.

Last but not least, not only are different criteria used in different countries for road taxation to reflect road costs (including road investment and maintenance, environment, congestion, accidents), but – as a rule – charges to reflect social and investment costs are not separated from taxes of a general revenue nature nor are they levied according to the territoriality principle.

Policy scenarios for road haulage in the year 2005

Two policy scenarios – a partial integration scenario identical to the reference scenario and a full integration scenario – have been designed to describe the impacts of transport policies on road freight production costs. In both policy scenarios, the completion of the single market deregulation programme for road freight transport is assumed to have been successfully implemented, including the freedom of cabotage.

In both scenarios it is also assumed that – within general rules for fair competition and monopoly control – road freight transport companies have become able to exploit the potential of an enlarged European market by strengthening regional and international networks and establishing strategic alliances and/or acquisitions.

The main difference between the two scenarios is that harmonization policies, as described in Section B.2 – are implemented only in the full integration scenario to remove distortions, to increase qualitative standards and to internalize the whole range of actual costs associated with road transport. Other things being equal in technical terms – such as weight and dimension of vehicles and emission standards – the harmonization of operating conditions in road haulage which is considered essential to avoid market distortion in the single European market, is fiscal and social in nature:

(a)   harmonization of financial and fiscal requirements for transport companies;
(b)   harmonization and upgrading of drivers' skills and driving hours;
(c)   harmonization of criteria for charging for the use of road infrastructure.

Harmonization of social standards

In the absence of a strong European commitment to reduce market distortions and to internalize production costs, the reference and partial integration scenarios describe a context in which companies specializing in value-added services will be in a position to increase profit margins by using abundant, cheap and relatively low-skilled labour in the market for road haulage.

Such a trend could be magnified in the presence of different technical, social and fiscal requirements in Eastern Europe – a contiguous market where labour costs are at about one-quarter and total operating costs at about three-quarters of those in the Union – which already discriminate against Western operators due to high border delays and poor infrastructures.

On the other hand, the full integration scenario describes a situation in which a set of measures is adopted – and enforced – in the Union which are designed to increase quality standards and drivers' skills, as well as to strengthen control over driving hours and working conditions. An increase in operating costs of road haulage is therefore assumed in which drivers' wages and working conditions reflect the social value of labour in transport operations – including new skills required by the introduction of ATT – and their share in productivity increases is captured.

Enforcement measures are therefore implemented in the full integration scenario using a mix of on-board and infrastructure devices to reduce the need for policing, most of which are implemented also with respect to the objective of levying direct charges for the use of road infrastructure.

B.3.2. Air transport

Figures published in 1996 by Airports Council International (see bibliography) show that Europe has experienced greater passenger growth than any other area of the world, except the Pacific region (the latter a 359 million passenger market in 1995): passenger numbers rose by 6.8% in 1995 up to 644 million.

In order to foresee the impact of the decision to deregulate civil aviation in Europe, results from air deregulation in the USA – by far the largest aviation market in the world with 1 billion passengers in 1995 – can be taken as benchmark. The benefits from civil aviation deregulation in the USA have been positive and well documented, the most dramatic one being experienced in terms of falling air rates (by some 50%) with aggregate welfare gains for consumers comprising between US$ 9 and 15 billion at 1990 prices. Following deregulation, airlines also changed their production patterns in a dramatic way, with hub-and-spoke operations allowing for both a significant reduction in costs and a lower degree of competition than expected.

The point is whether either the magnitude of benefits achieved in the USA or their distribution will be the same in Europe. Apart from differences in population, the structure of demand in Europe along with potential non-aviation competitors, are likely to limit the advantages.

(a)   Europe is larger than the USA in terms of population (347 million compared to 254 million in 1990), but it is geographically smaller.

(b)   The difference in size means that the length of trips is shorter in Europe (a stage length of 677 km compared to 1,016 km). Short stage length makes other transport modes more competitive, and especially highly subsidized conventional rail services and high speed ones.

(c)   Aggregate size of operators is also smaller. In 1991, the 24 largest operators in the USA (99% of traffic) generated 76,000 billion passenger-kilometres, while the 77 largest European ones (66% of traffic) generated only 49,000 billion.

(d)   European carriers are more internationally oriented: in 1995 international traffic accounted for 90% in scheduled services, of which 78% was on routes outside geographical Europe.

(e)   Charter travel is also more common in Europe (27% of total traffic versus 18% in the USA), and relatively low fares were charged for leisure traffic well before EU liberalization.

These structural components may explain why – despite each of the three packages for air liberalization in Europe which have progressively relaxed restriction on fares, an option which has started resulting in lower rates for domestic flights – fares have remained relatively high for international business travel – by far a less price-sensitive market than economy or leisure travel.

Other than higher quality in both airport and in-flight services than in the USA, the main compensation European air companies seem to offer to their customers willing to pay for convenient, flexible flight times and quick check-in facilities, are frequent flyer point schemes. As a whole, the European civil aviation sector at present shows high production costs and high tariffs for the flag carriers, while privatized companies (such as British Airways and KLM) are taking indirect advantage of limited competition and, due to lower costs, are making high profits.

Other measures designed to achieve a single market in civil aviation have not been effective so far. These include:

(a)   slot allocation regulation,
(b)   State aids,
(c)   accompanying conditions.

With some 20% of flights more than 15% behind schedule in 1995 (23 minutes on average), air congestion may become critical in terms of both terminal capacity and traffic control. To solve air congestion problems, the European Air Traffic Control Harmonization and Integration Programme is currently being implemented. This was decided on in 1990 by European Ministers for Transport in order to integrate 51 different computer languages across Europe. With cross-European planning of air traffic being centralized in Brussels, airlines and airport authorities would also have to re-design strategies in order to increase passenger terminal and runway capacity. If this proves difficult at main airports (as it may be also because of environmental concerns), the development of a more complex, wider network may have to be considered in order to integrate existing capacities at regional airports in Europe, in parallel with technology which is allowing the operation of larger aircraft.

These being the starting conditions, both the reference and the partial integration scenarios describe a situation in which cartelization, slot control at airports, enduring barriers to the entry of non-European low-cost new entrants may reduce the impact of air liberalization in Europe in the years to come. A reduction of fares is anyhow assumed as a result of liberalization of cabotage in 1997.

In the full integration scenario, a further reduction in air rates is assumed, due to strong competition and the adoption of competitive schemes to allocate slots.

Compared to 1991 levels, air rates are expected to decrease respectively by 20% in the reference and partial integration scenarios and by 35% in the full integration scenario.

B.3.3. The railway

In ECMT countries, passenger and freight transport by road has almost doubled since 1970 whereas the overall volume of rail traffic has remained virtually unchanged. Roads handle nearly 12 times the passenger-kms of the railway, while lorries have four times the tonne-km output of trains.

The traffic volumes and proportions involved show that there may not be an immediate possibility of mass transfer from road to rail, since a transfer to rail of 10% of road freight would amount to an increase of some 40% of the freight carried by rail which would be difficult to handle in rail links which are already operating close to capacity.

This is especially the case of rail links where different types of rail traffic – such as regional and IC passenger services and freight trains – compete for the use of the same track, making it impossible to operate high frequency trains at the same speed (an operating scheme which, in combination with advanced navigation systems, would increase capacity by 30%). Furthermore, rail output depends more on terminals than on capacity on the line.

In European regions where networks are quite dense, the construction of specialized rail links is under consideration – a substantial part of which is in the TEN programme – to allow for either high speed passenger or combined transport services being operated in a continuous and uniform way. Night operation of trains and parallel routes can also be considered an option to give additional capacity to freight services in the short run.

To deliver their benefits in terms of traffic diversion from congested corridor motorways, combined transport techniques would have to be operated along trunk links to ensure low costs, rapid transhipment of loads and sufficiently frequent services.

Directive 91/440/EEC: a legal framework to be turned into a reality

Member States are following a wide range of approaches in the adoption of the Rail Directive[12] to separate infrastructure from services and to restructure rail companies. Controversial issues are under discussion also at European level, with different options favoured for complementary directives currently in preparation.

---

[12]   See note 5 p. 33

Even assuming that the broad intention of expanding the market for rail services within Europe has been accepted, different players are reacting differently to liberalization due to different concerns but also to disparities in the previous existing situation in individual Member States. These include the relative importance of various national and international markets that are or may be served by the railway (e.g. bulk freight or intercity passenger); problems of overstaffing as well as the level of debt and subsidies. Also, the degree to which national railways need major investment to increase quality standards and/or improve network standard and capacity may vary in different countries as well as the commitment of national governments to make resources available for rail investment.

The reference solution and the partial integration scenario

As the European Union becomes more market-driven with wider competition also in the transport sector, the need for reshaping the railway into a market-sensitive transport entity is increasingly recognized as a vital objective. While detailed solutions and arrangements will vary from one country to another, technological specialization and different service requirements of different types of railway services – such as regional and passenger intercity or combined and bulk freight – will favour the adoption of *line of business-organization schemes*, resulting in more comprehensive business planning, more market and cost-sensitive decisions, and more responsive operations for each service.

Based on evidence from countries that have been pioneering the adoption of commercial approaches envisaged in Directive 91/440/EEC – such as the UK and Sweden – internal reorganization of management into business sectors has been successful in improving the financial performance of the system and reducing production costs without a significant reduction in services and traffic, but for route closures where alternative modes (coaches and lorries) can provide cheaper services of good quality (such as in sparsely populated rural areas).

Accompanying measures to prepare for commercialization of rail services include:

(a) outsourcing of workshops, cleaning and catering; extension of private ownership of wagons and transforming the stations into multi-management centres;
(b) provision of subsidies under Public Service Obligation (Directive 90/53 21/EEC);[13]
(c) to make the cost of infrastructure explicit by setting up a separate company to operate rail infrastructure.

Taking the European average as a benchmark for rates rail companies were able to charge in 1991/92, revenues are likely to balance the costs of restructured rail services in areas in which rail performances are equal or superior to those of other transport modes. As far as conventional rail services are concerned, potentially commercial services include:

(a) in passenger transport: Intercity and TEE;
(b) in freight transport, large volumes of bulk freight to be carried over long distance.

---

[13] Council Regulations 1191/60 and 1893/91 of 17 September 1990 on the procurement procedures of entities operating in the water, energy, transport and telecommunications sectors (OJ L 297, 29.10.1990, p. 1).

Other than for (heavily) subsidized high-volume services operated on regional rail networks (which are not considered in this study), some subsidies will be needed to allow rail transport to remain competitive with door-to-door road haulage in the high value freight transport, i.e. partial shipment and combined transport sector (in both cases, subsidies are provided in the UK on the basis of benefits respectively in terms of reduced congestion and environmental impacts).

Other things being equal in terms of the relative weight of different markets for rail services in different countries, the speed at which performances of national railways is expected to become aligned to the European average in 1991–92 will be strongly influenced by the departure situation from which the restructuring of each national rail will have to be started, and particularly staff numbers and level of deficit.

Reasons for assuming such a slow, complex process in reforming European railways are external to the rail industry, and are to be found in severe burdens to raise rail fares in areas in which the railway competes with liberalized industries, such as road freight (which in Europe is also the case in long-distance haulage) and air transport (whose further liberalization may affect profitability of new high speed rail services).

In a context in which any increase in rail fares could negatively affect internal goals to consolidate and to extend existing markets for rail services, incentives for rail managers to concentrate on cost reduction will become less stringent in the presence of governmental intervention to provide subsidies and to set up (or to cap) rail fares.

Evidence from a number of international studies on the efficiency of rail operators does confirm that variations in partial factor productivity can be associated with government policy. With indexes of managerial autonomy explaining almost one-third of variations between productivity levels, rather strong evidence is also available from international comparisons on the effect of subsidy on partial productivity measures: an increase in the subsidy ratio of 10% may reduce labour productivity by 1.2%, energy productivity by 1.3% and rolling stock by 0.8%.

In the assumption that the level of subsidies required to keep rail companies in the market will further delay the harmonization of national policies, the most likely dynamic impacts are to be expected in terms of missed opportunities for really international, commercial rail undertakings to become the driving force in order to achieve an integrated output at European scale (which is the main goal of Directive 91/440/EEC).

Within such a scenario of partial integration, present arrangements for existing European cross-border subsidiaries (such as Interfrigo, Intercontainer, Cemat) will be consolidated and possibly enlarged to meet the objective set by the European Union of enlarging the scale of rail operations in Europe by means of guaranteeing free access.

Also for high speed trains (HST) – where different national concepts for high value rail transport (TGV, ETR, ICE, X2000, IC 225) were not originally developed to be compatible – suitable arrangements will be found to allow for integrated operation of international services especially in case of contiguous networks (similar to those emerging for the high speed rail network connecting London–Paris–Brussels–Köln–Amsterdam).

To summarize, in both the reference scenario and the partial integration scenario a situation is described in which rail fares will continue to be set according to the principle of charging 'what traffic can bear' both in national and international services. On the basis of data and evidence available from European countries – including those that since the 1990s were committed to fragment national railways into business-like companies and to deregulate domestic road freight – rail fares in 2005 are expected to become aligned with the average rates charged in 1991/92 in the European Union.

The more the starting conditions (in the mid-1990s) lag behind those of the most commercially oriented/less subsidized railways in Europe, the slower the harmonization process will be.

Table B.7.   Rail traffic revenues and compensation

	Traffic revenue (million ECU)	Compensation by public bodies (million ECU)	Compensation/ revenue (%)
BR	3,990	1,037	26
SNCF	6,056	3,156	52
DB	7,475	4,776	64
RENFE	1,060	882	83
OBB	1,135	968	85
SNCB	670	1,297	195
FS	2,396	8,326	347
Source: UIC, 1990.			

Table B.8.   Performance indicators in selected European railways, 1995

	Network length (km)	Trains per day per km	Train km per staff member
BR	16,542	66.1	3,628
SNCF	31,893	37.5	2,454
DBAG	41,573	57.6	3,092
RENFE	12,610	33.2	4,194
OBB	5,672	62.5	2,171
SNCB	3,368	73.0	2,117
FS	16,005	54.2	2,608
Source: Railway Gazette International – Performance Survey, 1996.			

The full integration scenario

In the full integration scenario, a context is described in which railways are in a position to exploit competitive advantages on a European scale. The main reason for this is to be found in the adoption of harmonization measures 'to level the field' for competition within and between transport modes in the European Union by means of establishing conditions for actual transport costs to be passed through prices (including those imposed on other users and society).

In a context of fair competition between transport modes, the process of reforming national railways into commercially oriented companies is expected to be both faster and more transparent, once different business lines are able to recover their production costs by charging commercial rates in competition with other modes.

As soon as commercial restructuring results in cost reduction, average rates charged for commercial rail services in 1991 – IC passengers and freight services – are also used as a benchmark in the assumption that their harmonization across Europe will allow for break-even and reflect competitive pricing.

By sharing financial objectives and commercial freedom, rail companies will also be able to set up international undertakings to further explore competitive advantages on long- haul high density European corridors, where both theory and empirical evidence suggests that, in the short run, returns to scale are constant. Competitive advantages for rail can be summarized as follows:

(a)   economies of traffic density are achieved by large trains and better utilization of the equipment and crews other than by a better utilization of the fixed track allowing for larger trains and more direct train connections between an increasing number of terminals;

(b)   at the highest densities, average costs per car per km are about half those at the lowest density: 60% of these reductions are due to spreading crew costs over a larger number of cars, 10% to reduced marshalling and 30% to savings in car time (more direct services);

(c)   if the level of service is kept constant, these results do not seem to vary as a function of length of haul and network structure; if level of service is increased (more frequent services), the economies of scale are greater and correlate positively with the length of haulage.

Commercial companies will also be set up to operate passenger services in the dedicated high speed rail networks which come into operation in Europe by the year 2005. The fares they will charge will also have to recover infrastructure costs.

B.3.4. Waterborne transport

In response to increasingly international patterns in manufacture, seaborne trade – an 80 billion ECU industry world-wide in 1996 – is forecasted to double over the next 15 years. In the light of difficulties and delays experienced in both the Uruguay Round and World Trade Organization to deliver a liberalized framework for doing business in a sector which depends on free flows of world trade, most analysts would still agree on the fact that commercial pressures have already opened up the shipping market and that the adoption of a free trade agreement to substitute self-regulation within the industry – conference agreements to set cargo rates and capacity levels on important routes – would make little difference.

A variety of patterns in merchant fleet ownership have replaced those traditional in sea-faring nations, ranging from the large, predominantly Far Eastern corporations to single vessel companies. With yearly growth rates of about 10% in the last few years, container shipping – 17% of the world's seaborne tonnage but some 60% by value – has revolutionized the general cargo trade, extending the application of containers also to many low-cost commodities. With a stable market of oil tankers, demand for new vessels shows that demand for dry bulk carriers – such as coal and ore – has also been strong.

Also, current trends for maritime insurance, ship broking and ship finance indicate that – despite the industry having to cope with overcapacity in some sectors and pressure on costs to internalize increasingly high safety and environmental standards – the industry as a whole has been and is able to make profits by constantly adapting day-to-day operations and strategies to catch growth in different trade sectors, as well as currency movements.

Where competition is proving stronger – i.e. in container shipping as a result of mechanization of port operations activities cutting turn round times and improving profitability – instead of traditional, price-fixing conference arrangements, larger container groups have formed new consortium agreements in order to share expensive terminal facilities and to plan their timetables more cost-effectively (resulting in a substantial increase in scheduled services on densely trafficked lines). Participants in such alliances also combine to buy road and rail freight capacity at either end of the sea voyage.

The main reason behind the emerging joint purchasing strategies in the maritime industry is to be found in the steady decline of sea transport costs over years. Savings are being achieved by increases in both the size of container vessels (from 3,500 to 5,000 TEU and up to 6,000 and more) and the size of containers (from 20 to 40 feet), which should result in the further decline of transport unit costs.

Within its framework for fair trade and unrestricted competition, the European Commission has started watching over the series of takeovers and withdrawals taking place in the industry as well as over shipowners' control of the land leg of journeys (which may result in an unjustified extension of their influence over sea lines). The Commission is also exploring the potential for short sea shipping lines being established in Europe. Other things being equal in terms of geographical advantage – such as port location and coupling – competitive advantages in this area are currently associated with availability of suitable vessels (some 400 in the Union according to COM(95) 317 final, European Commission, 1995d) as well as availability of free capacity and quality of inland access network (road and rail). The spread in less restrictive working practices taking place in a number of regional ports is also expected to result in competitive advantages for short sea shipping.

Based on results from a sector study that was completed within the framework of this review (European Commission, 1997b) a competitive context is also assumed to characterize inland waterways. Dutch performances and tariffs are used in each scenario, estimated for the most competitive segment of international barge transport in Europe: transport on the Rhine. After the Treaty of Mannheim (1994), Rhine navigation is deregulated and freight rates are currently charged that cover the full cost sustained by master/barge owners (including wages and investment) while the tank transport (liquid cargo) at the moment is so depressed that full costs may not be completely met.

APPENDIX C

Theoretical structure, implementation and calibration of the Meplan model

C.1. Introduction

This appendix gives a fairly detailed description of the Meplan model and its mathematical structure in the context of regional economic and transport modelling in Europe; it also provides the actual implementation and calibration of the model, the key parameters used and the cost functions. For ease of reference it is treated as a self-contained introduction to the model.

C.2. Description of the model structure

Meplan is a computer software package designed to facilitate analyses of the interaction between economic activities and transport within a single, integrated framework. The software is used to forecast the effects of changes in transport on the regional economy and vice versa. The implementation is designed in such a way that it allows costs and benefits of different investment decisions to be calculated in a consistent manner.

Both the transport and the regional economic modelling capabilities of the software are used to quantify the impact of improvements in transport cost and service quality on the efficient functioning of the single market. An earlier version of this model was used in 1991 for the European Commission to analyse the regional economic effects in the European Community of the opening of the Channel Tunnel.

In this appendix, a very brief description is given of the model. Details of the mathematical structure, data use, parameter calibration and validation are provided.

C.3. Model calibration

This section presents the model implementation and calibration process, and provides key parameter values used in the model. It follows the same sequence as in Section C.2 above in describing the regional economic, interface and transport modules.

C.3.1. Regional economic module

Calibration of the regional economic module

Calibration of the regional economic module consists of the following tasks: first, definition of demand coefficients, including the technical coefficients between sectors of industry and demand for personal trips; second, estimation of the spatial allocation model.

Definition of demand coefficients: Use of Leontief input-output tables

The purpose of using Leontief input-output tables is to establish the demand-supply relationships between the final demand and the industries, and amongst the industries themselves. The input-output tables (IOTs) used in the regional economic model are the 59-

branch country-specific tables for the year 1985, published by Eurostat (Eurostat, 1995). Eurostat have also recently published the 1991 IOT for EUR-12, at the level of 25 branches (*ibid.*). The 1991 table, however, is not officially available at the country level and the industrial sectors are treated in a much more aggregated way. For example, it treats all energy industries, including coal, crude petroleum, refined petroleum products, gas and electricity as one branch. Whilst it may be appropriate to do so from the point of view of input-output analysis, this 25-branch table cannot be readily used in this study where the freight demand of the products need to be modelled separately. In other words, the 1985 tables appear to be, to date, the most appropriate source of IOTs for this study.

However, not all countries in the EUR-15 are covered by these 59-branch tables. For the purpose of this study, the existing tables are often used to cover a wider geographical area or to represent countries at a similar stage of development. Table C.1 shows the actual use of the IOTs.

Table C.1.   IOT used for each country group

Country group	Country group name	IOT used of
1	Germany/Austria	Former West Germany
2	Denmark/Sweden/Finland	Denmark
3	France	France
4	Italy	Italy
5	Benelux	Netherlands
6	Spain/Portugal/Greece	Spain
7	UK/Ireland	UK

In order to keep the number of factors within an appropriate and manageable dimension, some of the branches of the IOTs are amalgamated (Table C.2). Sectors that generate distinctive freight demand are kept separate. Transport services branches are also kept separate as in the original IOTs.

The technical coefficients, calculated for each of the seven IOTs, are presented in Tables C.3 to C.9.

Table C.2.   Definition of factors 11-44: amalgamation of NACE-Clio R59 branches

Factor number	NACE-Clio R59	Factor name	Unit
11	010	Agriculture, forestry and fishery products	million ECU 1991
12	031/033/050	Coal and coking	million ECU 1991
13	071	Crude petroleum	million ECU 1991
14	073	Petroleum products	million ECU 1991
15	075	Natural gas	million ECU 1991
16	095-110	Other power, water and manufactured gas	million ECU 1991
17	135-137	Ferrous and non-ferrous ores and metals	million ECU 1991
18	151/153/155	Cement, glass and ceramic products	million ECU 1991
19	157	Other non-metallic minerals and derived products	million ECU 1991
20	170	Chemical products	million ECU 1991
21	190	Metal products	million ECU 1991
22	210	Agricultural and industrial machinery	million ECU 1991
23	230	Office machines, etc.	million ECU 1991
24	250	Electrical goods	million ECU 1991
25	270/290	Transport equipment	million ECU 1991
26	310/330/350/370/390	Food, beverages, tobacco	million ECU 1991
27	410/430/450	Textile and clothing, leather, footwear	million ECU 1991
28	471/473	Paper and printing products	million ECU 1991
29	490	Rubber and plastic products	million ECU 1991
30	510	Other manufacturing products	million ECU 1991
31	530	Building and civil engineering works	million ECU 1991
32	550/570	Recovery, repair services, wholesale and retail trade	million ECU 1991
33	590	Lodging and catering services	million ECU 1991
34	611	Railway transport services	million ECU 1991
35	613	Road transport services	million ECU 1991
36	617	Inland waterways services	million ECU 1991
37	631	Maritime transport services	million ECU 1991
39	633	Air transport services	million ECU 1991
40	650	Auxiliary transport services	million ECU 1991
41	670	Communications	million ECU 1991
42	690	Credit and insurance	million ECU 1991
43	710/730/750/770/790	Other market services	million ECU 1991
44	810/850/890/930	Non-market services	million ECU 1991

Table C.3. Technical coefficients: West Germany

Factor	11	12	13	14	15	16	17	18	19	20	21	22	23	24	25	26	27	28	29	30	31	32	33	34	35	36	37	39	40	41	42	43	44
11	.0839	.0013	.0000	.0000	.0000	.0000	.0001	.0002	.0010	.0010	.0002	.0000	.0003	.0002	.0001	.2400	.0187	.0170	.0075	.0020	.0002	.0013	.0552	.0000	.0001	.0006	.0005	.0001	.0002	.0000	.0005	.0077	.0041
12	.0004	.2343	.0000	.0000	.0000	.1185	.0343	.0215	.0029	.0064	.0014	.0001	.0000	.0001	.0003	.0004	.0004	.0012	.0004	.0000	.0002	.0000	.0001	.0001	.0000	.0000	.0000	.0000	.0000	.0000	.0000	.0000	.0040
13	.0000	.0000	.0000	.3535	.0004	.0000	.0000	.0000	.0000	.0000	.0000	.0000	.0000	.0000	.0000	.0000	.0000	.0000	.0000	.0000	.0000	.0000	.0000	.0000	.0000	.0000	.0000	.0000	.0000	.0000	.0000	.0000	.0000
14	.0400	.0078	.0000	.0945	.0008	.0162	.0033	.0362	.0138	.0462	.0069	.0064	.0029	.0053	.0033	.0090	.0047	.0107	.0055	.0032	.0230	.0163	.0113	.0331	.1106	.1423	.0448	.1345	.0226	.0052	.0022	.0053	.0099
15	.0000	.0000	.0004	.0001	.0067	.1697	.0010	.0003	.0000	.0010	.0002	.0001	.0000	.0001	.0002	.0000	.0000	.0000	.0000	.0000	.0000	.0001	.0000	.0000	.0000	.0000	.0000	.0000	.0000	.0000	.0000	.0000	.0000
16	.0158	.0503	.0022	.0063	.0018	.1115	.0337	.0805	.0347	.0375	.0214	.0096	.0065	.0070	.0109	.0141	.0116	.0191	.0223	.0080	.0022	.0187	.0296	.1221	.0023	.0017	.0011	.0003	.0046	.0099	.0056	.0108	.0156
17	.0005	.0131	.0004	.0001	.0000	.0091	.4862	.0042	.0114	.0042	.1811	.0388	.0238	.0448	.0384	.0003	.0001	.0030	.0027	.0470	.0263	.0010	.0001	.0174	.0021	.0014	.0010	.0022	.0055	.0005	.0001	.0000	.0004
18	.0010	.0024	.0001	.0000	.0003	.0002	.0047	.0824	.0737	.0022	.0044	.0004	.0044	.0056	.0059	.0071	.0003	.0033	.0055	.0014	.0330	.0002	.0098	.0006	.0000	.0000	.0000	.0000	.0000	.0003	.0000	.0014	.0004
19	.0058	.0007	.0001	.0049	.0000	.0005	.0022	.0208	.1241	.0048	.0010	.0004	.0004	.0010	.0016	.0004	.0000	.0023	.0008	.0039	.0971	.0004	.0006	.0008	.0003	.0000	.0001	.0002	.0006	.0005	.0000	.0002	.0009
20	.0444	.0054	.0000	.0011	.0011	.0017	.0152	.0318	.0265	.2862	.0173	.0056	.0152	.0177	.0162	.0067	.0403	.0302	.1993	.0421	.0213	.0026	.0081	.0076	.0028	.0014	.0009	.0024	.0055	.0010	.0024	.0139	.0307
21	.0072	.0210	.0002	.0009	.0039	.0081	.0081	.0059	.0071	.0081	.0807	.0711	.0217	.0314	.0701	.0086	.0038	.0116	.0123	.0277	.0367	.0020	.0038	.0055	.0035	.0040	.0033	.0029	.0067	.0006	.0011	.0014	.0075
22	.0092	.0561	.0011	.0000	.0003	.0094	.0017	.0058	.0159	.0068	.0177	.1651	.0199	.0107	.0214	.0025	.0038	.0033	.0050	.0016	.0130	.0032	.0013	.0040	.0012	.0012	.0004	.0010	.0023	.0008	.0006	.0010	.0026
23	.0003	.0016	.0000	.0000	.0060	.0005	.0002	.0002	.0009	.0009	.0017	.0034	.0614	.0025	.0038	.0001	.0001	.0011	.0007	.0022	.0000	.0030	.0022	.0010	.0006	.0000	.0002	.0006	.0013	.0018	.0013	.0077	.0102
24	.0026	.0138	.0008	.0010	.0000	.0091	.0037	.0041	.0064	.0027	.0101	.0538	.0612	.0983	.0408	.0018	.0028	.0081	.0056	.0104	.0205	.0027	.0030	.0101	.0022	.0006	.0006	.0019	.0043	.0101	.0063	.0075	.0055
25	.0004	.0001	.0001	.0000	.0001	.0001	.0002	.0002	.0044	.0027	.0003	.0042	.0612	.0003	.1384	.0001	.0002	.0012	.0007	.0000	.0000	.0297	.0001	.0139	.0055	.0001	.0355	.0022	.0057	.0003	.0000	.0003	.0251
26	.0776	.0002	.0000	.0000	.0000	.0004	.0002	.0002	.0003	.0036	.0004	.0002	.0003	.0005	.0006	.1802	.0002	.0012	.0001	.0000	.0002	.0030	.2311	.0001	.0038	.0196	.0208	.0031	.0074	.0000	.0008	.0068	.0127
27	.0006	.0018	.0002	.0008	.0016	.0001	.0001	.0010	.0028	.0005	.0015	.0002	.0016	.0001	.0074	.0005	.2100	.0093	.0096	.0061	.0017	.0014	.0058	.0027	.0008	.0017	.0013	.0008	.0016	.0017	.0009	.0025	.0034
28	.0058	.0048	.0008	.0070	.0007	.0016	.0031	.0212	.0236	.0140	.0127	.0094	.0128	.0152	.0087	.0175	.0075	.2625	.0192	.0202	.0381	.0296	.0129	.0078	.0110	.0081	.0060	.0096	.0218	.0052	.0195	.0218	.0143
29	.0031	.0070	.0070	.0000	.0000	.0007	.0004	.0037	.0044	.0130	.0147	.0125	.0139	.0348	.0440	.0058	.0096	.0154	.0755	.0258	.0126	.0046	.0017	.0036	.0051	.0006	.0007	.0044	.0101	.0009	.0002	.0017	.0025
30	.0000	.0001	.0000	.0007	.0000	.0000	.0000	.0000	.0001	.0001	.0004	.0001	.0002	.0000	.0001	.0000	.0001	.0002	.0002	.0238	.0002	.0007	.0004	.0003	.0006	.0006	.0002	.0005	.0011	.0001	.0002	.0005	.0008
31	.0057	.0458	.0002	.0183	.0010	.0136	.0004	.0078	.0010	.0010	.0032	.0018	.0058	.0001	.0029	.0014	.0015	.0022	.0029	.0037	.0154	.0038	.0006	.0134	.0046	.0012	.0007	.0040	.0091	.0050	.0035	.0299	.0141
32	.0308	.0115	.0008	.0002	.0064	.0069	.0352	.0343	.0372	.0294	.0422	.0237	.0321	.0296	.0482	.0373	.0321	.0364	.0292	.0406	.0447	.0303	.0387	.0110	.0587	.0328	.0145	.0138	.0388	.0040	.0033	.0078	.0250
33	.0031	.0012	.0000	.0000	.0002	.0010	.0019	.0041	.0041	.0040	.0040	.0100	.0040	.0074	.0023	.0016	.0052	.0071	.0050	.0050	.0015	.0133	.0021	.0010	.0233	.0032	.0018	.0000	.0961	.0007	.0095	.0059	.0034
34	.0021	.0043	.0000	.0061	.0000	.0063	.0056	.0014	.0041	.0026	.0040	.0012	.0005	.0008	.0020	.0031	.0011	.0023	.0018	.0012	.0024	.0007	.0017	.0006	.0085	.0006	.0003	.0000	.0094	.0100	.0002	.0002	.0015
35	.0054	.0014	.0000	.0011	.0001	.0026	.0047	.0077	.0070	.0082	.0090	.0053	.0042	.0049	.0065	.0109	.0040	.0113	.0078	.0072	.0138	.0064	.0198	.0063	.0119	.0075	.0049	.0239	.0134	.0020	.0032	.0025	.0037
36	.0010	.0018	.0000	.0000	.0000	.0031	.0010	.0014	.0025	.0008	.0003	.0003	.0001	.0002	.0001	.0005	.0001	.0004	.0005	.0003	.0013	.0006	.0001	.0005	.0022	.0570	.0000	.0000	.0021	.0001	.0001	.0000	.0001
37	.0000	.0000	.0000	.0000	.0000	.0000	.0000	.0000	.0000	.0006	.0000	.0000	.0000	.0001	.0001	.0002	.0000	.0000	.0000	.0000	.0000	.0004	.0000	.0003	.0025	.0858	.2618	.0000	.0031	.0001	.0000	.0002	.0001
38	.0000	.0000	.0000	.0000	.0000	.0000	.0000	.0000	.0000	.0000	.0000	.0001	.0000	.0000	.0000	.0000	.0000	.0000	.0000	.0000	.0000	.0000	.0000	.0000	.0000	.0000	.0000	.0000	.0000	.0001	.0000	.0000	.0000
39	.0004	.0026	.0000	.0046	.0007	.0016	.0003	.0009	.0000	.0010	.0011	.0027	.0016	.0014	.0008	.0010	.0010	.0012	.0010	.0016	.0013	.0054	.0019	.0008	.0000	.0014	.0009	.1086	.0956	.0009	.0029	.0018	.0021
40	.0083	.0026	.0010	.0004	.0044	.0007	.0048	.0155	.0298	.0041	.0056	.0029	.0008	.0021	.0011	.0109	.0025	.0069	.0010	.0001	.0011	.0064	.0016	.0101	.0848	.0003	.0001	.1479	.0198	.0018	.0031	.0012	.0020
41	.0009	.0031	.0000	.0004	.0002	.0027	.0016	.0032	.0031	.0057	.0019	.0069	.0051	.0040	.0034	.0025	.0051	.0085	.0053	.0050	.0071	.0139	.0108	.0016	.0100	.0069	.0039	.0086	.0198	.0461	.0204	.0047	.0079
42	.0041	.0006	.0000	.0001	.0001	.0058	.0005	.0020	.0025	.0015	.0019	.0023	.0012	.0017	.0009	.0010	.0018	.0040	.0020	.0025	.0060	.0088	.0057	.0006	.0314	.0156	.0097	.0042	.0191	.0001	.6223	.0135	.0039
43	.0184	.0336	.0008	.0054	.0036	.0327	.0158	.0592	.0840	.0558	.0536	.0570	.0794	.0486	.0550	.0353	.0405	.0477	.0565	.0518	.0710	.1351	.0903	.0370	.0359	.0259	.0325	.0352	.0647	.0108	.1546	.0922	.1310
44	.0031	.0015	.0000	.0010	.0002	.0060	.0027	.0031	.0044	.0072	.0042	.0053	.0015	.0030	.0046	.0047	.0026	.0036	.0056	.0008	.0043	.0040	.0032	.0003	.0089	.0046	.0002	.0122	.0046	.0010	.0045	.0210	.1114

Table C.4. Technical coefficients: Denmark

Factor	11	12	13	14	15	16	17	18	19	20	21	22	23	24	25	26	27	28	29	30	31	32	33	34	35	36	37	39	40	41	42	43	44
11	.0970	.0000	.0000	.0000	.0000	.0002	.0000	.0000	.0005	.0008	.0002	.0001	.0002	.0001	.0003	.3406	.0135	.0163	.0029	.0008	.0050	.0004	.0327	.0001	.0000	.0000	.0001	.0005	.0002	.0003	.0003	.0002	.0030
12	.0013	.0000	.0000	.0000	.0000	.2316	.0000	.0226	.0113	.0001	.0003	.0000	.0000	.0000	.0000	.0023	.0000	.0007	.0000	.0000	.0000	.0000	.0000	.0000	.0000	.0000	.0000	.0000	.0000	.0000	.0000	.0000	.0000
13	.0000	.0000	.0000	.4070	.0000	.0435	.0000	.0000	.0000	.0000	.0000	.0000	.0000	.0000	.0000	.0000	.0000	.0000	.0000	.0000	.0000	.0000	.0000	.0000	.0000	.0000	.0000	.0000	.0000	.0000	.0000	.0000	.0000
14	.0234	.0000	.0019	.0077	.0000	.0979	.0000	.0426	.0141	.0242	.0046	.0047	.0016	.0035	.0019	.0103	.0046	.0046	.0100	.0034	.0130	.0142	.0078	.1419	.1186	.0000	.1449	.2021	.0082	.0132	.0052	.0039	.0097
15	.0000	.0000	.0000	.0000	.0000	.0000	.0000	.0000	.0000	.0000	.0000	.0000	.0000	.0000	.0000	.0000	.0000	.0000	.0000	.0000	.0000	.0000	.0000	.0000	.0000	.0000	.0000	.0000	.0000	.0000	.0000	.0000	.0000
16	.0088	.0000	.0000	.0017	.0000	.0222	.0152	.0323	.0120	.0090	.0079	.0038	.0027	.0043	.0023	.0072	.0041	.0088	.0115	.0055	.0030	.0101	.0179	.0126	.0040	.0000	.0005	.0025	.0034	.0093	.0114	.0050	.0173
17	.0000	.0000	.0000	.0000	.0000	.0000	.0689	.0056	.0198	.0009	.0904	.0325	.0143	.0236	.0215	.0010	.0002	.0019	.0017	.0148	.0041	.0004	.0000	.0001	.0000	.0000	.0000	.0005	.0000	.0000	.0000	.0002	.0002
18	.0000	.0000	.0000	.0001	.0000	.0000	.0049	.0487	.0722	.0029	.0013	.0008	.0008	.0013	.0013	.0037	.0001	.0044	.0020	.0010	.0220	.0009	.0000	.0000	.0000	.0000	.0000	.0000	.0000	.0000	.0000	.0000	.0004
19	.0015	.0000	.0000	.0001	.0000	.0002	.0011	.0090	.0779	.0147	.0033	.0015	.0002	.0005	.0015	.0007	.0004	.0016	.0011	.0034	.0798	.0001	.0010	.0004	.0000	.0000	.0001	.0001	.0001	.0001	.0001	.0000	.0006
20	.0592	.0000	.0004	.0016	.0000	.0046	.0055	.0246	.0302	.1451	.0261	.0101	.0157	.0150	.0065	.0087	.0242	.0218	.1883	.0422	.0375	.0075	.0037	.0071	.0036	.0000	.0014	.0185	.0013	.0019	.0018	.0030	.0125
21	.0010	.0000	.0003	.0002	.0000	.0017	.0105	.0045	.0210	.0095	.1096	.0557	.0163	.0267	.0360	.0132	.0031	.0138	.0074	.0205	.0669	.0056	.0002	.0031	.0000	.0000	.0004	.0170	.0007	.0006	.0006	.0004	.0018
22	.0305	.0000	.0012	.0009	.0000	.0068	.0105	.0092	.0157	.0040	.0239	.0812	.0166	.0212	.0347	.0025	.0019	.0047	.0038	.0085	.0206	.0054	.0007	.0126	.0000	.0000	.0014	.0156	.0028	.0021	.0020	.0012	.0034
23	.0001	.0000	.0000	.0000	.0000	.0003	.0001	.0005	.0005	.0002	.0035	.0061	.0398	.0088	.0025	.0002	.0002	.0044	.0005	.0013	.0025	.0004	.0001	.0004	.0000	.0000	.0000	.0018	.0001	.0001	.0001	.0007	.0029
24	.0021	.0000	.0009	.0006	.0000	.0049	.0064	.0064	.0089	.0026	.0088	.0274	.0627	.1033	.0160	.0018	.0012	.0024	.0036	.0088	.0246	.0070	.0006	.0083	.0001	.0000	.0011	.0070	.0021	.0018	.0019	.0031	.0046
25	.0065	.0000	.0001	.0001	.0000	.0006	.0011	.0008	.0018	.0004	.0050	.0100	.0011	.0034	.0391	.0002	.0002	.0004	.0018	.0027	.0019	.0137	.0001	.0536	.0092	.0000	.0336	.0016	.0011	.0002	.0002	.0006	.0122
26	.0989	.0000	.0003	.0001	.0000	.0010	.0002	.0047	.0036	.0419	.0009	.0007	.0010	.0008	.0003	.1365	.0037	.0038	.0027	.0025	.0008	.0019	.3336	.0007	.0000	.0000	.0005	.0024	.0009	.0016	.0019	.0010	.0110
27	.0008	.0000	.0001	.0000	.0000	.0004	.0001	.0006	.0008	.0024	.0021	.0006	.0011	.0011	.0012	.0003	.1986	.0116	.0036	.0119	.0027	.0008	.0015	.0003	.0001	.0000	.0002	.0103	.0002	.0005	.0006	.0007	.0019
28	.0028	.0000	.0017	.0002	.0000	.0078	.0015	.0226	.0182	.0141	.0171	.0078	.0129	.0104	.0057	.0201	.0087	.2386	.0198	.0442	.0658	.0213	.0060	.0044	.0011	.0000	.0041	.0180	.0067	.0124	.0182	.0341	.0144
29	.0018	.0000	.0005	.0001	.0000	.0009	.0003	.0040	.0051	.0093	.0088	.0114	.0101	.0084	.0038	.0038	.0048	.0042	.0446	.0147	.0080	.0061	.0012	.0034	.0001	.0000	.0004	.0071	.0011	.0016	.0010	.0008	.0044
30	.0002	.0000	.0001	.0000	.0000	.0005	.0005	.0047	.0011	.0006	.0010	.0008	.0018	.0009	.0004	.0005	.0027	.0015	.0009	.0744	.0015	.0008	.0004	.0004	.0000	.0000	.0003	.0009	.0004	.0006	.0006	.0005	.0013
31	.0140	.0000	.0035	.0000	.0000	.0834	.0011	.0047	.0033	.0024	.0027	.0025	.0032	.0027	.0017	.0023	.0014	.0029	.0020	.0031	.0025	.0175	.0294	.0946	.0027	.0000	.0029	.0076	.0202	.1147	.0167	.0690	.0261
32	.0593	.0000	.0008	.0004	.0000	.0117	.0794	.0308	.0504	.0135	.0496	.0394	.0253	.0263	.0162	.0197	.0339	.0459	.0135	.0422	.0610	.0508	.0558	.0524	.1409	.0000	.0047	.0366	.0139	.0156	.0042	.0070	.0151
33	.0009	.0000	.0003	.0001	.0000	.0025	.0005	.0018	.0024	.0019	.0015	.0017	.0022	.0016	.0007	.0011	.0011	.0022	.0014	.0013	.0022	.0031	.0028	.0015	.0006	.0000	.0013	.0056	.0027	.0047	.0111	.0037	.0058
34	.0019	.0000	.0000	.0001	.0000	.0001	.0008	.0006	.0009	.0018	.0013	.0006	.0004	.0007	.0001	.0025	.0007	.0013	.0005	.0003	.0008	.0037	.0001	.1210	.0040	.0000	.0000	.0002	.0124	.0110	.0005	.0017	.0044
35	.0019	.0000	.0001	.0002	.0000	.0019	.0016	.0140	.0337	.0037	.0059	.0031	.0023	.0028	.0008	.0075	.0056	.0159	.0055	.0039	.0321	.0377	.0009	.0005	.0002	.0000	.0011	.0018	.0321	.0015	.0036	.0017	.0074
36	.0000	.0000	.0000	.0000	.0000	.0000	.0013	.0050	.0017	.0017	.0010	.0000	.0000	.0000	.0000	.0013	.0005	.0003	.0021	.0001	.0000	.0000	.0001	.0000	.0064	.0000	.0000	.0002	.0028	.0002	.0005	.0002	.0008
37	.0000	.0000	.0768	.0002	.0000	.0000	.0000	.0000	.0000	.0000	.0000	.0000	.0000	.0000	.0000	.0000	.0000	.0000	.0000	.0000	.0000	.0000	.0000	.0000	.0000	.0000	.0000	.0000	.0000	.0000	.0000	.0000	.0000
38	.0000	.0000	.0000	.0000	.0000	.0000	.0000	.0000	.0000	.0000	.0000	.0000	.0000	.0000	.0000	.0000	.0000	.0000	.0000	.0000	.0000	.0000	.0000	.0000	.0000	.0000	.0000	.0000	.0000	.0000	.0000	.0000	.0000
39	.0004	.0000	.0082	.0000	.0000	.0012	.0003	.0008	.0012	.0014	.0012	.0012	.0020	.0020	.0004	.0007	.0006	.0025	.0015	.0014	.0019	.0028	.0014	.0007	.0003	.0000	.0044	.1589	.0104	.0107	.0055	.0019	.0015
40	.0037	.0000	.0012	.0001	.0000	.0004	.0013	.0045	.0044	.0050	.0058	.0047	.0042	.0033	.0028	.0043	.0058	.0063	.0046	.0057	.0017	.0172	.0004	.0003	.0001	.0000	.0288	.0178	.4094	.0035	.0016	.0007	.0043
41	.0023	.0000	.0008	.0001	.0000	.0011	.0011	.0045	.0063	.0049	.0039	.0044	.0056	.0041	.0017	.0030	.0028	.0058	.0037	.0032	.0058	.0080	.0074	.0038	.0017	.0000	.0033	.0146	.0070	.0123	.0289	.0097	.0153
42	.0043	.0000	.0021	.0001	.0000	.0030	.0010	.0058	.0052	.0037	.0031	.0035	.0031	.0034	.0020	.0022	.0034	.0049	.0033	.0028	.0034	.0071	.0049	.0034	.0000	.0000	.0130	.0109	.0035	.0055	.6423	.0087	.0016
43	.0215	.0000	.0086	.0004	.0000	.0314	.0056	.0220	.0312	.0243	.0193	.0221	.0276	.0209	.0085	.0149	.0146	.0332	.0189	.0162	.1209	.0417	.0508	.0200	.0088	.0000	.5049	.0710	.0359	.0614	.1386	.0703	.0872
44	.0000	.0000	.0000	.0000	.0000	.0001	.0000	.0000	.0001	.0001	.0001	.0001	.0001	.0001	.0000	.0001	.0001	.0001	.0001	.0000	.0001	.0002	.0001	.0001	.0001	.0000	.0001	.0003	.0001	.0002	.0005	.0002	.0039

Table C.5.   Technical coefficients: France

Factor	11	12	13	14	15	16	17	18	19	20	21	22	23	24	25	26	27	28	29	30	31	32	33	34	35	36	37	39	40	41	42	43	44
11	.1805	.0035	.0000	.0000	.0000	.0001	.0000	.0000	.0007	.0021	.0000	.0004	.0000	.0000	.0000	.3366	.0177	.0309	.0083	.0008	.0000	.0000	.0360	.0000	.0000	.0000	.0000	.0000	.0000	.0000	.0000	.0006	.0034
12	.0000	.2626	.0000	.0000	.0000	.0270	.0360	.0156	.0015	.0012	.0014	.0000	.0000	.0000	.0002	.0005	.0001	.0004	.0006	.0000	.0000	.0002	.0002	.0002	.0001	.0000	.0000	.0000	.0001	.0001	.0001	.0001	.0005
13	.0000	.0000	.0000	.4533	.0001	.0000	.0000	.0000	.0000	.0000	.0000	.0000	.0000	.0000	.0000	.0000	.0000	.0000	.0000	.0000	.0000	.0000	.0000	.0000	.0000	.0000	.0000	.0000	.0000	.0000	.0000	.0000	.0000
14	.0239	.0099	.0000	.0321	.3545	.0179	.0063	.0427	.0156	.0628	.0077	.0045	.0015	.0033	.0043	.0086	.0065	.0087	.0088	.0041	.0168	.0146	.0137	.0597	.1394	.1698	.1833	.1468	.0259	.0053	.0023	.0046	.0121
15	.0006	.0043	.0000	.0003	.0017	.0036	.0088	.0362	.0071	.0190	.0035	.0011	.0007	.0017	.0025	.0038	.0017	.0040	.0026	.0016	.0002	.0018	.0041	.0012	.0003	.0000	.0000	.0001	.0007	.0008	.0004	.0015	.0035
16	.0069	.0453	.0000	.0084	.0000	.2071	.0294	.0342	.0179	.0161	.0113	.0073	.0051	.0068	.0075	.0103	.0097	.0130	.0156	.0044	.0040	.0111	.0158	.0441	.0052	.0079	.0027	.0037	.0123	.0057	.0024	.0030	.0129
17	.0011	.0036	.0000	.0009	.0000	.0058	.2946	.0074	.0100	.0084	.1314	.0052	.0136	.0436	.0355	.0007	.0000	.0031	.0119	.0543	.0208	.0001	.0000	.0059	.0009	.0000	.0009	.0000	.0000	.0000	.0000	.0000	.0000
18	.0018	.0000	.0000	.0003	.0000	.0003	.0014	.0199	.0440	.0065	.0029	.0522	.0034	.0083	.0065	.0041	.0000	.0012	.0041	.0037	.0449	.0021	.0084	.0000	.0000	.0000	.0000	.0004	.0000	.0001	.0000	.0005	.0004
19	.0025	.0003	.0000	.0004	.0000	.0007	.0065	.0419	.0830	.0075	.0058	.0018	.0001	.0006	.0018	.0004	.0002	.0013	.0007	.0030	.0636	.0002	.0075	.0001	.0007	.0000	.0003	.0004	.0000	.0001	.0000	.0006	.0015
20	.0678	.0130	.0001	.0215	.0000	.0026	.0148	.0307	.0220	.1974	.0227	.0081	.0029	.0099	.0107	.0036	.0321	.0223	.2336	.0169	.0098	.0019	.0006	.0000	.0008	.0000	.0050	.0004	.0000	.0001	.0000	.0041	.0015
21	.0007	.0156	.0001	.0061	.0016	.0041	.0043	.0124	.0043	.0141	.1289	.0911	.0101	.0594	.0799	.0075	.0091	.0051	.0079	.0247	.0291	.0038	.0086	.0099	.0033	.0000	.0000	.0000	.0065	.0000	.0000	.0029	.0133
22	.0137	.0216	.0002	.0019	.0011	.0037	.0050	.0041	.0215	.0030	.0501	.0501	.0257	.0828	.0156	.0176	.0259	.0043	.0076	.0062	.0235	.0036	.0017	.0011	.0799	.0291	.0078	.0061	.0065	.0192	.0169	.0007	.0015
23	.0000	.0005	.0000	.0000	.0003	.0003	.0008	.0001	.0000	.0007	.0229	.0257	.0852	.0004	.0058	.0003	.0000	.0019	.0000	.0016	.0002	.0011	.0001	.0030	.0212	.0000	.0078	.0009	.0006	.0016	.0000	.0073	.0007
24	.0001	.0034	.0000	.0041	.0008	.0113	.0046	.0028	.0018	.0020	.0016	.0828	.0080	.0040	.1510	.0216	.0003	.0058	.0013	.0013	.0336	.0041	.0005	.0221	.0003	.0021	.0032	.0054	.0043	.0028	.0000	.0044	.0136
25	.0010	.0047	.0000	.0001	.0001	.0004	.0002	.0038	.0048	.0004	.0003	.0497	.0042	.0080	.1510	.0003	.0000	.0042	.0001	.0068	.0009	.0033	.0004	.0000	.0060	.0153	.0019	.0028	.0000	.0016	.0000	.0019	.0269
26	.0823	.0028	.0000	.0005	.0000	.0002	.0000	.0000	.0008	.0267	.0046	.1282	.0242	.0000	.0145	.1282	.0177	.0106	.0153	.0204	.0000	.0046	.1124	.0221	.0003	.0021	.0078	.0054	.0006	.0028	.0000	.0047	.0174
27	.0025	.0105	.0000	.0026	.0000	.0031	.0012	.0000	.0042	.0047	.0069	.0105	.0176	.0040	.0003	.0003	.2325	.0365	.0045	.0366	.0334	.0087	.0053	.0005	.0060	.0153	.0032	.0054	.0006	.0072	.0000	.0344	.0019
28	.0024	.0000	.0000	.0000	.0000	.0000	.0006	.0304	.0086	.0201	.0109	.0365	.0016	.0080	.1510	.0216	.0105	.2427	.0570	.0366	.0127	.0026	.0000	.0019	.0110	.0000	.0017	.0028	.0013	.0012	.0000	.0146	.0156
29	.0036	.0000	.0000	.0000	.0000	.0002	.0000	.0099	.0118	.0132	.0002	.0110	.0111	.0422	.0364	.0131	.0124	.0090	.0570	.0521	.0127	.0026	.0000	.0019	.0110	.0000	.0000	.0069	.0000	.0012	.0000	.0002	.0000
30	.0003	.0013	.0000	.0000	.0000	.0002	.0000	.0009	.0002	.0000	.0000	.0000	.0000	.0000	.0001	.0002	.0001	.0003	.0002	.0002	.0011	.0001	.0002	.0000	.0000	.0000	.0001	.0000	.0001	.0012	.0008	.0022	.0032
31	.0023	.0080	.0019	.0084	.0141	.0175	.0009	.0014	.0020	.0012	.0012	.0007	.0016	.0010	.0016	.0004	.0008	.0003	.0007	.0004	.0004	.0012	.0012	.0017	.0007	.0001	.0001	.0000	.0041	.0013	.0281	.0032	.0278
32	.0425	.0067	.0002	.0013	.0001	.0076	.0414	.0298	.0504	.0178	.0214	.0393	.0111	.0197	.0251	.0276	.0231	.0365	.0246	.0178	.0436	.0393	.0581	.0162	.0502	.0296	.0017	.0048	.0055	.0060	.0044	.0146	.0057
33	.0005	.0006	.0000	.0005	.0012	.0001	.0004	.0009	.0011	.0007	.0012	.0120	.0017	.0007	.0007	.0006	.0009	.0005	.0005	.0006	.0010	.0120	.0145	.0045	.0007	.0000	.0000	.0151	.0009	.0007	.0001	.0067	.0042
34	.0038	.0055	.0001	.0007	.0004	.0022	.0065	.0026	.0029	.0031	.0022	.0016	.0006	.0006	.0019	.0014	.0003	.0022	.0014	.0004	.0022	.0084	.0025	.0005	.0006	.0000	.0000	.0000	.0006	.0043	.0003	.0004	.0016
35	.0020	.0028	.0000	.0085	.0118	.0038	.0048	.0278	.0462	.0170	.0147	.0071	.0076	.0149	.0052	.0055	.0068	.0068	.0015	.0065	.0207	.0452	.0010	.0130	.0131	.0270	.0147	.0000	.0442	.0042	.0023	.0022	.0020
36	.0000	.0014	.0000	.0000	.0000	.0001	.0014	.0013	.0031	.0000	.0003	.0000	.0000	.0000	.0000	.0000	.0012	.0000	.0000	.0012	.0012	.0000	.0000	.0000	.0000	.0000	.0022	.0000	.0015	.0000	.0001	.0000	.0001
37	.0000	.0000	.0000	.0000	.0000	.0000	.0000	.0000	.0000	.0000	.0000	.0000	.0000	.0000	.0000	.0000	.0001	.0000	.0000	.0000	.0000	.0000	.0000	.0000	.0000	.0000	.0395	.0000	.0079	.0000	.0000	.0000	.0000
38	.0000	.0000	.0000	.0000	.0000	.0000	.0000	.0000	.0000	.0000	.0012	.0000	.0064	.0042	.0009	.0000	.0006	.0003	.0000	.0029	.0000	.0020	.0000	.0000	.0000	.0000	.0000	.0182	.0214	.0048	.0008	.0054	.0043
39	.0001	.0031	.0000	.0003	.0005	.0010	.0001	.0001	.0000	.0026	.0049	.0032	.0058	.0039	.0039	.0018	.0033	.0349	.0017	.0119	.0052	.0071	.0000	.0039	.0000	.0100	.0000	.1014	.0730	.0009	.0008	.0053	.0008
40	.0002	.0018	.0000	.0051	.0047	.0016	.0068	.0196	.0407	.0049	.0106	.0037	.0107	.0052	.0037	.0025	.0034	.0078	.0035	.0051	.0043	.0123	.0059	.0039	.0064	.0111	.0039	.0061	.0030	.0243	.0213	.0175	.0104
41	.0002	.0001	.0001	.0009	.0022	.0046	.0035	.0006	.0017	.0053	.0101	.0077	.0087	.0093	.0071	.0053	.0082	.0063	.0042	.0059	.0260	.0106	.0034	.0143	.0283	.0111	.0373	.0144	.0082	.0243	.0154	.0069	.0020
42	.0085	.0590	.0001	.0028	.0002	.0030	.0045	.0087	.0125	.0087	.0526	.0990	.0619	.0771	.0727	.0442	.0469	.0434	.0639	.0567	.1247	.0508	.0439	.0816	.0300	.0307	.1223	.0580	.0352	.0404	.6154	.0971	.0629
43	.0143	.0000	.0006	.0358	.0232	.0569	.0131	.0472	.0544	.0579	.0000	.0000	.0000	.0000	.0000	.0000	.0000	.0000	.0000	.0000	.0000	.0000	.0000	.0000	.0000	.0000	.0000	.0000	.0000	.0000	.1509	.0000	.0000
44	.0000	.0000	.0000	.0000	.0000	.0000	.0000	.0000	.0000	.0000	.0000	.0000	.0000	.0000	.0000	.0000	.0000	.0000	.0000	.0000	.0000	.0000	.0000	.0000	.0000	.0000	.0000	.0000	.0000	.0000	.0000	.0000	.0000

Table C.6. Technical coefficients: Italy

Factor	44	43	42	41	40	39	37	36	35	34	33	32	31	30	29	28	27	26	25	24	23	22	21	20	19	18	17	16	15	14	13	12	11
11	.0030	.0003	.0001	.0003	.0000	.0024	.0047	.0000	.0000	.0010	.0548	.0000	.0004	.0081	.0199	.0154	.0199	.3143	.0008	.0003	.0001	.0000	.0000	.0034	.0014	.0029	.0002	.0000	.0000	.0000	.0000	.0000	.1672
12	.0001	.0000	.0000	.0000	.0000	.0000	.0000	.0000	.0000	.0003	.0002	.0000	.0000	.0000	.0000	.0000	.0000	.0000	.0000	.0000	.0000	.0001	.0003	.0005	.0003	.0115	.0194	.0296	.0000	.0000	.0000	.3427	.0000
13	.0000	.0097	.0016	.0070	.0202	.1633	.2046	.3271	.1768	.0000	.0117	.0238	.0118	.0037	.0091	.0085	.0055	.0078	.0071	.0027	.0016	.0034	.0058	.0380	.0088	.0000	.0000	.0000	.0000	.0000	.0000	.0000	.0000
14	.0150	.0002	.0000	.0001	.0001	.0000	.0000	.0000	.0000	.0739	.0044	.0010	.0000	.0063	.0019	.0037	.0017	.0036	.0026	.0006	.0004	.0008	.0047	.0137	.0017	.0416	.0079	.1883	.0003	.5048	.0001	.0000	.0188
15	.0011	.0000	.0000	.0001	.0000	.0000	.0001	.0000	.0041	.0007	.0195	.0094	.0032	.0065	.0263	.0163	.0127	.0112	.0070	.0053	.0094	.0081	.0181	.0178	.0029	.0416	.0099	.0555	.0029	.0172	.0000	.0000	.0003
16	.0101	.0089	.0042	.0118	.0081	.0046	.0039	.0000	.0003	.0605	.0195	.0034	.0399	.3126	.0159	.0038	.0007	.0042	.0499	.0745	.0249	.0823	.2273	.0057	.0279	.0396	.0415	.0951	.0019	.0001	.0000	.0461	.0075
17	.0015	.0000	.0000	.0000	.0000	.0000	.0022	.0000	.0003	.0049	.0004	.0005	.0865	.0076	.0037	.0055	.0004	.0085	.0063	.0113	.0050	.0014	.0062	.0052	.0425	.0136	.2574	.0012	.0009	.0039	.0001	.0003	.0007
18	.0015	.0003	.0000	.0000	.0000	.0000	.0018	.0000	.0001	.0013	.0077	.0001	.0538	.0101	.0005	.0017	.0001	.0004	.0008	.0008	.0001	.0005	.0033	.0186	.0696	.0271	.0127	.0004	.0001	.0001	.0000	.0005	.0005
19	.0001	.0000	.0000	.0000	.0000	.0000	.0006	.0000	.0000	.0003	.0024	.0025	.0155	.0133	.2614	.0404	.0546	.0065	.0097	.0158	.0049	.0082	.0145	.2805	.1293	.1117	.0029	.0005	.0001	.0000	.0000	.0005	.0005
20	.0151	.0100	.0006	.0005	.0036	.0015	.0043	.0080	.0011	.0068	.0077	.0025	.0155	.0133	.0165	.0112	.0034	.0061	.0689	.0339	.0305	.1251	.0629	.0042	.0145	.0553	.0198	.0060	.0001	.0002	.0000	.0051	.0364
21	.0038	.0029	.0010	.0029	.0083	.0000	.0051	.0080	.0014	.0212	.0024	.0134	.0471	.0338	.0165	.0112	.0034	.0061	.0689	.0339	.0305	.1251	.0629	.0042	.0140	.0051	.0104	.0067	.0028	.0042	.0006	.0057	.0007
22	.0063	.0010	.0005	.0000	.0003	.0000	.0015	.0027	.0102	.0000	.0000	.0032	.0138	.0018	.0029	.0023	.0017	.0013	.0259	.0176	.0061	.1033	.0101	.0022	.0040	.0110	.0044	.0065	.0019	.0002	.0002	.0057	.0014
23	.0043	.0010	.0000	.0016	.0010	.0000	.0028	.0000	.0004	.0046	.0000	.0012	.0029	.0002	.0010	.0007	.0003	.0002	.0059	.0057	.0910	.0050	.0007	.0009	.0011	.0005	.0003	.0009	.0003	.0002	.0000	.0000	.0000
24	.0046	.0020	.0011	.0096	.0049	.0009	.0031	.0000	.0023	.0075	.0015	.0113	.0308	.0094	.0043	.0011	.0003	.0005	.0302	.1429	.0427	.0275	.0072	.0022	.0021	.0025	.0034	.0125	.0008	.0003	.0000	.0046	.0002
25	.0194	.0003	.0000	.0014	.0010	.0413	.0674	.0904	.0100	.0511	.0000	.0179	.0000	.0001	.0007	.0000	.0000	.0000	.0942	.0005	.0001	.0017	.0007	.0001	.0013	.0005	.0001	.0000	.0000	.0001	.0000	.0000	.0014
26	.0109	.0004	.0004	.0000	.0000	.0091	.0124	.0000	.0000	.0075	.2313	.0001	.0000	.0010	.0004	.0011	.0222	.1280	.0000	.0005	.0000	.0000	.0007	.0137	.0000	.0005	.0012	.0000	.0000	.0000	.0000	.0000	.0719
27	.0025	.0009	.0055	.0049	.0025	.0015	.0015	.0000	.0017	.0215	.0029	.0028	.0016	.0046	.0211	.0123	.2985	.0006	.0043	.0012	.0023	.0010	.0021	.0012	.0031	.0008	.0012	.0000	.0002	.0000	.0000	.0003	.0015
28	.0176	.0116	.0055	.0109	.0125	.0115	.0136	.0053	.0064	.0215	.0126	.0182	.0350	.0160	.0169	.3063	.0067	.0145	.0068	.0114	.0087	.0086	.0115	.0153	.0127	.0318	.0040	.0014	.0001	.0003	.0000	.0019	.0006
29	.0029	.0025	.0001	.0010	.0017	.0013	.0009	.0000	.0305	.0052	.0009	.0057	.0115	.0131	.0781	.0146	.0183	.0059	.0346	.0274	.0173	.0181	.0068	.0113	.0058	.0082	.0017	.0015	.0017	.0001	.0000	.0000	.0011
30	.0008	.0004	.0001	.0008	.0001	.0024	.0009	.0000	.0001	.0016	.0001	.0001	.0002	.0053	.0010	.0005	.0007	.0002	.0006	.0012	.0095	.0003	.0003	.0007	.0023	.0030	.0054	.0000	.0007	.0000	.0000	.0000	.0003
31	.0273	.0273	.0051	.0494	.0183	.0074	.0028	.0027	.0027	.1562	.0062	.0028	.0280	.0007	.0028	.0018	.0014	.0011	.0020	.0025	.0035	.0024	.0023	.0024	.0084	.0037	.0054	.0174	.0007	.0011	.0000	.0008	.0003
32	.0165	.0146	.0053	.0166	.0252	.0122	.0296	.0372	.0703	.0781	.0843	.0495	.0310	.0401	.0681	.0525	.0554	.0455	.0388	.0506	.0346	.0534	.0705	.0403	.0690	.0849	.1118	.0051	.0013	.0012	.0001	.0049	.0332
33	.0023	.0079	.0032	.0094	.0067	.0026	.0111	.0000	.0113	.0003	.0000	.0060	.0035	.0017	.0025	.0019	.0019	.0012	.0031	.0054	.0048	.0045	.0038	.0034	.0046	.0044	.0030	.0012	.0020	.0012	.0000	.0011	.0000
34	.0006	.0005	.0007	.0130	.0016	.0004	.0003	.0000	.0006	.0368	.0002	.0005	.0006	.0005	.0006	.0009	.0004	.0009	.0011	.0005	.0004	.0009	.0012	.0011	.0009	.0023	.0021	.0032	.0007	.0075	.0000	.0023	.0002
35	.0052	.0045	.0015	.0080	.0488	.0065	.0669	.0080	.0052	.0231	.0094	.0056	.0218	.0154	.0169	.0119	.0101	.0171	.0133	.0144	.0138	.0168	.0198	.0137	.0346	.0322	.0291	.0032	.0014	.0075	.0002	.0105	.0061
36	.0000	.0000	.0000	.0000	.0002	.0000	.0001	.0000	.0001	.0000	.0001	.0001	.0003	.0002	.0001	.0002	.0001	.0001	.0003	.0001	.0002	.0001	.0002	.0007	.0002	.0013	.0004	.0004	.0000	.0000	.0000	.0016	.0001
37	.0008	.0000	.0000	.0001	.0061	.0000	.0000	.0000	.0004	.0000	.0003	.0002	.0007	.0002	.0013	.0004	.0002	.0001	.0005	.0007	.0008	.0007	.0022	.0022	.0014	.0019	.0011	.0004	.0002	.0008	.0000	.0022	.0002
38	.0000	.0000	.0000	.0000	.0000	.0000	.0000	.0000	.0000	.0000	.0000	.0000	.0000	.0000	.0000	.0000	.0000	.0001	.0000	.0007	.0000	.0007	.0017	.0007	.0002	.0013	.0000	.0000	.0000	.0000	.0000	.0000	.0000
39	.0006	.0009	.0003	.0106	.0025	.0000	.0000	.0000	.0001	.0000	.0002	.0009	.0003	.0006	.0014	.0009	.0007	.0006	.0017	.0017	.0025	.0017	.0017	.0025	.0006	.0017	.0024	.0004	.0004	.0006	.0000	.0000	.0000
40	.0009	.0006	.0006	.0060	.0261	.1546	.2612	.0239	.0737	.0306	.0036	.0129	.0025	.0013	.0029	.0032	.0020	.0024	.0041	.0045	.0041	.0073	.0071	.0049	.0046	.0044	.0051	.0001	.0014	.0008	.0000	.0000	.0000
41	.0104	.0059	.0129	.0055	.0121	.0272	.0051	.0053	.0061	.0033	.0074	.0107	.0026	.0026	.0037	.0048	.0039	.0014	.0039	.0044	.0054	.0059	.0046	.0050	.0048	.0057	.0047	.0038	.0011	.0006	.0003	.0003	.0097
42	.0070	.0102	.6391	.0073	.0261	.0083	.0202	.0133	.0232	.0046	.0017	.0171	.0099	.0058	.0051	.0117	.0083	.0050	.0038	.0061	.0039	.0096	.0106	.0048	.0045	.0056	.0060	.0026	.0037	.0021	.0001	.0011	.0011
43	.0629	.0635	.1737	.0566	.0721	.0346	.0364	.0186	.0409	.0052	.0403	.0719	.0419	.0238	.0295	.0296	.0263	.0195	.0356	.0407	.0438	.0317	.0374	.0412	.0480	.0274	.0276	.0105	.0033	.0022	.0000	.0016	.0033
44	.0002	.0000	.0000	.0000	.0000	.0000	.0000	.0000	.0000	.0000	.0000	.0000	.0000	.0000	.0000	.0000	.0000	.0000	.0000	.0000	.0000	.0000	.0000	.0000	.0000	.0000	.0000	.0000	.0000	.0000	.0000	.0000	.0000

Table C.7. Technical coefficients: Netherlands

Factor	11	12	13	14	15	16	17	18	19	20	21	22	23	24	25	26	27	28	29	30	31	32	33	34	35	36	37	39	40	41	42	43	44
11	.0991	.0000	.0000	.0007	.0003	.0033	.0004	.0009	.0010	.0017	.0006	.0005	.0010	.0005	.0004	.3413	.0037	.0025	.0019	.0011	.0010	.0015	.0179	.0055	.0021	.0006	.0005	.0027	.0055	.0003	.0004	.0024	.0028
12	.0000	.0000	.0000	.0032	.0000	.0250	.0217	.0013	.0007	.0004	.0000	.0000	.0000	.0000	.0000	.0000	.0000	.0000	.0000	.0000	.0000	.0000	.0000	.0000	.0000	.0000	.0000	.0000	.0000	.0000	.0000	.0000	.0000
13	.0000	.0000	.0000	.4053	.0000	.0000	.0000	.0000	.0000	.0000	.0000	.0000	.0000	.0000	.0000	.0000	.0000	.0000	.0000	.0000	.0000	-.0037	.0000	.0000	.0000	.0000	.0000	.0000	.0000	.0000	.0000	.0000	.0000
14	.0099	.0000	.0000	.0108	.0002	.0066	.0018	.0049	.0046	.0469	.0028	.0015	.0005	.0015	.0014	.0012	.0006	.0011	.0011	.0022	.0134	.0000	.0023	.0105	.0909	.2114	.2489	.2221	.0119	.0033	.0021	.0030	.0078
15	.0000	.0000	.0000	.0533	.0521	.3760	.0053	.0189	.0043	.0326	.0000	.0000	.0000	.0000	.0000	.0018	.0000	.0034	.0000	.0000	.0000	.0123	.0000	.0000	.0000	.0000	.0000	.0000	.0000	.0000	.0000	.0000	.0000
16	.0252	.0000	.0000	.0031	.0021	.0836	.0284	.0277	.0198	.0141	.0093	.0038	.0016	.0046	.0029	.0089	.0053	.0070	.0113	.0079	.0020	.0009	.0283	.0934	.0069	.0000	.0000	.0032	.0126	.0027	.0062	.0093	.0105
17	.0002	.0000	.0000	.0001	.0001	.0035	.1265	.0052	.0194	.0025	.1170	.0274	.0166	.0150	.0149	.0013	.0001	.0001	.0029	.0000	.0000	.0013	.0000	.0000	.0000	.0000	.0010	.0000	.0002	.0000	.0003	.0003	.0012
18	.0005	.0000	.0000	.0002	.0002	.0001	.0042	.0385	.0730	.0020	.0046	.0006	.0016	.0026	.0009	.0052	.0000	.0006	.0033	.0037	.0230	.0018	.0009	.0000	.0000	.0000	.0000	.0000	.0000	.0000	.0001	.0008	.0006
19	.0024	.0000	.0000	.0001	.0079	.0000	.0018	.0176	.0642	.0058	.0009	.0002	.0010	.0007	.0016	.0005	.0319	.0030	.0006	.0016	.0688	.0129	.0000	.0133	.0000	.0000	.0000	.0000	.0000	.0000	.0016	.0005	.0023
20	.0196	.0000	.0000	.0032	.0050	.0052	.0074	.0213	.0103	.2017	.0096	.0019	.0000	.0067	.0121	.0082	.0083	.0154	.1495	.0284	.0104	.0054	.0022	.0022	.0017	.0116	.0014	.0011	.0015	.0014	.0017	.0113	.0060
21	.0120	.0000	.0000	.0027	.0094	.0059	.0077	.0062	.0166	.0073	.1086	.0390	.0192	.0117	.0312	.0115	.0014	.0060	.0039	.0200	.0548	.0080	.0001	.0376	.0004	.0105	.0007	.0010	.0048	.0002	.0021	.0017	.0155
22	.0008	.0000	.0000	.0026	.0000	.0091	.0060	.0054	.0086	.0033	.0117	.0805	.0099	.0058	.0368	.0018	.0000	.0028	.0052	.0056	.0138	.0029	.0007	.0315	.0018	.0000	.0017	.0051	.0185	.0247	.0018	.0010	.0055
23	.0000	.0000	.0000	.0000	.0067	.0000	.0000	.0000	.0000	.0000	.0000	.0000	.0099	.0000	.0446	.0000	.0005	.0017	.0034	.0000	.0000	.0260	.0000	.0000	.0016	.0006	.0002	.0000	.0000	.0000	.0071	.0003	.0000
24	.0006	.0000	.0000	.0009	.0004	.0142	.0034	.0009	.0011	.0018	.0112	.0317	.2568	.0937	.0010	.0010	.0001	.0020	.0005	.0186	.0296	.0163	.0027	.0072	.0032	.0000	.0148	.0120	.0045	.0064	.0006	.0070	.0175
25	.0010	.0000	.0000	.0002	.0001	.0001	.0007	.0000	.0003	.0001	.0004	.0039	.0005	.0005	.0001	.1705	.0050	.0059	.0004	.0175	.0020	.0077	.0000	.0000	.0000	.0614	.0050	.0329	.0021	.0021	.0004	.0003	.0117
26	.1591	.0000	.0000	.0000	.0001	.0000	.0001	.0000	.0001	.0066	.0000	.0000	.0000	.0005	.0026	.0006	.1217	.2451	.0058	.0006	.0004	.0085	.2347	.0000	.0021	.0000	.0024	.0186	.0000	.0000	.0002	.0094	.0128
27	.0014	.0000	.0000	.0003	.0028	.0024	.0008	.0006	.0014	.0010	.0014	.0002	.0016	.0042	.0063	.0234	.0034	.0128	.0179	.0026	.0007	.0336	.0028	.0022	.0048	.0022	.0024	.0014	.0031	.0031	.0001	.0010	.0025
28	.0025	.0000	.0000	.0012	.0083	.0024	.0043	.0153	.0209	.0129	.0104	.0035	.0073	.0090	.0121	.0078	.0132	.0005	.0622	.0306	.0368	.0088	.0121	.0105	.0096	.0022	.0002	.0058	.0141	.0141	.0139	.0223	.0186
29	.0023	.0000	.0000	.0010	.0001	.0044	.0060	.0129	.0188	.0095	.0106	.0084	.0208	.0020	.0026	.0003	.0005	.0042	.0007	.0096	.0155	.0032	.0006	.0061	.0008	.0000	.0005	.0005	.0007	.0005	.0004	.0017	.0026
30	.0002	.0000	.0000	.0004	.0002	.0017	.0010	.0007	.0004	.0005	.0013	.0010	.0005	.0016	.0010	.0016	.0009	.0353	.0030	.0281	.0013	.0085	.0102	.0011	.0180	.0006	.0095	.0027	.0022	.0006	.0010	.0021	.0040
31	.0060	.0000	.0000	.0014	.0015	.0024	.0033	.0052	.0053	.0027	.0034	.0013	.0042	.0315	.0404	.0460	.0133	.0018	.0262	.0031	.2109	-.0703	.0285	.0757	.0821	.0266	.0197	.0066	.0312	.0461	.0115	.0176	.0354
32	.0333	.0000	.0000	.0061	.0000	.0111	.0472	.0351	.0571	.0291	.0504	.0386	.0977	.0022	.0016	.0010	.0007	.0001	.0010	.0281	.0698	.0126	.0176	.0436	.0026	.0072	.0012	.0181	.0173	.0082	.0167	.0168	.0213
33	.0003	.0000	.0000	.0011	.0008	.0004	.0006	.0019	.0019	.0017	.0024	.0024	.0057	.0001	.0001	.0001	.0000	.0020	.0001	.0026	.0004	.0014	.0000	.0044	.0005	.0066	.0005	.0029	.0077	.0023	.0072	.0065	.0052
34	.0000	.0000	.0000	.0002	.0001	.0000	.0003	.0000	.0001	.0002	.0001	.0001	.0005	.0008	.0005	.0004	.0001	.0000	.0003	.0002	.0000	.0605	.0005	.0144	.0291	.0006	.0010	.0005	.0008	.0023	.0001	.0001	.0014
35	.0002	.0000	.0000	.0009	.0000	.0001	.0002	.0000	.0006	.0010	.0008	.0007	.0016	.0000	.0000	.0000	.0000	.0000	.0000	.0009	.0028	.0081	.0005	.0044	.0004	.0011	.0002	.0006	.0037	.0006	.0017	.0011	.0027
36	.0000	.0000	.0000	.0000	.0001	.0000	.0000	.0000	.0000	.0000	.0000	.0000	.0000	.0005	.0004	.0002	.0001	.0005	.0000	.0000	.0004	.0002	.0000	.0006	.0002	.0476	.0640	.0003	.0017	.0004	.0000	.0000	.0001
37	.0000	.0000	.0000	.0000	.0105	.0000	.0000	.0000	.0000	.0000	.0000	.0000	.0000	.0003	.0002	.0001	.0000	.0004	.0002	.0000	.0000	.0025	.0000	.0011	.0002	.0028	.0014	.0003	.0006	.0003	.0000	.0000	.0001
38	.0000	.0000	.0000	.0000	.0020	.0001	.0002	.0006	.0003	.0003	.0003	.0005	.0010	.0026	.0014	.0016	.0018	.0077	.0001	.0006	.0001	.0271	.0003	.0122	.0018	.0000	.0531	.0000	.0000	.0000	.0000	.0000	.0000
39	.0000	.0000	.0000	.0001	.0134	.0000	.0001	.0002	.0003	.0003	.0001	.0002	.0005	.0005	.0009	.0012	.0012	.0114	.0017	.0002	.0002	.0143	.0072	.0088	.0102	.0006	.0095	.0222	.0009	.0025	.0004	.0001	.0004
40	.0000	.0000	.0000	.0008	.0019	.0063	.0011	.0028	.0043	.0028	.0034	.0024	.0052	.0026	.0014	.0016	.0018	.0486	.0160	.0050	.0021	.0130	.0118	.0022	.0074	.0454	.0043	.0448	.0735	.0021	.0018	.0004	.0006
41	.0032	.0000	.0000	.0014	.0105	.0063	.0011	.0028	.0043	.0028	.0034	.0024	.0052	.0026	.0014	.0016	.0018	.0077	.0017	.0050	.0021	.0143	.0072	.0088	.0102	.0089	.0095	.0084	.0214	.0080	.0817	.0096	.0085
42	.0060	.0000	.0000	.0003	.0020	.0014	.0006	.0011	.0014	.0012	.0016	.0014	.0010	.0005	.0009	.0012	.0012	.0114	.0160	.0014	.0036	.0130	.0118	.0022	.0074	.0116	.0043	.0050	.0111	.0001	.5960	.0040	.0074
43	.0197	.0000	.0000	.0337	.0134	.0193	.0353	.0531	.0641	.0514	.0473	.0430	.1045	.0422	.0324	.0422	.0280	.0486	.0259	.0551	.0464	.1053	.0938	.0448	.0715	.0321	.2417	.1868	.1037	.0409	.0572	.0826	.0768
44	.0012	.0000	.0000	.0035	.0019	.0200	.0023	.0028	.0047	.0047	.0035	.0035	.0047	.0033	.0026	.0033	.0025	.0058	.0029	.0067	.0036	.0111	.0132	.0138	.0071	.0050	.0017	.0006	.0099	.0075	.0072	.0107	.0285

Table C.8. Technical coefficients: Spain

Factor	44	43	42	41	40	39	37	36	35	34	33	32	31	30	29	28	27	26	25	24	23	22	21	20	19	18	17	16	15	14	13	12	11
11	.0030	.0011	.0000	.0000	.0000	.0000	.0006	.0000	.0000	.0000	.0437	.0001	.0002	.0014	.0233	.0553	.0250	.3848	.0000	.0000	.0000	.0000	.0000	.0064	.0000	.0001	.0000	.0000	.0000	.0000	.0000	.0000	.1540
12	.0040	.0002	.0003	.0001	.0000	.0000	.0002	.0000	.0000	.0019	.0004	.0000	.0005	.0004	.0003	.0004	.0003	.0004	.0002	.0001	.0000	.0002	.0018	.0039	.0007	.0336	.0317	.1226	.0000	.0000	.0000	.1562	.0000
13	.0000	.0000	.0000	.0000	.0000	.0000	.0000	.0000	.0000	.0000	.0000	.0000	.0000	.0000	.0000	.0000	.0000	.0000	.0000	.0000	.0011	.0000	.0000	.0000	.0000	.0000	.0000	.0000	.0000	.5889	.0011	.0000	.0000
14	.0122	.0080	.0008	.0029	.0105	.1963	.2285	.0000	.1990	.0927	.0247	.0059	.0255	.0017	.0072	.0160	.0074	.0098	.0041	.0032	.0002	.0024	.0066	.0229	.0549	.0537	.0130	.0489	.0009	.0444	.0003	.0107	.0358
15	.0003	.0003	.0001	.0001	.0009	.0000	.0000	.0000	.0000	.0000	.0018	.0013	.0001	.0002	.0021	.0014	.0021	.0005	.0001	.0009	.0000	.0002	.0018	.0057	.0010	.0050	.0023	.0165	.0853	.0000	.0000	.0000	.0000
16	.0178	.0053	.0081	.0093	.0087	.0013	.0017	.0000	.0033	.1103	.0298	.0226	.0033	.0057	.0249	.0248	.0164	.0088	.0101	.0100	.0011	.0054	.0205	.0434	.0353	.0666	.0471	.1220	.0034	.0053	.0006	.0388	.0229
17	.0000	.0000	.0000	.0001	.0028	.0000	.0000	.0000	.0009	.0000	.0000	.0000	.0300	.0472	.0158	.0048	.0007	.0014	.0880	.0871	.0092	.0608	.2423	.0101	.0247	.0109	.4423	.0006	.0000	.0000	.0019	.0047	.0003
18	.0003	.0002	.0000	.0001	.0031	.0006	.0027	.0000	.0005	.0000	.0033	.0030	.0744	.0016	.0018	.0015	.0002	.0092	.0084	.0073	.0002	.0008	.0032	.0055	.1038	.0302	.0058	.0007	.0000	.0000	.0004	.0001	.0003
19	.0000	.0000	.0000	.0000	.0024	.0000	.0000	.0000	.0000	.0000	.0000	.0000	.0706	.0020	.0000	.0015	.0002	.0005	.0002	.0010	.0002	.0006	.0028	.0277	.0961	.0165	.0035	.0002	.0000	.0000	.0007	.0000	.0003
20	.0150	.0084	.0014	.0006	.0022	.0004	.0035	.0000	.0014	.0005	.0151	.0110	.0160	.0395	.2591	.0482	.0783	.0091	.0158	.0293	.0015	.0053	.0182	.1633	.0242	.0441	.0193	.0022	.0001	.0003	.0002	.0082	.0533
21	.0072	.0006	.0007	.0003	.0095	.0009	.0074	.0000	.0023	.0044	.0059	.0038	.0372	.0080	.0046	.0099	.0019	.0130	.0779	.0280	.0092	.0708	.0577	.0108	.0097	.0031	.0011	.0042	.0000	.0022	.0001	.0048	.0047
22	.0174	.0013	.0002	.0007	.0004	.0006	.0009	.0000	.0007	.0007	.0001	.0003	.0092	.0035	.0122	.0044	.0076	.0036	.0831	.0068	.0009	.0831	.0086	.0034	.0269	.0133	.0128	.0173	.0021	.0028	.0007	.0158	.0164
23	.0156	.0032	.0030	.0033	.0031	.0024	.0085	.0000	.0004	.0358	.0008	.0013	.0017	.0009	.0010	.0003	.0004	.0006	.0025	.0017	.1340	.0021	.0004	.0000	.0001	.0001	.0003	.0015	.0000	.0000	.0000	.0005	.0001
24	.0066	.0012	.0002	.0060	.0061	.0002	.0008	.0000	.0024	.0000	.0004	.0126	.0271	.0189	.0008	.0007	.0006	.0003	.0428	.0695	.0832	.0261	.0042	.0009	.0008	.0029	.0049	.0146	.0000	.0001	.0000	.0039	.0007
25	.0195	.0004	.0000	.0001	.0050	.0615	.0431	.0000	.0250	.3233	.0000	.0338	.0001	.0002	.0002	.0009	.0312	.0000	.1332	.0000	.0000	.0043	.0000	.0000	.0000	.0000	.0000	.0000	.0000	.0000	.0000	.0000	.0030
26	.0060	.0028	.0002	.0000	.0020	.0036	.0036	.0000	.0000	.0009	.2192	.0025	.0008	.0002	.0001	.0009	.2033	.0738	.0000	.0000	.0009	.0000	.0000	.0169	.0000	.0000	.0000	.0000	.0000	.0000	.0000	.0000	.1335
27	.0052	.0007	.0002	.0012	.0145	.0022	.0041	.0000	.0013	.0081	.0062	.0155	.0176	.0094	.0188	.0056	.0091	.0009	.0089	.0007	.0002	.0005	.0039	.0029	.0029	.0007	.0004	.0001	.0000	.0000	.0000	.0027	.0019
28	.0103	.0127	.0079	.0093	.0004	.0032	.0024	.0000	.0018	.0006	.0019	.0104	.0113	.0267	.0149	.2201	.0221	.0180	.0053	.0062	.0038	.0026	.0084	.0220	.0059	.0257	.0008	.0013	.0003	.0001	.0001	.0095	.0003
29	.0016	.0012	.0003	.0001	.0011	.0001	.0025	.0000	.0350	.0006	.0004	.0004	.0005	.0305	.0141	.0071	.0009	.0136	.0550	.0214	.0064	.0087	.0091	.0143	.0000	.0051	.0006	.0006	.0006	.0000	.0000	.0000	.0036
30	.0029	.0009	.0033	.0007	.0299	.0022	.0002	.0000	.0003	.2456	.0001	.0129	.0000	.1662	.0305	.0029	.0028	.0007	.0004	.0009	.0003	.0009	.0011	.0305	.0011	.0011	.0003	.0001	.0001	.0000	.0000	.0001	.0000
31	.0114	.0601	.0129	.0005	.0124	.0007	.0008	.0000	.0013	.0297	.0281	.0174	.0261	.0023	.0022	.0420	.0035	.0019	.0021	.0017	.0015	.0013	.0024	.0018	.0057	.0037	.0030	.0038	.0044	.0004	.0007	.0453	.0015
32	.0099	.0076	.0034	.0042	.0026	.0098	.0148	.0000	.0741	.0007	.0656	.0017	.0104	.0225	.0245	.0100	.0254	.0172	.0051	.0186	.0115	.0137	.0331	.0140	.0239	.0231	.0549	.0099	.0018	.0022	.0003	.0083	.0192
33	.0072	.0059	.0083	.0004	.0010	.0366	.0055	.0000	.0070	.0000	.0002	.0004	.0021	.0069	.0109	.0008	.0120	.0046	.0068	.0081	.0023	.0069	.0067	.0086	.0200	.0063	.0025	.0089	.0040	.0054	.0000	.0035	.0011
34	.0028	.0001	.0003	.0120	.0088	.0006	.0006	.0000	.0006	.0428	.0138	.0032	.0339	.0003	.0008	.0180	.0004	.0006	.0009	.0003	.0001	.0003	.0008	.0008	.0012	.0007	.0018	.0013	.0000	.0001	.0000	.0000	.0005
35	.0062	.0022	.0021	.0075	.0000	.0084	.0068	.0000	.0070	.0000	.0000	.0002	.0000	.0126	.0154	.0004	.0125	.0197	.0126	.0063	.0022	.0090	.0134	.0195	.0224	.0175	.0179	.0059	.0005	.0012	.0007	.0149	.0148
36	.0000	.0000	.0000	.0000	.0012	.0000	.0000	.0000	.0000	.0025	.0002	.0002	.0011	.0006	.0007	.0000	.0004	.0002	.0005	.0002	.0001	.0002	.0007	.0008	.0041	.0028	.0000	.0000	.0000	.0000	.0000	.0000	.0000
37	.0004	.0001	.0001	.0012	.0000	.0010	.0224	.0000	.0005	.0000	.0000	.0000	.0000	.0000	.0000	.0021	.0000	.0000	.0000	.0000	.0000	.0000	.0000	.0000	.0000	.0000	.0000	.0000	.0000	.0000	.0000	.0010	.0004
39	.0000	.0000	.0000	.0000	.0036	.0000	.0000	.0000	.0000	.0001	.0001	.0007	.0015	.0008	.0023	.0028	.0013	.0011	.0012	.0006	.0006	.0008	.0011	.0021	.0019	.0036	.0016	.0038	.0002	.0001	.0000	.0018	.0000
40	.0020	.0015	.0036	.0036	.0059	.0389	.0090	.0000	.0002	.0150	.0006	.0015	.0009	.0011	.0032	.0039	.0026	.0020	.0017	.0022	.0002	.0011	.0022	.0017	.0011	.0022	.0006	.0018	.0006	.0005	.0004	.0032	.0001
41	.0003	.0007	.0006	.0003	.0181	.1630	.0064	.0000	.0964	.0081	.0188	.0114	.0040	.0027	.0035	.0123	.0031	.0019	.0032	.0088	.0046	.0028	.0042	.0039	.0061	.0033	.0033	.0015	.0016	.0016	.0001	.0008	.0026
42	.0077	.0070	.0233	.0160	.0088	.0048	.2024	.0000	.0050	.0065	.0069	.0070	.0125	.0093	.0272	.0191	.0136	.0047	.0100	.0287	.0098	.0075	.0136	.0120	.0093	.0083	.0056	.0067	.0040	.0030	.0002	.0082	.0003
43	.0002	.0040	.7608	.0017	.0489	.0035	.0165	.0000	.0166	.0846	.0189	.0568	.0445	.0289	.0430	.0000	.0190	.0125	.0275	.0000	.0000	.0192	.0209	.0260	.0238	.0173	.0103	.0165	.0104	.0144	.0052	.0263	.0013
44	.0842	.0496	.1258	.0332	.0000	.0436	.0638	.0000	.0167	.0000	.0000	.0000	.0000	.0000	.0000	.0000	.0000	.0000	.0000	.0000	.0000	.0000	.0000	.0000	.0000	.0000	.0000	.0000	.0000	.0000	.0000	.0000	.0180

Table C.9. Technical coefficients: UK

Factor	11	12	13	14	15	16	17	18	19	20	21	22	23	24	25	26	27	28	29	30	31	32	33	34	35	36	37	39	40	41	42	43	44
11	.1591	.0000	.0000	.0000	.0000	.0000	.0000	.0000	.0000	.0009	.0001	.0000	.0000	.0000	.0000	.2261	.0195	.0080	.0114	.0001	.0001	.0025	.0237	.0000	.0001	.0000	.0012	.0000	.0000	.0000	.0000	.0009	.0014
12	.0002	.0193	.0000	.0001	.0000	.1934	.0253	.0251	.0111	.0042	.0024	.0005	.0000	.0007	.0009	.0009	.0009	.0010	.0007	.0001	.0036	.0000	.0005	.0000	.0000	.0000	.0000	.0000	.0000	.0000	.0000	.0001	.0009
13	.0000	.0000	.0264	.5392	.0000	.1866	.0000	.0004	.0000	.0033	.0000	.0000	.0000	.0000	.0000	.0000	.0000	.0000	.0000	.0000	.0007	.0000	.0009	.0000	.0000	.0000	.0000	.0000	.0000	.0000	.0000	.0003	.0000
14	.0309	.0146	.0000	.0615	.0000	.0412	.0040	.0154	.0401	.0759	.0033	.0029	.0005	.0013	.0029	.0044	.0024	.0027	.0050	.0011	.0090	.0148	.0026	.0228	.1048	.0000	.0923	.1771	.0020	.0068	.0014	.0045	.0108
15	.0000	.0000	.0000	.0000	.0000	.0000	.0000	.0000	.0000	.0000	.0000	.0000	.0000	.0000	.0000	.0000	.0000	.0000	.0000	.0000	.0000	.0000	.0000	.0000	.0000	.0000	.0000	.0000	.0000	.0000	.0000	.0000	.0000
16	.0170	.0711	.0006	.0040	.0000	.0506	.0276	.0641	.0360	.0308	.0203	.0107	.0028	.0073	.0119	.0141	.0089	.0131	.0219	.0063	.0075	.0292	.0262	.0326	.0044	.0000	.0027	.0050	.0015	.0157	.0185	.0102	.0136
17	.0014	.0789	.0000	.0002	.0000	.0021	.2171	.0141	.0152	.0113	.1910	.0584	.0085	.0446	.0378	.0001	.0001	.0049	.0115	.0535	.0202	.0000	.0011	.0055	.0077	.0000	.0000	.0000	.0000	.0028	.0000	.0003	.0005
18	.0033	.0000	.0000	.0001	.0000	.0007	.0058	.0551	.1061	.0026	.0061	.0022	.0004	.0051	.0039	.0084	.0002	.0014	.0047	.0018	.0312	.0013	.0012	.0043	.0023	.0000	.0000	.0009	.0002	.0005	.0000	.0001	.0015
19	.0007	.0000	.0005	.0001	.0000	.0013	.0015	.0015	.0263	.2015	.0060	.0020	.0020	.0000	.0048	.0001	.0001	.0008	.0015	.0001	.0695	.0003	.0001	.0000	.0000	.0000	.0000	.0000	.0000	.0003	.0000	.0000	.0003
20	.0694	.0146	.0029	.0109	.0000	.0036	.0131	.0300	.0263	.0185	.0142	.0082	.0030	.0131	.0097	.0092	.0417	.0234	.1905	.0189	.0089	.0065	.0036	.0023	.0036	.0000	.0003	.0011	.0007	.0007	.0026	.0026	.0219
21	.0034	.0090	.0291	.0027	.0000	.0075	.0104	.0086	.0111	.0185	.0766	.0588	.0100	.0222	.0415	.0236	.0044	.0081	.0150	.0197	.0301	.0072	.0009	.0026	.0015	.0000	.0001	.0014	.0003	.0009	.0023	.0008	.0027
22	.0073	.0777	.0000	.0012	.0000	.0059	.0122	.0204	.0227	.0059	.0233	.1118	.0016	.0146	.0292	.0070	.0090	.0096	.0108	.0083	.0179	.0075	.0008	.0003	.0002	.0000	.0000	.0000	.0002	.0006	.0035	.0015	.0108
23	.0000	.0018	.0131	.0000	.0000	.0004	.0004	.0004	.0048	.0012	.0002	.0005	.0220	.0038	.0014	.0007	.0002	.0005	.0002	.0004	.0002	.0009	.0001	.0012	.0004	.0000	.0003	.0012	.0000	.0011	.0020	.0028	.0054
24	.0007	.0257	.0000	.0003	.0000	.0178	.0042	.0026	.0043	.0001	.0092	.0350	.0751	.1494	.0429	.0008	.0008	.0021	.0000	.0348	.0066	.0064	.0012	.0055	.0109	.0000	.0003	.0047	.0003	.0392	.0046	.0014	.0167
25	.0056	.0010	.0131	.0000	.0000	.0007	.0004	.0015	.0041	.0001	.0037	.0057	.0000	.0012	.1135	.0008	.0001	.0004	.0005	.0014	.0007	.0198	.0011	.0787	.0461	.0000	.0120	.0370	.0012	.0029	.0004	.0024	.0390
26	.1292	.0063	.0001	.0005	.0000	.0005	.0002	.0021	.0002	.0095	.0002	.0005	.0000	.0003	.0001	.1629	.0120	.0011	.0006	.0011	.0004	.0112	.1517	.0017	.0001	.0000	.0105	.0133	.0017	.0001	.0030	.0002	.0078
27	.0057	.0117	.0000	.0001	.0000	.0043	.0002	.0017	.0048	.0009	.0016	.0010	.0000	.0006	.0076	.0000	.2074	.0092	.0119	.0108	.0040	.0165	.0146	.0081	.0031	.0000	.0000	.0021	.0007	.0022	.0043	.0011	.0045
28	.0059	.0172	.0041	.0008	.0000	.0033	.0040	.0328	.0273	.0226	.0197	.0122	.0646	.0148	.0122	.0327	.0107	.2506	.0259	.0288	.0322	.0397	.0084	.0049	.0132	.0000	.0022	.0065	.0213	.0127	.0508	.0112	.0106
29	.0064	.0003	.0001	.0009	.0000	.0014	.0017	.0036	.0017	.0151	.0113	.0117	.0107	.0152	.0226	.0159	.0115	.0144	.0644	.0314	.0078	.0122	.0044	.0009	.0327	.0000	.0008	.0027	.0005	.0036	.0032	.0019	.0015
30	.0006	.0000	.0000	.0000	.0000	.0007	.0006	.0006	.0007	.0005	.0023	.0018	.0009	.0012	.0010	.0022	.0003	.0006	.0008	.0293	.0015	.0059	.0013	.0023	.0073	.0000	.0005	.0000	.0005	.0002	.0035	.0018	.0077
31	.0064	.0276	.0000	.0049	.0000	.0014	.0012	.0021	.0041	.0210	.0609	.0456	.0252	.0289	.0358	.0313	.0241	.0312	.0206	.0318	.2121	-.0122	.0025	.0392	.0847	.0000	.0082	.0257	.0141	.0639	.0189	.0193	.0263
32	.0247	.0000	.0041	.0005	.0000	.0018	.1118	.0229	.0341	.0058	.0000	.0000	.0006	.0013	.0010	.0017	.0000	.0035	.0010	.0019	.0203	.0013	.0132	.0009	.0002	.0000	.0004	.0145	.0000	.0004	.0016	.0031	.0082
33	.0004	.0001	.0279	.0016	.0000	.0100	.0047	.0066	.0000	.0016	.0029	.0018	.0014	.0036	.0000	.0153	.0000	.0006	.0000	.0010	.0000	.0013	.0022	.0006	.0002	.0000	.0032	.0002	.0000	.0038	.0016	.0031	.0019
34	.0007	.0070	.0031	.0055	.0000	.0023	.0145	.0652	.0063	.0032	.0134	.0064	.0024	.0000	.0022	.0000	.0009	.0035	.0010	.0019	.0004	.0005	.0018	.0023	.0006	.0000	.0019	.0008	.0002	.0005	.0001	.0004	.0030
35	.0063	.0000	.0002	.0016	.0000	.0016	.0190	.0000	.0034	.0022	.0000	.0000	.0001	.0036	.0055	.0044	.0059	.0136	.0136	.0046	.0062	.0319	.0000	.0000	.0114	.0000	.0015	.0000	.0000	.0017	.0000	.0012	.0000
36	.0000	.0027	.0036	.0013	.0000	.0041	.0000	.0039	.0027	.0032	.0028	.0030	.0014	.0026	.0021	.0013	.0003	.0022	.0009	.0011	.0012	.0060	.0003	.0006	.0011	.0000	.0015	.0437	.0009	.0051	.0080	.0011	.0012
37	.0038	.0179	.0000	.0055	.0000	.0100	.0190	.0000	.0063	.0058	.0041	.0024	.0024	.0000	.0031	.0035	.0035	.0063	.0043	.0038	.0024	.0005	.0015	.0009	.0015	.0000	.0000	.0045	.0003	.0017	.0000	.0000	.0011
38	.0000	.0031	.0031	.0022	.0000	.0100	.0000	.0000	.0000	.0000	.0000	.0000	.0000	.0000	.0000	.0052	.0003	.0000	.0000	.0000	.0024	.0000	.0003	.0006	.0000	.0000	.0015	.0437	.0009	.0051	.0000	.0000	.0000
39	.0013	.0028	.0031	.0089	.0000	.0023	.0011	.0026	.0034	.0016	.0013	.0005	.0001	.0006	.0005	.0013	.0014	.0022	.0009	.0011	.0000	.0060	.0022	.0032	.0011	.0000	.1560	.0828	.0218	.0014	.0080	.0011	.0012
40	.0041	.0016	.0279	.0002	.0000	.0016	.0011	.0032	.0027	.0032	.0028	.0030	.0014	.0026	.0021	.0052	.0023	.0036	.0026	.0026	.0034	.0106	.0067	.0049	.0129	.0000	.0046	.0063	.0010	.0408	.0117	.0026	.0009
41	.0045	.0045	.0002	.0002	.0000	.0041	.0011	.0034	.0043	.0022	.0052	.0055	.0024	.0041	.0018	.0017	.0023	.0087	.0037	.0071	.0035	.0251	.0055	.0023	.0079	.0000	.0071	.0136	.0010	.0041	.0539	.0135	.0155
42	.0105	.0048	.0002	.0022	.0000	.0084	.0061	.0150	.0128	.0143	.0151	.0145	.0058	.0116	.0104	.0163	.0080	.0164	.0129	.0121	.0047	.0303	.0162	.0069	.0253	.0000	.0012	.0011	.0000	.0119	.5421	.0123	.0057
43	.0059	.0196	.0036	.0454	.0000	.0160	.0104	.0274	.0319	.0252	.0298	.0283	.0679	.0236	.0179	.0302	.0124	.0321	.0259	.0242	.0570	.0888	.0294	.0058	.0210	.0000	.0001	.0008	.0000	.0030	.0945	.0429	.0220
44	.0186	.0001	.0000	.0000	.0000	.0001	.0001	.0000	.0000	.0000	.0001	.0001	.0000	.0000	.0001	.0001	.0000	.0002	.0000	.0000	.0146	.0137	.0000	.0000	.0217	.0000	.0000	.0000	.0000	.0000	.0682	.0104	.0213

For each factor and each zone, an existing level of production (i.e. of 1991) is estimated. This is done through the following steps:

(a)   the total level of production of each factor, for each country whose IOT is available, is taken from the IOT;

(b)   the total level of production of each factor is expanded to its equivalent in 1991, using the observed GDP growth rates available from Eurostat's New Cronos database;

(c)   this total production is then distributed to zones according to the distribution of the value-added of 1991 at the NUTS1 level, the data of which is available from Eurostat's Regio database. The value added data is available at the level of 17 branches, thus it was necessary for some factors to use the distribution of the nearest branch in the data. Occasionally, employment data were used to supplement gaps that exist in the value-added data, and for zones that are subdivisions of NUTS1 regions.

For countries whose IOT is not available, a simple assumption is made: for each of these countries the per capita production for each factor is assumed to be the same as that used for the country from which it borrows the IOT coefficients (see Table C.3). This enables the level of production to be estimated from the population size of the zone, which is available as a consistent dataset from Eurostat. This estimation is not expected to be entirely accurate; yet it is a simple assumption which is consistent with the wider usage of existing IOTs. Before country specific IOTs become available for all Member States, this approach is likely to remain a practicable option without resorting to extensive data processing.

Private consumption, as a final demand, is modelled in terms of per capita demand. The coefficients are derived in the following way.

(a)   Private consumption of each factor is taken from each of the 1985 country tables, and divided by the population of 1985 of that country, to give the average consumption per capita in national currency. Based on the above definition, the technical coefficients are calculated for each of the seven IOTs. These are presented in Table C.10.

(b)   The average consumption is expanded to the 1991 level, using harmonized Eurostat national accounts data for private consumption between 1985 and 1991, and then converted to 1991 ECU. These coefficients are shown in Table C.10, for all seven countries whose IOTs are available.

Other final demands, such as public/collective consumption, capital formation, change in stocks, and export, were expanded to their 1991 equivalent through a similar process using Eurostat harmonized national accounts data. These items of final consumption, however, are not modelled on a per capita basis; rather, they are distributed as a lump sum for each factor. For public/collective consumption, capital formation and change of stocks, the total for each factor is distributed as a lump sum to each zone according to the existing level of total production; for export, the total is distributed as a lump sum amongst the external zones according to the distribution in 1991 of export found in the Eurostat TREX database. Import from external zones is similarly established. For countries whose IOT is not available, the totals are derived using the per capita estimation approach described above.

At the end of this expansion process, a multi-regional input-output model is established, using the technical coefficients from the 1985 tables, yet all final demand and import values are expanded to their equivalent in 1991.

Table C.10. Private consumption: demand coefficients ('000 ECU per person in 1991 value) derived from Eurostat IOTs

Factor	D (W)	DK	F	I	NL	E	UK
11	.2337	.1911	.2698	.3618	.1517	.2139	.1403
12	.0162	.0024	.0096	.0008	.0002	.0092	.0257
13	.0000	.0000	.0000	.0000	.0000	.0000	.0000
14	.5061	.3987	.4647	.3310	.2237	.3260	.1140
15	.0000	.0000	.0994	.0888	.0000	.0025	.0000
16	.3823	.3477	.2796	.1715	.3815	.1322	.3881
17	.0037	.0005	.0021	.0000	.0004	.0000	.0003
18	.0332	.0171	.0106	.0131	.0164	.0106	.0152
19	.0253	.0041	.0026	.0068	.0036	.0002	.0081
20	.1557	.1125	.2292	.2828	.1426	.1748	.1022
21	.0574	.0433	.0273	.0384	.0456	.0477	.0302
22	.0067	.0606	.0042	.0068	.0059	.0004	.0075
23	.0566	.0201	.0482	.0422	.0012	.0241	.0196
24	.1866	.0910	.1214	.1513	.1550	.0859	.1128
25	.4195	.5214	.3426	.2581	.2943	.1968	.1809
26	1.5056	1.4108	1.2303	1.1450	1.0245	1.1584	1.0109
27	.6216	.3911	.4276	.7479	.4364	.3837	.3599
28	.3712	.2253	.2591	.2583	.2857	.1316	.1816
29	.0756	.0393	.0399	.0499	.0297	.0223	.0308
30	.0802	.0665	.0932	.0908	.0787	.0613	.0779
31	.0300	.0000	.0911	.0243	.0553	.0256	.0779
32	1.7240	1.6496	1.9027	2.1465	1.8759	1.5161	1.7526
33	.4241	.4048	.6181	.8942	.4075	1.2216	.6741
34	.0449	.1189	.1171	.0276	.0399	.0200	.0476
35	.1294	.0842	.0610	.2151	.0705	.1895	.1207
36	.0019	.0000	.0000	.0021	.0059	.0000	.0000
37	.0015	.0165	.0039	.0107	.0035	.0094	.0393
38	.0000	.0000	.0000	.0000	.0000	.0000	.0000
39	.0208	.0641	.0477	.0161	.0512	.0306	.1001
40	.0473	.0517	.0346	.0502	.0243	.0255	.0039
41	.2046	.1456	.1811	.1104	.1464	.0652	.1498
42	.3653	.1628	.2126	.0560	.3190	.0518	.2649
43	2.3763	2.4127	2.1995	1.9258	3.5478	1.4070	.2103
44	.1720	.2813	.2776	.1177	.1318	.1306	1.4402
Total	**10.2794**	**9.3354**	**9.7083**	**9.6419**	**9.9559**	**7.6746**	**7.6875**

An important aspect in setting up the supply-demand relationships is the treatment of transport services. Since, in the Meplan model, the transport module will be used to estimate the monetary transport costs, those costs of transport services as estimated in the input-output table need to be replaced. The following procedure is implemented:

(a) Set the unit cost of transport services branches to zero (the original unit cost being 1.0). Thus, whilst retaining the technical coefficients, so that the total volume of output is generated consistently with the input-output matrices, the hire-and-reward transport cost element is no longer included in the production costs. Some residual transport cost element is still retained in the remainder of the table, yet the residual is unlikely to significantly affect the evaluation results where only the cost differences are extracted.

(b) Introduce the transport costs estimated by the transport model to the input-output matrices, on an origin-destination pair basis, for each type of goods and services.

(c)   Verify that the output unit cost averages close to 1.0 for each branch, in the 12-country area for which the input-output table was originally estimated.

In this manner the production cost of goods and services will reflect the changes in overall cost related to transport, capturing the impact of both direct and indirect costs.

Definition of demand coefficients: other demand coefficients

The only other demand coefficients used in the regional economic model are those of demand for personal travel. These coefficients are estimated based on the UK National Travel Survey 1989/1991 (UK Department of Transport, 1993). The UK National Travel Survey gives the average number of journeys per person per year by trip length and purpose in the country (Table C.11). These are used in conjunction with the overseas passenger trips to derive the travel demand coefficients.

The per capita demand for passenger travel derived from the table above is assumed to be representative for all zones in the study area. This simplification was made owing to the need to avoid extensive data processing, which would have been necessary because of the lack of travel demand data defined on a consistent basis in the countries of the EU.

Business travel demand is then converted into a demand parameter in terms of trips per million ECU of service trade which generates such journeys. Using total trip-generating service trade volumes originating from the UK, the travel demand is calculated at 413.6 trips per million ECU of trade, which is then applied to all service generating trades in all zones (see Section C.3.2).

The total per capita demand for independent travel is split into two categories of trips (Independent A and B), according to the average value of time assumed for personal travellers in each country of the EU. Table C.14 gives the demand parameters for each country. For the split procedure, see Section C.3.3.

Demand for inclusive tours derived from Table C.11 is used in the model, assuming half of the total journeys as 'out' trips and the other half 'return' trips.

Definition of the spatial allocation model

The second task is to define the spatial allocation model, which primarily involves the estimation of the activity distribution parameters for each transportable factor, so that the trade volumes between each pair of zones are simulated in a way that they reflect the current observed patterns of domestic and inter-country trade. Of the four λ parameters the spatial activity distribution depends critically on λ_2, which is the focus of the procedure. Other parameters were pre-set. Due to lack of consistent freight and business passenger matrices no formal estimation procedure was undertaken; instead an approximate two-step approach was adopted.

(a)   For a number of representative destination zones, the λ_2 value is adjusted so that the average trip length of the trade of supply falls within the expected range for the commodity type that is associated with the trade. For freight-related factors, the expected ranges were estimated from the Eurostat New Cronos database for tonnes and tonne-kms by mode for 24 groups of goods; for business travel related factors, the likely range of average trip length is derived from the UK NTS. This factor-by-factor procedure gives the starting values of λ_2 for each individual trade.

(b)   These starting values of λ_2 are then applied to the regional economic model. Trade matrices are generated, which are then converted into passenger and freight matrices that are used in the transport model. The average trip lengths by flow and mode are compared with limited observed data (i.e. Eurostat data are reasonably comprehensive for road, rail and inland waterway modes, yet lack infomation on shipping, which makes calculation of overall trip length difficult), and the modelled passenger- and tonne-kilometres are then compared with the control totals from the DG VII Transport Database. The λ_2 values are then fine-tuned for a group of factors at a time that are related to a given flow (see Table 4.4 on the relationship between factors and flows); in other words all λ_2 of the factor group are adjusted by a same proportion (whilst maintaining the variations of the starting values within the group), so that the trip lengths and overall volume-km totals compare reasonably with the observed data.

The parameters for personal trips were estimated in a similar manner. The actual values of the parameters are shown in Table C.13.

Validation of the regional economic model

The regional economic model is built upon the harmonized ESA national accounts data, taken from the Eurostat New Cronos database, for its estimation of economic activities. The interrelationship amongst industries and estimation of final demand are consistent with the 1985 Eurostat input-output tables (the latest edition available) at a level of detail appropriate for the study.

The estimated distribution of trade in space needs to be checked. In theory, once the interregional and international trade data are processed in categories corresponding to the production factors used in the model, the modelled and observed matrices may be compared to check how close the simulation is. In practice, however, both the inter regional and international trade matrices and passenger matrices come in a variety of definitions, and demand substantial processing and harmonization before they can be used meaningfully.

For this study a simpler approach is taken, which is to condense the trade matrices into passenger and freight matrices, and some overall comparisons are made with regard to the trip lengths and/or total p-kms and t-kms by passenger and freight types. Such comparisons imply an overall degree of accuracy of fit, between the modelled transport demand and the observed. Such data are presented along with the results of the transport model in the base year of 1991. In any case, the aim of this study is to gauge the overall impact of the policies and infrastructure projects; to this end, the aggregate comparisons would seem to meet the requirements.

Table C.11. Derivation of passenger travel demand

Purpose	40–80 km	80–160 km	> 160 km	Total
Commuting	6.7	1.8	0.3	8.8
Business	3.5	2.0	1.1	6.6
Education	0.4	0.1	-	0.5
Escort – Commuting	0.1	-	-	0.1
Escort – Education	0.1	0.1	-	0.2
Shopping	2.5	0.4	0.1	3.0
Other personal business	3.0	1.1	0.4	4.5
Social/entertainment	7.4	3.5	2.1	13.0
Holiday/other	3.9	2.8	2.0	8.7
All domestic	27.6	11.8	6.0	45.4
Domestic journeys included in the model				
Business	3.5	2.0	1.1	6.6
All personal	17.4	8.0	4.6	29.2
Total domestic to include in the model	20.9	10.0	5.7	35.8
Business trips: domestic				6.6
Business trips: overseas				0.1
Total business trips				6.7
Inclusive personal trips: domestic	0.6	0.4	0.4	1.4
Inclusive personal trips: overseas				0.2
Total inclusive personal trips				1.6
Independent personal trips: domestic	16.8	7.6	4.2	28.6
Independent personal trips: overseas				0.3
Total independent personal trips				28.9

Notes:

1   The source of the per capita journeys by length and purpose in the top half of this table is the UK National Travel Survey (NTS) 1989/1991 (UK Department of Transport, 1993, p52). Journey length ranges were originally defined in miles, and are converted into km here. The table above reports only journeys greater than 40 km, which is the definition used in the model for medium- to long-distance passenger travel.

2   NTS covers only journeys within the UK, and thus journeys overseas made by the population in the UK need to be added to give total per capita demand. The total number of trips overseas by purpose (business, inclusive tours, and others) by sea and air in 1991 is provided by Transport Statistics Great Britain 1992 (UK Department of Transport, 1992, pp. 22–23), which are converted into per capita demand above.

3   Long-distance domestic commuting journeys are excluded in the modelled demand; business journeys are treated as one separate group; domestic inclusive tours (i.e. coach tours) are assumed to be 15% of the total of 'holiday/other' trips under 160 km, and 20% above 160 km; the rest is grouped as independent personal travel.

Table C.12.   Per capita demand for independent trips (trips per capita per year)

	Independent A	Independent B	Total
Belgium/Luxembourg	5.3	9.1	14.5
Denmark	3.6	10.9	14.5
Germany	7.8	6.7	14.5
Greece	0.0	14.5	14.5
Spain	0.0	14.5	14.5
France	7.7	6.7	14.5
Ireland	2.2	12.2	14.5
Italy	5.5	9.0	14.5
Netherlands	4.3	10.2	14.5
Portugal	0.0	14.5	14.5
United Kingdom	1.8	12.7	14.5
Finland	3.4	11.0	14.5
Sweden	5.3	9.2	14.5
Austria	7.8	6.7	14.5

Note: Different from Table C.11, the travel demand in this table is presented in terms of the out journey only. For example, the total demand for out-journeys is 14.5, whereas the sum of out and return journeys is 28.9.

Table C.13.   Activity distribution parameter values

Factor	Factor name	λ_1	λ_2	λ_3	λ_4
11	Agriculture, forestry and fishery products	1.0	2.0	0.5	0.4
12	Coal and coking	1.0	10.0	0.5	0.3
13	Crude petroleum	0.1	5,000.0	0.5	0.4
14	Petroleum products	1.0	35.0	0.1	0.8
15	Natural gas	0.1	5,000.0	0.1	0.5
16	Other power, water and manufactured gas	0.1	5,000.0	0.1	0.5
17	Ferrous and non-ferrous ores and metals	1.0	50.0	0.5	0.5
18	Cement, glass and ceramic products	1.0	12.0	0.5	0.5
19	Other non-metallic minerals and derived products	1.0	9.0	0.5	0.5
20	Chemical products	1.0	25.0	0.3	0.5
21	Metal products	1.0	28.0	0.3	0.5
22	Agricultural and industrial machinery	1.0	6.0	0.3	0.5
23	Office machines, etc.	1.0	3.2	0.3	0.5
24	Electrical goods	1.0	3.2	0.3	0.5
25	Transport equipment	1.0	6.0	0.3	0.5
26	Food, beverages, tobacco	1.0	3.0	0.3	0.5
27	Textile and clothing, leather, footwear	1.0	4.0	0.3	0.5
28	Paper and printing products	1.0	9.0	0.3	0.5
29	Rubber and plastic products	1.0	3.2	0.3	0.5
30	Other manufacturing products	1.0	3.2	0.3	0.5
31	Building and civil engineering works	0.1	4,000.0	0.1	0.5
32	Recovery, repair services, wholesale and retail trade	1.0	11.0	0.3	0.5
33	Lodging and catering services	0.1	200.0	0.1	0.5
34	Railway transport services	0.1	200.0	0.1	0.5
35	Road transport services	0.1	200.0	0.1	0.5
36	Inland waterways services	0.1	200.0	0.1	0.5
37	Maritime transport services	0.1	200.0	0.1	0.5
39	Air transport services	0.1	200.0	0.1	0.5
40	Auxiliary transport services	0.1	200.0	0.1	0.5
41	Communications	1.0	11.0	0.3	0.5
42	Credit and insurance	1.0	7.6	0.3	0.5
43	Other market services	1.0	7.6	0.3	0.5
44	Non-market services	1.0	7.6	0.3	0.5
61	Inclusive personal tours	0.0	715.0	1.0	0.5
63	Independent personal travel A	0.0	170.0	0.5	0.5
64	Independent personal travel B	0.0	55.0	0.5	0.7

Notes:
1   λ_1, λ_3 and λ_4 are pre-set, and the estimation procedure focused on λ_2.
2   Factors 13, 16, 17, 31 and 33 through 40 do not generate transport demand; thus their parameters are only nominal.

C.3.2 Interface module

Table C.14.   Volume to value ratios and their application by factor and flow type

	Factor	Flow	tonne/million ECU	Yearly to daily conversion	Remarks
Bulk freight	12	7	6,556.3	Yes	One way, in the direction of trade
	14	6	2,625.3	Yes	One way, in the direction of trade
	17	7	710.9	Yes	One way, in the direction of trade
	18	8	13,974.4	Yes	One way, in the direction of trade
	19	7	45,471.4	Yes	One way, in the direction of trade
	20	8	2,131.2	Yes	One way, in the direction of trade
	21	8	2,332.5	Yes	One way, in the direction of trade

	Factor	Flow	feu/million ECU	Yearly to daily conversion	Remarks
General freight	11	9	102.1	Yes	One way, in the direction of trade
	22	10	22.6	Yes	One way, in the direction of trade
	23	10	77.3	Yes	One way, in the direction of trade
	24	10	77.3	Yes	One way, in the direction of trade
	25	10	22.6	Yes	One way, in the direction of trade
	26	9	80.5	Yes	One way, in the direction of trade
	27	10	46.1	Yes	One way, in the direction of trade
	28	10	13.7	Yes	One way, in the direction of trade
	29	10	77.3	Yes	One way, in the direction of trade
	30	10	77.3	Yes	One way, in the direction of trade

	Factor	Flow	trip/million ECU	Yearly to daily conversion	Remarks
Business travel	32	2	413.6	Yes	Both 'out' and 'return'
	41	2	413.6	Yes	Both 'out' and 'return'
	42	1	413.6	Yes	Both 'out' and 'return'
	43	1	413.6	Yes	Both 'out' and 'return'
	44	1	413.6	Yes	Both 'out' and 'return'

	Factor	Flow	trip/demanded trip	Yearly to daily conversion	Remarks
Personal travel	61	5	1.0	Yes	Both 'out' and 'return'
	63	3	1.0	Yes	Both 'out' and 'return'
	64	4	1.0	Yes	Both 'out' and 'return'

Calibration of the interface module

The factor-flow relationship having been defined, the tasks of calibration of the interface module are basically the estimation of volume to value ratios and the time period conversion factor. The volume to value ratios for freight in this study are estimated from the total freight tonnes information of the tonnes by mode statistics in the Eurostat New Cronos database, in conjunction with the total trade values estimated in the regional economic model. This is done for broad freight categories.

For freight, the annual trade volumes produced by the regional economic model also need to be scaled down to daily volumes of traffic, after the value-volume conversion. A simple scaling factor is set at 300, which means the typical daily freight traffic on the European transport networks is 1/300 of the annual volume.

For passengers, because the demand generated in the regional economic model is defined in terms of trips per year, the same time scaling factor applies.

Correct estimation of the parameters of the interface module is a prerequisite for the validation of the regional economic and transport modules. For this reason, no independent validation is performed on the interface module. In other words, the interface module estimation will be checked indirectly through the two modules that it connects.

C.3.3. Multimodal transport module

Implementation of the multimodal transport model

Transport cost and tariff functions

The perceived cost functions may represent either a cost faced by an operator or a tariff charged to a user. The model requires user cost/tariff information and uses this information in the modal split algorithm.

Apart from cars, the perceived cost functions for passengers have been derived from fares using linear regression analysis. The perceived cost function for cars has been considered equal to the operating cost of running the vehicle: the out-of-pocket money spent for gasoline and lubricants and the use of tolled motorways.

(a)   *Cars* The perceived cost function is based on network operating costs. It is related to distance and distinguishes different fuel prices and different tolls currently applied in each country across Europe (Tables C.15 and C.16).

(b)   *Coaches* The perceived cost function is based on tariffs for both national and international long distance trips in different European countries. An average value for all Europe has been used and the fare is linear with distance (Table C.17).

(c)   *Train* Actual fares for each European country were implemented on the basis of a survey study conducted by the Italian Railways. The function is distance-based and allows for distinction among different flows (business and personal trips) on the basis of a different mix of first- and second-class tickets (Table C.18).

(d)   *High Speed Train* As for train mode, actual fares for each European country where a high speed train service is in operation were implemented. The distance-based function allows for distinction among different flows (business and personal trips) on the basis of a different mix of first- and second-class tickets (Table C.19).

(e)   *Air* On the basis of a study conducted for the European Commission (1997a) by the Cranfield Institute for Air Transport different cost functions were used to differentiate between domestic and international flights. All functions have a fixed component and a component related to distance. Specific domestic functions were implemented for France, Germany, Italy, Spain and the UK (Table C.20).

The perceived cost functions for freight were derived by using different criteria for different modes; in some cases they were calculated on the basis of operating costs while in other cases official fares have been implemented using linear regression analysis. When published fares appear not to be realistic (such as for freight or rail), they were adjusted on the basis of the average revenues per tonne.

(a) *Road* Tariffs for lorry transport were derived from the operating costs of the vehicles plus an additional quota which allows for the profit. The cost terms were divided into a number of separate components: distance specific costs: lubricants and oils, tyres, repair/maintenance, variable depreciation, fuel (differentiated by country) and other variable costs; time specific costs: vehicle tax (differentiated by country), interest, fixed depreciation, insurance and drivers' cost (differentiated by country); fixed costs, which are the annual non-trip-dependent costs of administering the transport firm. The costs implemented are the same all over Europe and were calculated as a weighted average of different European values. They are related to distance and time and distinguish between different tolls currently applied in each country across Europe. On the basis of the distinction among the operating costs of different specialized trucks, separate values for each flow were derived (Table C.21).

(b) *Rail* For bulk flows (liquid, solid and semi-bulk) data collected from different European rail operators was readjusted using average revenues per tonne-km of the major European operators (FS, BR, DB, SNCF, RENFE) from the Strategic Studies Department of the Italian Railways. Specific cost functions (fixed term plus a distance term) were implemented for five groups of countries. Further to the cost function applied to the journey from origin to destination, other costs were included for terminal operations. For containerized flows (general cargo and high value freight) data from national companies offering international services for intermodal swap bodies and containers were found to be reliable and thus were used to estimate a unique function across Europe. The cost function is distance based and in its fixed term also includes terminal traction costs (Table C.22).

(c) *Bulk and container ships* As for other freight modes, operating cost based tariffs were applied for bulk and container ships for both short sea and deep sea shipping. The ships' consignment costs were distinguished in ship costs and port costs: the first group includes the costs related to the ship in movement and to the ship in port, while the second group makes reference to port activities, such as movement of goods, loading and unloading of the ships. Data sources vary from specialized consultancy (Ocean Shipping Consultants Ltd) to commercial brokers of import export companies. Three different functions were implemented: one for port activities (fixed coefficient) one for the ship in port (time-related term) and one for the ship in navigation (a fixed term plus a time-related term) (Table C.23).

(d) *Inland waterways* The estimation of cost function was based on the brief report *Inland waterway tariffs and cost structure* commissioned by NEI Transport. The function implemented has two terms, one related to distance and one related to time (Table C.24).

Table C.15.   Car operating costs

Year	Country	Fuel costs	Total perceived costs
Base year (1991/92),	Austria	0.6402	0.0629
2005 base scenario and	Belgium	0.7362	0.0723
2005 partial integration scenario	France	0.6257	0.0615
	Germany	0.6211	0.0610
	Netherlands	0.6022	0.0591
	Italy	0.9461	0.0929
	Portugal	0.7341	0.0721
	Spain	0.6653	0.0653
	United Kingdom	0.6194	0.0608
	Switzerland	0.4943	0.0486
2005 full integration scenario	All EU	0.9461	0.0929

Notes:
1   All estimated costs are in 1991/92 ECU.
2   In the base year (1991/92), 2005 base scenario and 2005 partial integration scenario: fuel costs are differentiated by country; other perceived costs are given as fuel costs +10%.
3   In the 2005 full integration scenario: fuel costs are the Italian ones; other perceived costs are given as fuel costs +10%.

Table C.16.   Motorway tolls

Year	Country	Toll per km	
		Cars	Heavy vehicles
Base year (1991/92),	Austria	0.152	0.884
2005 base scenario and	France	0.055	0.107
2005 partial integration scenario	Greece	0.014	0.066
	Italy	0.043	0.097
	Portugal	0.050	0.107
	Spain	0.085	0.133
2005 full integration scenario	All EU	0.152	0.245

Notes:
1   All estimated costs are in 1991/92 ECU.
2   In the base year (1991/92), 2005 base scenario and 2005 partial integration scenario: tolls are differentiated by country.
3   In the 2005 full integration scenario: Tolls for cars are unified at Austrian levels on all motorways, TEN projects and other congested main roads; Tolls for lorries are unified at EU weighted average on all motorways, TEN projects and other congested main roads.

Table C.17.   Coach cost

Year	Country	Distance related cost
Base year (1991/92), 2005 base scenario, 2005 partial integration scenario and 2005 full integration scenario	All EU	0.041

Notes: All estimated costs are in 1991/92 ECU.

Table C.18.   Rail passengers

Years	Country	Fare per km
Base year (1991/92)	Austria	0.0779
	Belgium	0.0882
	Denmark	0.0567
	UK	0.0992
	Finland	0.0636
	France	0.0798
	Germany	0.1177
	Greece	0.0640
	Netherlands	0.0872
	Italy	0.0447
	Portugal	0.0404
	Spain	0.0530
	Sweden	0.1158
	Switzerland	0.1137
	Norway	0.1217
2005 base scenario and 2005 partial integration scenario	Austria	0.0770
	Belgium	0.0821
	Denmark	0.0664
	UK	0.0876
	Finland	0.0698
	France	0.0779
	Germany	0.0969
	Greece	0.0700
	Netherlands	0.0816
	Italy	0.0604
	Portugal	0.0582
	Spain	0.0645
	Sweden	0.0959
	Switzerland	0.1137
	Norway	0.1217
2005 full integration scenario	All EU	0.0760

Notes:
1   All estimated costs are in 1991/92 ECU.
2   In the base year (1991/92) fares are differentiated by country.
3   In the 2005 base scenario and 2005 partial integration scenario fares are by country increased/decreased by 50% of the difference between each country and the EU average.
4   In the 2005 full integration scenario fares are unified to the EU level.

Table C.19.   High speed fares

Years	Country	Fare per km
Base year (1991/92)	France	0.104
	Germany	0.147
	Italy	0.056
	Spain	0.067
2005 base scenario and	Belgium	0.103
2005 partial integration scenario	France	0.097
	Germany	0.121
	Netherlands	0.102
	Italy	0.075
	Spain	0.081
	UK (Channel Tunnel)	0.110
2005 full integration scenario	Belgium	0.103
	France	0.103
	Germany	0.103
	Netherlands	0.103
	Italy	0.103
	Spain	0.103
	UK (Channel Tunnel)	0.103

Notes:
1   All estimated costs are in 1991/92 ECU.
2   In the base year (1991/92) fares are differentiated by country.
3   In the 2005 base scenario and 2005 partial integration scenario fares are by country 25% higher than conventional IC trains.
4   In the 2005 full integration scenario fares are by country 35% higher than conventional IC trains.

Table C.20.   Air tariffs

Years	Country	Fixed part	Variable with distance
Base year (1991/92)	France	99.453	0.149
	Germany	91.089	0.1931
	Italy	107.21	0.0956
	Spain	52.705	0.1173
	UK	93.919	0.1182
	International routes	128	0.2026
2005 base scenario and	France	79.5624	0.1192
2005 partial integration scenario	Germany	72.8712	0.15448
	Italy	85.768	0.07648
	Spain	42.164	0.09384
	UK	75.1352	0.09456
	International routes	102.4	0.16208
2005 full integration scenario	France	64.64445	0.0968
	Germany	59.20785	0.125515
	Italy	69.686	0.06214
	Spain	34.25825	0.076245
	UK	61.04735	0.07683
	International routes	83.2	0.13169

Notes:
1   All estimated costs are in 1991/92 ECU.
2   In the base year (1991/92) fares are differentiated by country.
3   In the 2005 base scenario and 2005 partial integration scenario fares are by country 20% less than in 1991.
4   In the 2005 full integration scenario fares are by country 35% less than in 1991.

Table C.21. Lorry costs

Year	Country	Flow	Distance related cost	Time related costs
Base year (1991/92)	All EU and other countries	Average	0.535	25.837
		General freight A	0.519	25.081
		General freight B	0.530	25.578
		Liquid bulk	0.585	28.271
		Semi-bulk	0.536	25.896
		Solid bulk	0.536	25.896
2005 base scenario and 2005 partial integration scenario	All EU and other countries	Average	0.535	23.822
		General freight A	0.519	23.125
		General freight B	0.530	23.583
		Liquid bulk	0.585	26.067
		Semi-bulk	0.536	23.877
		Solid bulk	0.536	23.877
2005 full integration scenario	All EU and other countries	Average	0.614	27.364
		General freight A	0.596	26.564
		General freight B	0.608	27.090
		Liquid bulk	0.672	29.943
		Semi-bulk	0.616	27.427
		Solid bulk	0.616	27.427

Notes:

1   All estimated costs are in 1991/92 ECU.

2   Distance (km) related costs include:

Costs of oil and lubricants	European average
Costs of tyres	European average
Costs of repair and maintenance	European average
Variable depreciation costs	European average
Fuel costs	By country in base year (1991/92), 2005 base and partial integration scenario unified at UK level in 2005 full integration scenario
Other variable costs	European average.

3   Time (hours) related costs include:

Vehicle tax	By country in base year (1991/92), 2005 base and partial integration scenario unified at UK level in 2005 full integration scenario
Interest costs	European average
Fixed depreciation costs	European average
Insurance costs	European average
Driver's costs	By country in base year (1991/92), by country – 10% in 2005 base and partial integration scenario by country + 5% in 2005 full integration scenario.

4   Management costs are 10% of total costs.

Table C.22a. Rail freight costs – Liquid/solid bulk and semi-bulk

Year	Country	Liquid and solid bulk		Semi-bulk	
		Fixed part	Variable with distance	Fixed part	Variable with distance
Base year (1991/92)	Austria	3.93	0.0261	7.85	0.0521
	Belgium	3.93	0.0603	7.85	0.1207
	France	3.93	0.0175	7.85	0.0349
	Germany	3.93	0.0289	7.85	0.0577
	Netherlands	3.93	0.0306	7.85	0.0612
	Italy	3.93	0.0102	7.85	0.0205
	Spain	3.93	0.0151	7.85	0.0302
	UK	3.93	0.0228	7.85	0.0455
	Switzerland	3.93	0.0546	7.85	0.1092
2005 base scenario and 2005 partial integration scenario	Austria	3.93	0.0248	7.85	0.0495
	Belgium	3.93	0.0419	7.85	0.0838
	France	3.93	0.0205	7.85	0.0410
	Germany	3.93	0.0262	7.85	0.0524
	Netherlands	3.93	0.0270	7.85	0.0541
	Italy	3.93	0.0169	7.85	0.0337
	Spain	3.93	0.0193	7.85	0.0386
	UK	3.93	0.0231	7.85	0.0462
	Switzerland	3.93	0.0546	7.85	0.1092
2005 full integration scenario	All EU	3.93	0.0235	7.85	0.0470

Notes:
1 All estimated costs are in 1991/92 ECU and reduced by 45% to equal average revenues per tonne.
2 In the 2005 base scenario and 2005 partial integration scenario costs by country increased/decreased by 50% of the difference between each country and the EU average.
3 In the 2005 full integration scenario fares are unified to the EU average.

Table C.22b. Rail freight costs – General freight A and B (combined transport)

Year	Country	Fixed part	Variable with distance	Terminal costs
Base year (1991/92) and 2005 base scenario	All EU	134.61	0.609	509.0
2005 partial integration and 2005 full integration scenarios	All EU	134.61	0.609	458.1

Notes:
1 All estimated costs are in 1991/92 ECU per feu.
3 In 2005 partial integration and 2005 full integration scenarios there is a 10% reduction in terminal costs.

Table C.23. Short sea shipping costs

Year	Flow	Port activities	Ship in port	Ship in navigation	
			Variable with time	Fixed part	Variable with time
Base year (1991/92)	Liquid bulk (tonnes)		0.1528	2.3655	0.1359
	Solid bulk (tonnes)	5.41	0.0815	6.8078	0.0329
	Semi-bulk (tonnes)	27.03	0.1019	8.5115	0.0411
	General freight A (feu)	139.92	1.4078	78.3702	0.8462
	General freight B (feu)	139.92	1.4078	78.3702	0.8462
2005 base scenario,	Liquid bulk (tonnes)		0.1528	2.3655	0.1359
2005 partial integration and	Solid bulk (tonnes)	4.32	0.0815	6.8078	0.0329
2005 full integration scenarios	Semi-bulk (tonnes)	21.62	0.1019	8.5115	0.0411
	General freight A (feu)	111.94	1.4078	78.3702	0.8462
	General freight B (feu)	111.94	1.4078	78.3702	0.8462

Notes: All estimated costs are in 1991/92 ECU per feu.

Table C.24. Inland waterway costs

Year	Country	Flow	Distance related cost	Time related costs
Base year (1991/92),	All EU	Liquid bulk (tonnes)	0.00071	0.04235
2005 base scenario,	and other	Solid bulk (tonnes)	0.00067	0.03952
2005 partial integration scenario and	countries	Semi-bulk (tonnes)	0.00069	0.04705
2005 full integration scenario		General freight (feu)	0.01957	1.16352

Notes: All estimated costs are in 1991/92 ECU.

Calibration of the multimodal transport module

The transport operating costs and tariffs having been determined, the tasks of transport module calibration are basically estimation of the network capacities, capacity restraint functions for certain link types, definition of path choice parameters, and modal choice parameters.

Network capacities and capacity restraint functions

In principle, network capacities and capacity restraint functions may be defined for all links included in the multi modal transport network. In practice, time and resource constraints mean that link capacities and capacity restraint function are likely to be implemented only for a selection of link types. Road links are obvious candidates. There exist certain bottlenecks on the rail and inland waterway networks and at some ports, yet in the general European context it would appear that the capacity problem is not as critical as on road. There is evidence of congestion of air space and traffic throughput at certain airports, yet the complex nature of the issues is perhaps beyond the scope of the current study. In particular, according to Eurocontrol (1996), some EATCHIP initiatives have shown remarkable results in capacity improvements amidst traffic growth in the study area. For these reasons, two different methods were adopted:

(a)   for road links, link capacities are estimated and capacity restraint functions are developed based on previous experience in road traffic modelling;

(b)   for all other links, no specific capacity restraint is applied; rather, the link loads produced by the model are closely examined to make sure that no excessive loads are generated beyond the practical capacities on these links, in order to safeguard the validity of the results.

When building the road network the daily capacity of each link was input as one of the link characteristics. Where a link represents one single motorway or road, the capacity of that motorway/road is coded; very often, however, a modelled road link represents a few road links that are approximately in parallel to one another, and in this case an appropriate corridor capacity is calculated according to the network connectivity.

Table C.31 presents the parameters of the capacity restraint functions that are used in this study. The parameters are derived from a previous study of interurban transport in the UK (Williams, 1994). The capacity restraint functions are defined for each link type, yet the capacity of each specific link is taken into account when the calculation is carried out for its speed under a given volume/capacity ratio.

Table C.25.   Parameters for capacity restraint functions

	ParA	ParB	ParC	ParD	ParE
All motorway link types	0.342	3.71	0.924667	16	8.4
All dual carriageway link types	0.297	3.46	0.836333	16	5.4
All single carriageway link types	0.454	1.29	0.323778	16	4.2

On road, however, the interurban traffic, which is the subject of this study, is usually a very small proportion of the total traffic, and it is the local traffic that is dominant. In order to represent correctly the link capacities, the volume of local traffic has to be estimated. The procedure for this estimation is:

(a)   code on each link the observed total traffic load in passenger car unit (pcu); apply the capacity restraint function and, in conjunction with the overall capacity, work out the link speed under the observed load;

(b)   assign the modelled interurban traffic on the links, using the link speed already derived;

(c)   subtract the assigned interurban traffic from the total observed traffic, to give the study estimation of local traffic; this local traffic is then pre-loaded by the transport module in the base year before modelled traffic is assigned, to give the correct overall volume of traffic, and hence the correct network time.

In future model periods, both the link capacity and the local traffic may be expanded, using appropriate growth rates. The observed traffic volumes used for this procedure were collected from the UN Census of Motorway Traffic of 1990. For a small number of roads not covered by the UN data, study estimates were made.

Table C.26.   Path choice function parameters

Flow	Mode	λ_p	Value of time (ECU/hour)
Business travel A	Car	0.10	37.00
Business travel B	Car	0.15	27.75
Independent personal A	Car	0.15	15.00
	Coach	0.15	15.00
Independent personal B	Car	0.15	6.50
	Coach	0.15	6.50
Inclusive personal	Coach	0.50	6.50
Liquid bulk	Lorry	1.00	12.50
Solid bulk	Lorry	1.00	12.50
Semi-bulk	Lorry	1.00	12.50
General freight A	Lorry	150.00	12.50
General freight B	Lorry	100.00	12.50

Note: For value of time, see discussion under Modal Choice in C.3.3.

Path choice

At present, path choice is implemented in a detailed way only on road, for car, coach and lorry.

For modes which are not used door-to-door, the model parameters are adjusted such that the journey length of the auxiliary mode is kept to a minimum. In other words, the main mode is used at the earliest opportunity as the flow originates from the centroid.

For car and lorry the operating cost is used in conjunction with value of time of travel in determining the minimum path. For coach and other modes, a time-based function is used, which determines the minimum path according to journey time. Then the path choice parameter λ_p is estimated such that most of the traffic from an origin zone to a destination zone uses the minimum path on the strategic network, while a small proportion (typically around 10-15%) is spread amongst the alternative paths. The actual spread, however, depends on the specific connectivity in the part of the network. Table C.26 gives the path choice parameters for road modes for each flow type.

Modal choice

Modal choice calibration was carried out for each of the transport flows. This involves the estimation of value of time and the modal constant in the disutility function, and the modal choice parameter λ_m. As there are no systematic origin-destination data available, a two-tiered approximation approach is adopted in place of a direct formal calibration procedure (such as the maximum likelihood method).

(a)   For each flow, a value of time is assumed based on existing knowledge (detailed below). Note this value of time is defined to depict the user choice behaviour, i.e. the trade-off between tariff (or in the case of car, perceived car operating costs) and journey time.

(b)   The modal choice parameter and the modal constants are then estimated. For passenger flows, an initial maximum likelihood estimation was carried out on a small dataset obtained from an interurban transport study in Italy. The modal choice parameters and the constants are then readjusted for each individual flow type, based on known relativities of the parameters. For freight, modal choice parameters are estimated against the overall modal shares, and then fine-tuned through readjustments of modal constants. The estimated functions are then examined in a series of sensitivity tests on elasticity with respect to cost and time changes.

Table C.27 presents the process in which the passenger values of time are determined. It also shows the value-of-time basis on which the two independent travel groups are divided for each country or country group. The principal sources have been the CAA London airport surveys and the EURET study, though other available studies such as *Segmentation of the travel market in London: estimates of elasticities and values of travel time* (ITS, 1993) were consulted in the process.

The values of time derived above are slightly modified before inputting into the model. This modification concerns only coach: based on previous modelling experience, the value of time on coach is increased by 15% for flows 3 and 4, and by 200% for flow 5, to reflect the relative more severe discomfort of travelling by coach. The actual values of time input to the transport model are presented in Table C.28.

The modal choice hierarchy for passenger travel is set in the form of a two-tiered tructure for the first four flows: HST and Train form a lower hierarchy, whilst the Car, Coach (where applicable), Air and Train Group forms the higher hierarchy. This is to represent the relative higher degree of similarity between HST and conventional train, amongst the modal choices. For inclusive personal travel, only one hierarchy is necessary between two available choices: Coach and Air.

A maximum likelihood estimation was carried out on a small dataset from an interurban transport study in Italy, which provided the modal choice parameters and mode-specific constants for Independent Personal Travel Group A. The modal choice parameters and modal constants for other passenger flow types were then estimated, using the results for Independent A as a starting point. The λ_m values used in the model are presented in Table C.29, and the modal constants in Table C.28.

For freight transport, study estimates were made concerning the value of time. The results are presented in Table C.30. The values of time for freight are estimated in terms of possible savings on direct transport costs that may be made through faster delivery. It is useful to note that faster delivery often means not only lower inventory carrying expenses on interest charges, but also a more reliable and flexible service that could lower other logistics costs. This is because journey time is frequently related to the ability to deliver on time, and to deliver more promptly on request. In other words, the shorter the journey time, the more reliable and more flexible the transport service is likely to be. This is particularly the case for general freight. For bulk freight, the main objective is usually meeting a fixed delivery schedule, the actual journey time being of little or no relevance.

Table C.27.   Value of time for passengers: general definitions

	Business travel		Personal travel					
	Sector A	Sector B	EURET values		Independent tours			Inclusive tours
			1990 ECU	1991 ECU	50% wk time	% Group A	% Group B	
	(ECU/ hour)	(ECU/ hour)	(ECU/ hour)	(ECU/hour)	(ECU/hour)	(ECU/hour)	(ECU/hour)	(ECU/hour)
Belgium/ Luxembourg	37	27.75	18.65	19.25	9.62	37%	63%	6.50
Denmark	37	27.75	16.83	17.23	8.62	25%	75%	6.50
Germany	37	27.75	21.39	22.13	11.07	54%	46%	6.50
Greece	37	27.75	5.58	6.67	6.50	0%	100%	6.50
Spain	37	27.75	11.18	11.85	6.50	0%	100%	6.50
France	37	27.75	21.39	22.08	11.04	53%	47%	6.50
Ireland	37	27.75	15.12	15.60	7.80	15%	85%	6.50
Italy	37	27.75	18.28	19.43	9.71	38%	62%	6.50
Netherlands	37	27.75	17.35	18.02	9.01	30%	70%	6.50
Portugal	37	27.75	9.47	10.50	6.50	0%	100%	6.50
UK	37	27.75	14.26	15.10	7.55	12%	88%	6.50
Finland	37	27.75	16.47	17.04	8.52	24%	76%	6.50
Sweden	37	27.75	18.54	19.18	9.59	36%	64%	6.50
Austria	37	27.75	21.39	22.13	11.07	54%	46%	6.50

Notes:

1   According to CAA surveys of London Airports (CAA, 1991, various surveys), in 1991 the average personal income for UK and non-UK travellers was UK £49,500; this when converted into ECU using ECU 1 = UK £0.688934 (Eurostat official exchange rate for June 1991), gives a personal income of ECU 71,850. Assuming that there are 240 working days in a year and 8 hours in a working day, this gives an hourly income of ECU 37 per hour. For Sector A business trips, the full hourly income is assumed to be the value of time.

2   For Sector B business trips, the value of time is assumed to be 75% of that for Sector A. This implies an annual income of ECU 53,800. This income level is found in between the average income for business travellers in London Airports, and that found through small sample surveys in rail-ferry terminals and car-ferry terminals in the UK.

3   The values of time are assumed to be the same for travellers from all EU countries for sectors A and B.

4   The EURET values of time are those 'illustrative' values per person per hour, derived based on 1990 GDP per head of the working population per working hour (European Commission, 1994, p. 139). These values are updated to 1991 ECU using Eurostat's General Consumer Price Index. Independent tours are assumed to have a 50% share of the working time according to normal practice. However, a minimum value of ECU 6.5 is set.

5   It is then assumed that there exist two groups of independent travellers, one having a value of time at ECU 15, the other at ECU 6.5. The proportions for each country are then determined through the average value of time derived from EURET.

6   Inclusive tours are assumed to have this minimum value of time of ECU 6.5.

Table C.28.   Value of time for passengers and mode-specific constants by flow and mode

Flow	Mode	Value of time	Modal constant
Business travel A	Car	37.0	100.0
	HST	37.0	100.0
	Train	37.0	105.0
	Air	37.0	100.0
Business travel B	Car	27.8	100.0
	HST	27.8	100.0
	Train	27.8	105.0
	Air	27.8	100.0
Independent personal A	Car	15.0	100.0
	Coach	17.3	140.0
	HST	15.0	105.0
	Train	15.0	110.0
	Air	15.0	100.0
Independent personal B	Car	6.5	100.0
	Coach	7.5	125.0
	HST	6.5	105.0
	Train	6.5	107.5
	Air	6.5	100.0
Inclusive personal	Coach	19.5	100.0
	Air	6.5	100.0

Table C.29.   Modal hierarchy and λ_m parameters

Flow	Modal hierarchy	λ_m
Business travel A	Car, Train group, Air	0.040
	HST, Train	0.080
Business travel B	Car, Train group, Air	0.040
	HST, Train	0.080
Independent personal A	Car, Coach, Train group, Air	0.030
	HST, Train	0.050
Independent personal B	Car, Coach, Train group, Air	0.045
	HST, Train	0.050
Inclusive personal	Coach, Air	0.030

Based the above judgement, the values of time are estimated for each flow as follows:

(a)   For liquid bulk, the value of time is set to zero. This is based on the belief that interurban transport of petroleum products is primarily based on a fixed schedule, rather than time-sensitive delivery (local distribution, which is usually short distance, would be a different matter, yet local distribution is not the focus of the model). A similar set-up is implemented for bulk and semi-bulk flows; the small values of time are only nominal, implying that a small benefit in general logistics may result from savings of time.

(b)   For general freight types A and B, the set-up needs to be rather different. There is an increasing volume of documented evidence which demonstrates in very detailed terms the benefits that the user and freight shipper may derive from savings of journey time. Savings of time not only reduce the inventory interest charges, which for certain products could amount to a substantial sum, but also help improve the reliability and flexibility that have become central to time-sensitive delivery. The contribution of time savings to reduction of indirect logistics costs, though it may be calculated for a given user or freighter, is difficult to determine at the aggregate level at which the model operates. While recognizing that this is a task for much more extensive research, the study team have attempted to provide some initial values of time for general freight, which are used in this study. The estimation starts from the European Logistics – Quality and Productivity Survey, carried out in this study by A.T. Kearney. The survey noted that there is a marked difference between the logistics costs incurred by an average firm and a firm that is at the leading edge in logistics optimization. The inventory carrying, administration, warehousing and direct transport costs for a leading company are, respectively, 45%, 37%, 30% and 30% less than those for an average company, in terms of percentage of total revenue. The general reduction of logistics costs as a percentage of revenue could be a result of overall efficiency improvements, which might also contribute to increasing revenue with respect to cost in general. However, a conservative estimate could be made on the potential optimization benefits by observing the larger savings in inventory carrying and administration costs of the leading company. This could be assumed to be the savings that could be made under optimized arrangements, for which reliable and flexible delivery is generally essential. In numerical terms, this implies a saving of 0.6% in terms of the total revenue, or 20% of the direct transport costs currently incurred by an average company. Taking into account the fact that not all firms are able to optimize to the extent that has been achieved by the leaders, we could assume that the potential indirect transport cost savings could range from 10% to 20% of the direct transport costs currently incurred. From this viewpoint, the values of time for general freight is assumed to be ECU 8/hour for Type A and ECU 12.5/hour for Type B, which are approximately 10% and 15% of an hour's worth of user's direct transport costs by lorry.

(c)   The general level of values of time having been derived, some modal modifications were carried out. These concern only rail and shipping, the modes on which time sensitive delivery is largely not yet an issue. The lower value of time for rail, and the zero value of time for shipping imply that on these modes the main objective is to deliver regularly according to a fixed schedule, rather than deliver promptly on request. For short sea shipping, the situation may change in the future as new, high-speed vessel types are developed and put into use. For this reason, in 2005 runs a small value of time is input for the shipping modes.

The actual values of time that are input into the model are presented in Table C.30. The modal choice hierarchies for freight flows are all defined as simple, one-level structures. The modal choice parameters and modal constants are adjusted to fit the overall modal shares, derived from the freight tonnes data from Eurostat's New Cronos database. The modal choice parameters are presented in Table C.31 and the modal constants in Table C.30.

Validation of the transport module

The transport module was validated in terms of its representation of the base year situation and its sensitivity to potential policy changes. The former verification was done through comparing the average distances and overall modal split where available. The Eurostat passenger matrices from the tourism data and the freight matrices from the *Carriage of goods* data has served this purpose.

The elasticity tests, which demonstrate the sensitivity of the model to changes of cost and time, were done by running the model under modified inputs or parameters, and comparing the changes between model runs to see if the model sensitivities to change fall within the known ranges of values that exist in the transport studies, especially those commissioned by the European Commission.

Table C.30.   Value of time and modal constants for freight by flow and mode

Flow	Mode	Value of time	Modal constant
Liquid bulk	Road	0.0	30.0
	Rail	0.0	47.5
	Shipping	0.0	22.5
	Water	0.0	42.5
Solid bulk	Road	0.1	5.0
	Rail	0.1	10.0
	Shipping	0.0	5.0
	Water	0.1	12.0
Semi-bulk	Road	0.2	50.0
	Rail	0.2	67.5
	Shipping	0.0	20.0
	Water	0.2	75.0
General freight A	Road	8.0	200.0
	Rail	4.0	225.0
	Shipping	0.0	225.0
	Water	8.0	450.0
General freight B	Road	12.5	500.0
	Rail	12.5	750.0
	Shipping	0.0	250.0

Table C.31. Modal choice hierarchy for freight by flow type

Flow	Modal hierarchy	λ_m
Liquid bulk	Road, rail, shipping and water	0.100
Solid bulk	Road, rail, shipping and water	0.500
Semi-bulk	Road, rail, shipping and water	0.050
General freight A	Road, rail, shipping and water	0.006
General freight B	Road, rail, shipping and water	0.003

C.4. Analysis of the base year results

As mentioned above, in the base year the model is to be checked in its capability in reproducing a cross-sectional picture depicted by the known data, and in its sensitivity with respect particularly to changes in transport cost and time.

Table C.32 compares the transport results from the model against observed data. Since this is a comparison of both transport demand and model choice, it checks both the regional economic model and the transport model. The aggregate observed statistics are independent from the calibration process. It shows that the model is capable of reproducing the observed patterns of demand and modal choice within reasonable limits.

Table C.33 presents the elasticities of the passenger and freight flows with respect to changes in cost and time for a number of modes. Over the years a large number of estimates have been undertaken for passenger travel. However, the studies were carried out under quite different circumstances, and any comparison needs to be treated with caution. Yet on the whole the modelled elasticities compare fairly well with existing analyses of cost and time elasticities. The modelled elasiticities are particularly important for modes like air and rail, where the modal share in the future could mean success or failure of the business. Oum, Waters and Yong (World Bank, 1990) carried out a general review of price elasticities for transport. The price elasticity for air travel is given to be within -0.4 to -1.2 for business travel and between -1.1 to -2.7 for leisure ravel. Intercity rail travel has a range of -0.3 to -1.2 For time elasticities British Rail's studies on HST gave an estimate of -0.9, whilst SNCF gave a higher figure of -1.4. Elasticities on freight transport are harder to find and compare; these aspects are being investigated in some ongoing FPIV research projects.

Table C.32.   Comparison of 1991 transport results with known data

Passengers		Modelled				Observed			
		Av. distance (km)	Annual volume (million trips)	Annual p-km (billion)	Modal choice	Av. distance (km)	Annual volume (million trips)	Annual p-km (billion)	Modal choice
Business travel	Car	136	2,889	393	82				
	HST	619	27	17	1				
	Train	359	306	110	9				
	Air	3,829	313	1,197	9				
	All	486	3,535	1,716	100				
Personal travel	Car	78	9,010	705	81				
	Coach	108	428	46	4				
	HST	294	36	10	0				
	Train	89	1,225	109	11				
	Air	552	421	232	4				
	All	99	11,118	1, 102	100				
All passengers	Car	92	11,900	1,098	81			1,117	
	Coach	108	428	46	3			54	
	HST	433	63	27	0		54.5(1992)	(included below)	
	Train	143	1,531	219	10			194	
	Air	1,949	733	1,429	5				
	All	192	14,653	2,818	100				

Table C.32.   Comparison of 1991 transport results with known data (continued)

Freight		Modelled				Observed			
		Av. distance (km)	Annual volume (million trips)	Annual p-km (billion)	Modal choice	Av. Distance (km)	Annual volume (million trips)	Annual p-km (billion)	Modal choice
Liquid bulk	Road	119	535	64	67				63
	Rail	275	65	18	8				7
	Shipping	2,308	146	336	18				22
	Water	647	55	35	7				8
	All	566	800	453	100		746		100
Solid bulk	Road	52	3,686	192	89				85
	Rail	217	235	51	6				6
	Shipping	2,442	109	265	3				3
	Water	585	135	79	3				5
	All	141	4,165	587	100		4,033		99
Semi-bulk	Road	159	1,962	311	75				74
	Rail	331	279	92	11				8
	Shipping	2,392	308	736	12				16
	Water	546	67	36	3				2
	All	450	2,615	1,176	100		2,350		100
General freight A	Road	232	1,717	399	73				79
	Rail	403	104	42	4				7
	Shipping	2,998	474	1,422	20				12
	Water	513	49	25	2				2
	All	806	2,344	1,888	100		2,277		100
General freight B	Road	194	1,572	305	73				75
	Rail	453	112	51	5				5
	Shipping	2,815	460	1,296	21				20
	All	770	2,144	1,651	100		2,143		100
All freight	Road	134	9,472	1,271	78			938	
	Rail	319	794	254	7			236	
	Shipping	2,710	1,496	4,055	12				
	Water	576	305	176	3			108	
	All	477	12,068	5,755	100		11,549		

Notes:

1   The modelled data include both movements within the EU and to/from the rest of the world, which is compatible with the observed data under comparison.

2   The total passenger and freight km data are taken from the DG VII Transport Database, unless noted otherwise. For freight, these are total t-kms, since the model includes freight movements of all distances; for passengers, the total p-kms are, respectively, 35%, 15%, and 72.5% of the total p-kms on car, coach/bus and train, the percentages being estimated shares of interregional travel.

3   The observed annual volume for HST was taken from *High Speed Europe* (p. 32), published by the High Level Group on the European HST Network.

4   Note that the model output for a given user mode includes the passenger-km and tonne-km travelled on auxiliary modes; thus for those modes that use auxiliary modes extensively, the model tends to give figures that are higher than the figures found in observed data.

Table C.33.   Cost elasticity tests

	Test	Flow No	Flow name	Own elasticity
Passenger	Car cost +10%	1	Business A	-0.058
		2	Business B	-0.028
		3	Independent A	-0.034
		4	Independent B	-0.043
	Coach tariff +10%	3	Independent A	-0.128
		4	Independent B	-0.158
		5	Inclusive	-0.032
	HST tariff +10%	1	Business A	-1.566
		2	Business B	-1.015
		3	Independent A	-0.909
		4	Independent B	-0.972
	Train tariff +10%	1	Business A	-0.694
		2	Business B	-0.384
		3	Independent A	-0.218
		4	Independent B	-0.249
	Air tariff +10%	1	Business A	-0.618
		2	Business B	-0.948
		3	Independent A	-1.713
		4	Independent B	-2.478
		5	Inclusive	-0.183
Freight	Lorry tariff +10%	6	Liquid	-0.483
		7	Bulk	-1
		8	Semi-bulk	-0.245
		9	General A	-0.698
		10	General B	-0.37
	Rail freight tariff +10%	6	Liquid	-1.028
		7	Bulk	-1.196
		8	Semi-bulk	-0.71
		9	General A	-4.236
		10	General B	-2.164
	Shipping tariff +10%	6	Liquid	-0.499
		7	Bulk	-0.406
		8	Semi-bulk	-0.486
		9	General A	-0.347
		10	General B	-0.274
	Inland water tariff +10%	6	Liquid	-0.119
		7	Bulk	-0.196
		8	Semi-bulk	-0.117
		9	General A	-0.306

Notes:

1 The values of elasticity were calculated using the approximation formula [(Base volume – Test volume)/Base volume]/[(Base tariff – Test tariff)/Base tariff]. A value which is greater in its absolute value indicates a strong propensity for changing modes. The negative sign indicates that the modal volume is inversely related to cost changes.

2 All tests were performed with the 1991 modelled matrix, which is fixed in the origins and destinations of trips. In this way it is possible to isolate the modal shift effect, which is what is presented here.

3 All calculations are performed on the total volume of each flow.

Table C.34. Time elasticity tests

	Test	Flow no	Flow name	Own elasticity
Passenger	Car time -10%	1	Business A	-0.758
		2	Business B	-0.772
		3	Independent A	-0.48
		4	Independent B	-0.316
	Bus time -10%	3	Independent A	-1.421
		4	Independent B	-0.789
		5	Inclusive	-0.604
	Train time -10%	1	Business A	-2.704
		2	Business B	-1.825
		3	Independent A	-0.579
		4	Independent B	-0.309
	Airport waiting -10%	1	Business A	-0.25
		2	Business B	-0.072
		3	Independent A	-0.762
		4	Independent B	-0.571
		5	Inclusive	-0.039
Freight	Lorry time -10%	9	General A	-0.097
		10	General B	-0.066
	Rail freight time -10%	9	General A	-0.511
		10	General B	-0.494

Notes:

1 The values of elasticity were calculated using the approximation formula [(Base volume – Test volume)/Base volume]/[(Base time – Test time)/Base time]. A value which is greater in its absolute value indicates a strong propensity for changing modes. The negative sign indicates that the modal volume is inversely related to cost changes.

2 All tests were performed with the 1991 modelled matrix, which is fixed in the origins and destinations of trips. In this way it is possible to isolate the modal shift effect, which is what is presented here.

3 All calculations are performed on the total volume of each flow.

APPENDIX D

Meplan model results

D.1. General notes

These general notes apply to the results in this appendix:

1   The acronyms of the policy scenarios represent, respectively:

     PI   Partial Integration

     FI   Full Integration

     CC   Full Integration with Congestion Charging

     RQI   Sensitivity test: Rail Service Quality Improvement (a variation of CC scenario)

2   Figures may not add on occasions due to rounding.

D.2. Results from the regional economic model

The results from the land use model include, by sector and by geographical area: total production, production cost, production disutility, consumption cost, consumption disutility. The tables are presented below, using aggregate sectors (agriculture, heavy industries, other manufacturing, services, and all branches total) and aggregate geographical areas. The purpose of the aggregation is to enable the reader to inspect, with relative ease, the broad impact of the policy scenarios, as output by the model. All production volumes are measured in million ECU (1991 value) per annum; all policy scenario production volumes are scaled by the sectoral totals of the 2005, and costs and disutilities are scaled by the study area average of the 2005 base, to facilitate reading and comparison with the tables in the main report.

Table D.1.   Regional economic model – Total production: agriculture

Area	1991	2005 base	PI	FI	CC	RQI
Cohesion countries	49,822	72,120	72,280	72,613	73,049	72,967
New Member States	31,534	47,185	47,324	47,825	47,855	47,799
Rest of EUR-15	247,333	341,109	340,810	339,976	339,510	339,648
Belgium/Luxembourg	7,127	10,022	10,009	9,978	9,852	9,868
Denmark	9,074	13,453	13,444	13,477	13,330	13,344
Former West Germany	45,579	61,860	61,850	61,852	61,294	61,398
Former East Germany	4,864	7,092	7,072	7,095	7,016	7,031
Greece	3,022	4,749	4,770	4,822	4,855	4,848
Spain	43,415	62,225	62,330	62,602	62,975	62,906
France	72,245	100,439	100,125	98,953	99,214	99,232
Ireland	796	1,236	1,255	1,269	1,274	1,272
Italy	59,765	80,346	80,259	80,232	80,597	80,572
Netherlands	18,945	26,573	26,642	26,665	26,566	26,600
Austria	5,481	7,863	7,870	7,779	7,666	7,663
Finland	8,910	13,484	13,557	13,808	13,914	13,887
Portugal	2,919	4,458	4,476	4,482	4,512	4,505
Sweden	15,172	22,699	22,750	23,048	23,077	23,052
UK	31,375	43,914	44,005	44,351	44,272	44,235
Total regions	**328,689**	**460,414**	**460,414**	**460,414**	**460,414**	**460,414**

Table D.2.   Regional economic model – Total production: heavy industries

Area	1991	2005 base	PI	FI	CC	RQI
Cohesion countries	118,276	156,795	156,950	155,906	156,596	156,183
New Member States	62,645	83,725	83,750	84,061	84,032	83,566
Rest of EUR-15	857,414	1,102,193	1,102,013	1,102,746	1,102,085	1,102,964
Belgium/Luxembourg	14,108	19,187	19,171	19,269	19,110	19,225
Denmark	10,348	13,596	13,585	13,665	13,715	13,719
Former West Germany	267,419	327,625	328,151	329,058	328,065	328,056
Former East Germany	34,305	40,608	40,464	40,885	40,703	40,674
Greece	6,976	9,698	9,687	9,757	9,784	9,797
Spain	100,498	132,447	132,590	131,400	131,994	131,672
France	153,963	197,163	196,559	195,179	195,533	196,567
Ireland	4,383	5,441	5,490	5,502	5,528	5,510
Italy	169,153	221,003	220,583	221,563	222,391	222,233
Netherlands	37,531	50,550	50,455	50,376	50,357	50,541
Austria	32,793	42,124	42,133	42,143	41,937	41,735
Finland	10,020	14,863	14,879	14,929	14,979	14,685
Portugal	6,729	9,642	9,616	9,686	9,732	9,658
Sweden	17,267	23,265	23,264	23,445	23,551	23,490
UK	172,840	235,501	236,087	235,855	235,332	235,153
Total regions	**1,038,335**	**1,342,713**	**1,342,713**	**1,342,713**	**1,342,713**	**1,342,713**

Table D.3. Regional economic model – Total production: other manufacturing

Area	1991	2005 base	PI	FI	CC	RQI
Cohesion countries	270,684	414,759	413,392	414,445	417,953	417,199
New Member States	241,191	394,196	394,391	395,770	394,682	393,627
Rest of EUR-15	2,601,322	3,905,479	3,906,652	3,904,219	3,901,799	3,903,608
Belgium/Luxembourg	44,164	68,707	68,762	69,521	68,847	68,837
Denmark	48,729	79,530	79,376	79,871	79,034	78,767
Former West Germany	850,806	1,276,384	1,286,445	1,290,588	1,278,524	1,282,797
Former East Germany	111,529	179,208	177,035	179,523	177,868	178,600
Greece	15,981	26,251	25,966	26,099	26,298	26,278
Spain	230,107	350,887	349,844	350,511	353,458	352,730
France	475,478	711,713	708,870	702,005	705,359	704,870
Ireland	9,899	16,094	16,280	16,402	16,581	16,522
Italy	569,609	864,386	862,961	857,139	864,840	862,936
Netherlands	117,449	178,351	177,762	178,287	179,961	180,416
Austria	104,559	167,079	166,954	165,018	162,731	162,509
Finland	47,412	78,703	78,927	80,291	81,130	80,965
Portugal	15,425	22,984	22,768	22,914	23,096	23,137
Sweden	81,495	133,234	133,183	135,037	135,528	134,949
UK	390,556	560,924	559,302	561,229	561,179	560,120
Total regions	**3,113,197**	**4,714,434**	**4,714,434**	**4,714,434**	**4,714,434**	**4,714,434**

Table D.4. Regional economic model – Total production: other services

Area	1991	2005 base	PI	FI	CC	RQI
Cohesion countries	515,831	767,221	765,885	745,607	746,916	747,430
New Member States	444,829	642,129	641,927	644,948	642,506	640,494
Rest of EUR-15	4,635,845	6,561,344	6,562,881	6,580,139	6,581,272	6,582,770
Belgium/Luxembourg	99,313	140,536	141,110	143,601	141,063	141,310
Denmark	108,070	160,736	160,414	160,994	160,278	159,360
Former West Germany	1,281,121	1,799,787	1,798,913	1,809,105	1,798,214	1,805,929
Former East Germany	183,863	286,948	284,977	282,693	285,094	283,427
Greece	30,371	46,151	46,085	38,826	38,900	39,404
Spain	435,823	646,740	646,096	637,570	638,481	638,255
France	966,149	1,352,261	1,348,889	1,347,354	1,353,176	1,352,594
Ireland	20,510	31,001	30,738	29,719	29,962	29,881
Italy	926,287	1,298,994	1,296,821	1,295,194	1,300,716	1,299,139
Netherlands	264,031	373,322	375,834	377,286	382,070	381,803
Austria	159,087	224,314	224,659	223,706	220,746	219,983
Finland	103,388	153,008	152,898	154,110	154,458	154,187
Portugal	29,340	43,652	43,289	39,831	39,918	40,230
Sweden	180,223	261,716	261,289	263,799	263,914	263,003
UK	808,930	1,151,527	1,158,683	1,166,906	1,163,703	1,162,191
Total regions	**5,596,505**	**7,970,694**	**7,970,694**	**7,970,694**	**7,970,694**	**7,970,694**

Table D.5.   Regional economic model – Total production: all branches

Area	1991	2005 base	PI	FI	CC	RQI
Cohesion countries	954,613	1,410,895	1,408,507	1,388,572	1,394,514	1,393,779
New Member States	780,199	1,167,235	1,167,392	1,172,603	1,169,075	1,165,486
Rest of EUR-15	8,341,914	11,910,125	11,912,356	11,927,080	11,924,666	11,928,990
Belgium/Luxembourg	164,713	238,451	239,052	242,369	238,871	239,240
Denmark	176,220	267,316	266,819	268,007	266,357	265,191
Former West Germany	2,444,925	3,465,657	3,475,359	3,490,602	3,466,097	3,478,181
Former East Germany	334,561	513,856	509,547	510,196	510,681	509,731
Greece	56,350	86,849	86,508	79,504	79,837	80,327
Spain	809,844	1,192,299	1,190,859	1,182,084	1,186,909	1,185,562
France	1,667,834	2,361,577	2,354,443	2,343,492	2,353,282	2,353,263
Ireland	35,589	53,773	53,764	52,891	53,345	53,185
Italy	1,724,815	2,464,728	2,460,624	2,454,128	2,468,545	2,464,880
Netherlands	437,957	628,796	630,692	632,614	638,954	639,360
Austria	301,919	441,380	441,617	438,646	433,081	431,890
Finland	169,730	260,058	260,262	263,138	264,482	263,724
Portugal	54,413	80,736	80,149	76,913	77,258	77,530
Sweden	294,156	440,914	440,485	445,329	446,070	444,494
UK	1,403,700	1,991,867	1,998,077	2,008,342	2,004,486	2,001,699
Total regions	**10,076,726**	**14,488,255**	**14,488,255**	**14,488,255**	**14,488,255**	**14,488,255**

Table D.6.   Regional economic model – Total value added

Area	1991	2005 base	PI	FI	CC	RQI
Cohesion countries	532,272	785,711	784,313	770,825	773,768	773,637
New Member States	438,737	644,756	644,666	648,135	646,291	644,203
Rest of EUR-15	4,715,597	6,692,646	6,694,134	6,704,153	6,703,054	6,705,273
Belgium/Luxembourg	97,283	139,166	139,558	141,641	139,514	139,690
Denmark	105,312	156,442	156,131	156,958	156,020	155,234
Former West Germany	1,309,931	1,863,255	1,868,055	1,878,042	1,864,582	1,871,179
Former East Germany	179,623	279,580	277,351	277,299	277,814	277,154
Greece	31,360	48,328	48,166	43,191	43,361	43,708
Spain	450,353	662,021	661,311	655,665	658,019	657,407
France	990,651	1,390,263	1,386,334	1,380,544	1,386,157	1,386,015
Ireland	20,304	30,734	30,572	30,036	30,289	30,198
Italy	973,337	1,372,059	1,369,850	1,367,280	1,374,884	1,372,896
Netherlands	258,675	366,752	367,849	368,927	373,046	373,201
Austria	161,789	236,857	237,002	235,709	232,671	231,976
Finland	101,222	151,281	151,340	153,030	153,791	153,370
Portugal	30,255	44,628	44,264	41,933	42,098	42,324
Sweden	175,726	256,618	256,324	259,396	259,828	258,857
UK	800,785	1,125,129	1,129,006	1,133,462	1,131,038	1,129,905
Total regions	**5,686,606**	**8,123,113**	**8,123,113**	**8,123,113**	**8,123,113**	**8,123,113**

Table D.7.   Regional economic model – Trade volumes by industry by region

Industry	From region	To region	1991	2005 base	PI	FI	CC	RQI
Agriculture	Cohesion countries	Cohesion countries	21,876	27,156	26,923	26,857	26,937	26,922
		New Member States	3,133	5,256	5,297	5,390	5,436	5,426
		Rest of EU	23,919	38,599	38,952	39,269	39,573	39,519
	New Member States	Cohesion countries	3,595	5,939	5,954	6,063	6,086	6,077
		New Member States	8,885	10,815	10,773	10,916	10,958	10,942
		Rest of EU	16,390	26,310	26,468	26,665	26,624	26,597
	Rest of EU	Cohesion countries	24,746	40,062	40,215	40,375	40,513	40,476
		New Member States	14,557	23,619	23,793	23,892	23,851	23,822
		Rest of EU	203,903	272,515	271,895	270,844	270,294	270,491
	Total		321,004	450,271	450,271	450,271	450,271	450,271
Heavy industries	Cohesion countries	Cohesion countries	71,286	93,786	93,598	93,877	94,161	94,066
		New Member States	3,101	4,505	4,488	4,416	4,434	4,344
		Rest of EU	33,412	46,633	47,087	46,149	46,415	46,310
	New Member States	Cohesion countries	2,898	4,231	4,217	4,190	4,202	4,188
		New Member States	29,604	39,017	38,891	39,281	39,455	38,739
		Rest of EU	23,343	32,597	32,785	32,456	32,228	32,334
	Rest of EU	Cohesion countries	37,727	54,517	54,769	53,924	54,065	54,058
		New Member States	26,214	36,499	36,751	36,273	35,993	35,905
		Rest of EU	738,953	950,335	949,533	951,556	951,168	952,177
	Total		966,538	1,262,120	1,262,120	1,262,120	1,262,120	1,262,120
Other manufacturing	Cohesion countries	Cohesion countries	183,059	238,283	234,727	236,609	237,065	237,594
		New Member States	4,783	9,062	9,178	9,291	9,415	9,357
		Rest of EU	43,872	85,246	87,859	87,811	89,195	88,433
	New Member States	Cohesion countries	11,593	24,125	24,287	24,633	24,688	24,581
		New Member States	127,967	160,474	158,342	160,860	162,825	162,759
		Rest of EU	58,531	116,930	119,443	117,137	114,695	114,132
	Rest of EU	Cohesion countries	83,213	167,270	170,868	169,058	169,362	168,425
		New Member States	54,206	100,297	102,361	100,043	97,910	97,723
		Rest of EU	2,050,401	2,853,180	2,847,804	2,849,425	2,849,711	2,851,862
	Total		2,617,625	3,754,867	3,754,867	3,754,867	3,754,867	3,754,867
Services	Cohesion countries	Cohesion countries	341,039	488,806	485,840	463,897	464,588	465,893
		New Member States	9,871	15,109	15,083	15,412	15,440	15,361
		Rest of EU	141,873	207,877	209,780	212,715	213,254	212,324
	New Member States	Cohesion countries	16,181	28,711	28,580	29,282	29,325	29,149
		New Member States	263,374	341,383	339,997	339,587	341,401	340,761
		Rest of EU	126,735	187,603	189,274	191,221	186,811	185,633
	Rest of EU	Cohesion countries	221,079	363,755	367,060	371,744	372,171	371,078
		New Member States	115,702	167,250	168,593	170,363	167,452	167,283
		Rest of EU	4,074,883	5,487,344	5,483,631	5,493,618	5,497,395	5,500,356
	Total		5,310,737	7,287,838	7,287,838	7,287,838	7,287,838	7,287,838

Table D.8.   Regional economic model – Production cost: all branches

Area	1991	2005 base	PI	FI	CC	RQI
Cohesion countries	1.024	1.026	1.025	1.031	1.032	1.031
New Member States	0.991	0.982	0.982	0.986	0.987	0.986
Rest of EUR-15	1.004	0.998	0.998	1.003	1.004	1.003
Belgium/Luxembourg	1.000	0.988	0.988	0.993	0.994	0.993
Denmark	0.978	0.960	0.960	0.965	0.966	0.965
Former West Germany	1.012	1.008	1.008	1.014	1.015	1.015
Former East Germany	1.022	1.024	1.023	1.031	1.033	1.032
Greece	1.068	1.082	1.081	1.087	1.088	1.087
Spain	1.015	1.011	1.011	1.016	1.017	1.016
France	1.000	0.995	0.995	0.999	1.000	0.999
Ireland	1.024	1.027	1.023	1.033	1.034	1.033
Italy	1.002	0.997	0.997	1.002	1.002	1.001
Netherlands	1.001	0.989	0.989	0.993	0.995	0.994
Austria	1.014	1.012	1.011	1.017	1.019	1.018
Finland	0.970	0.952	0.952	0.955	0.955	0.955
Portugal	1.043	1.044	1.043	1.053	1.054	1.053
Sweden	0.975	0.957	0.957	0.961	0.961	0.961
UK	0.994	0.985	0.985	0.990	0.991	0.990
Total regions	**1.005**	**1.000**	**1.000**	**1.005**	**1.006**	**1.005**

Table D.9.   Regional economic model – Production disutility: all branches

Area	1991	2005 base	PI	FI	CC	RQI
Cohesion countries	1.030	1.004	1.002	1.006	1.007	1.004
New Member States	0.995	0.980	0.979	0.979	0.980	0.977
Rest of EUR-15	1.011	1.001	1.000	1.003	1.005	1.000
Belgium/Luxembourg	0.900	0.890	0.888	0.889	0.894	0.889
Denmark	0.873	0.856	0.855	0.855	0.857	0.855
Former West Germany	1.080	1.065	1.064	1.065	1.068	1.062
Former East Germany	1.159	1.125	1.125	1.128	1.130	1.126
Greece	1.175	1.124	1.121	1.137	1.138	1.133
Spain	1.008	0.984	0.981	0.986	0.987	0.983
France	0.937	0.934	0.932	0.936	0.937	0.933
Ireland	1.162	1.132	1.133	1.132	1.133	1.131
Italy	1.006	1.003	1.001	1.006	1.007	1.002
Netherlands	0.891	0.882	0.880	0.880	0.882	0.879
Austria	1.159	1.142	1.140	1.143	1.148	1.144
Finland	0.886	0.877	0.876	0.876	0.877	0.875
Portugal	1.122	1.089	1.088	1.099	1.100	1.097
Sweden	0.880	0.865	0.864	0.863	0.865	0.863
UK	1.007	1.001	0.999	1.002	1.005	1.001
Total regions	**1.011**	**1.000**	**0.999**	**1.001**	**1.003**	**0.999**

Table D.10. Regional economic model – Consumption cost: all branches

Area	1991	2005 base	PI	FI	CC	RQI
Cohesion countries	1.033	1.061	1.060	1.082	1.083	1.081
New Member States	0.978	0.987	0.987	0.998	1.000	0.998
Rest of EUR-15	0.980	0.992	0.992	1.004	1.006	1.004
Belgium/Luxembourg	0.997	1.010	1.009	1.023	1.029	1.026
Denmark	0.981	0.994	0.994	1.008	1.011	1.010
Former West Germany	0.985	0.996	0.996	1.008	1.012	1.010
Former East Germany	1.007	1.027	1.027	1.047	1.051	1.048
Greece	1.181	1.248	1.247	1.299	1.300	1.296
Spain	1.000	1.012	1.012	1.024	1.025	1.024
France	0.976	0.986	0.986	0.997	0.998	0.997
Ireland	1.041	1.070	1.057	1.084	1.086	1.082
Italy	0.979	0.991	0.991	1.003	1.003	1.002
Netherlands	0.994	1.008	1.007	1.020	1.022	1.020
Austria	0.989	1.001	1.001	1.014	1.018	1.017
Finland	0.966	0.974	0.974	0.982	0.983	0.982
Portugal	1.095	1.121	1.119	1.165	1.165	1.161
Sweden	0.975	0.988	0.987	0.998	0.999	0.998
UK	0.963	0.972	0.972	0.982	0.985	0.984
Total regions	**0.986**	**1.000**	**1.000**	**1.013**	**1.015**	**1.014**

Table D.11. Regional economic model – Consumption disutility: all branches

Area	1991	2005 base	PI	FI	CC	RQI
Cohesion countries	1.134	1.097	1.095	1.095	1.095	1.093
New Member States	1.039	1.017	1.015	1.016	1.018	1.014
Rest of EUR-15	0.996	0.983	0.981	0.983	0.986	0.980
Belgium/Luxembourg	0.988	0.982	0.979	0.976	0.983	0.976
Denmark	1.012	0.988	0.987	0.987	0.992	0.988
Former West Germany	0.955	0.946	0.943	0.944	0.947	0.941
Former East Germany	1.018	1.002	1.002	1.003	1.006	1.000
Greece	1.263	1.167	1.166	1.161	1.161	1.161
Spain	1.102	1.065	1.064	1.065	1.065	1.062
France	1.002	0.987	0.987	0.991	0.991	0.987
Ireland	1.183	1.163	1.150	1.147	1.148	1.146
Italy	1.011	0.994	0.993	0.998	0.998	0.993
Netherlands	0.990	0.981	0.977	0.977	0.978	0.972
Austria	1.034	1.021	1.019	1.023	1.027	1.022
Finland	1.048	1.021	1.019	1.018	1.018	1.013
Portugal	1.187	1.172	1.171	1.169	1.170	1.168
Sweden	1.025	0.995	0.993	0.993	0.995	0.991
UK	1.035	1.020	1.018	1.018	1.022	1.017
Total regions	**1.015**	**1.000**	**0.998**	**1.000**	**1.002**	**0.997**

D.3. Results from the transport model

The results from the transport model are: general operating statistics by flow and mode (i.e. average distances, costs, times, and modal share, total volumes and volume-kilometres), and summary of travel consumer surplus output by factor and flow type. More results may be derived from the general operating statistics, such as revenue (as product of average cost and volume), energy use, and emissions. For brevity these derived statistics are omitted here, since the overall results are already presented in the main report.

The flow names are self-explanatory; yet the short-hand form of some mode names may need a little explanation: 'HST' stands for High Speed Train, 'Train' in the tables stands for conventional passenger train, 'Shipping' for short-sea shipping, and 'Water' for inland waterways.

All distance, cost and time values are presented in terms of the whole journey, door to door. In other words, the figures under one mode often include operations of auxiliary journey stages. For this reason the statistics need to be interpreted with caution.

All volumes for passengers are in million trips, and for freight, million tonnes per year. Volume-kms for passengers are measured in billion passenger-km, and for freight, billion tonne-km per year. All distances are in km, time in hours, and cost in ECU (1991 value) per trip for passenger travel and per tonne for freight. This applies to general freight as well, by using a simple conversion rate of 25 tonnes per 40-foot container unit (which is the unit used within the model).

Table D.12.   Multimodal transport model – Base year 1991

Flow	Mode	Distance	Cost	Time	Modal share	Volume	Volume-km
Business travel A	Car	142	8	3	85%	2,078	295
	HST	641	97	8	1%	20	13
	Train	357	51	6	8%	201	72
	Air	947	333	7	6%	140	132
	All	210	31	3	100%	2,438	512
Business travel B	Car	114	6	2	87%	784	89
	HST	560	55	7	1%	8	4
	Train	284	27	5	10%	90	26
	Air	1,127	355	7	2%	17	19
	All	153	15	3	100%	898	138
Independent personal A	Car	86	2	2	85%	2,945	254
	Coach	105	14	5	2%	58	6
	HST	299	36	5	1%	19	6
	Train	100	13	3	12%	432	43
	Air	423	97	7	0%	17	7
	All	91	4	2	100%	3,471	316
Independent personal B	Car	73	1	2	86%	6,037	443
	Coach	89	14	5	3%	180	16
	HST	287	32	5	0%	17	5
	Train	82	12	3	11%	789	65
	Air	348	78	7	0%	8	3
	All	76	3	2	100%	7,031	531
Inclusive personal	Coach	124	12	5	33%	188	23
	Air	558	91	6	67%	388	217
	All	417	65	6	100%	576	240
Liquid bulk	Road	114	6	3	74%	521	59
	Rail	530	16	21	7%	52	28
	Shipping	2,079	43	212	12%	85	176
	Water	653	3	66	7%	48	31
	All	417	11	33	100%	707	295
Solid bulk	Road	40	2	1	93%	3,535	143
	Rail	676	17	27	4%	145	98
	Shipping	2,188	40	215	1%	40	88
	Water	555	3	59	2%	85	47
	All	99	3	6	100%	3,805	376
Semi-bulk	Road	115	6	3	86%	1,697	194
	Rail	227	17	9	10%	204	46
	Shipping	2,706	95	229	3%	52	141
	Water	540	3	59	2%	30	16
	All	201	9	10	100%	1,983	398
General freight A	Road	221	12	5	75%	1,573	348
	Rail	885	49	33	4%	88	78
	Shipping	2,977	59	158	20%	412	1,225
	Water	519	3	57	2%	33	17
	All	792	22	36	100%	2,106	1,668
General freight B	Road	141	9	3	80%	1,150	162
	Rail	425	38	16	4%	59	25
	Shipping	2,893	59	155	16%	226	652
	All	585	18	27	100%	1,434	839

Table D.13.   Multimodal transport model – Base scenario 2005

Flow	Mode	Distance	Cost	Time	Modal share	Volume	Volume-km
Business travel A	Car	141	9	3	86%	2,717	383
	HST	514	91	7	1%	22	11
	Train	241	37	5	6%	179	43
	Air	925	270	7	8%	242	224
	All	209	31	3	100%	3,160	661
Business travel B	Car	111	6	2	89%	1,119	124
	HST	455	52	6	1%	11	5
	Train	196	21	4	7%	87	17
	Air	1,096	289	7	3%	36	40
	All	148	16	3	100%	1,253	185
Independent personal A	Car	95	2	2	89%	6,818	645
	Coach	88	14	5	1%	80	7
	HST	294	34	5	1%	42	12
	Train	97	13	3	9%	679	66
	Air	499	88	7	1%	43	21
	All	98	4	2	100%	7,661	751
Independent personal B	Car	77	1	2	87%	5,485	424
	Coach	88	14	5	2%	140	12
	HST	283	31	5	0%	20	6
	Train	85	12	3	10%	641	55
	Air	375	67	7	0%	13	5
	All	80	3	2	100%	6,298	501
Inclusive personal	Coach	130	13	5	39%	342	44
	Air	570	89	6	61%	542	309
	All	400	60	6	100%	884	353
Liquid bulk	Road	117	6	3	73%	757	89
	Rail	451	17	18	7%	69	31
	Shipping	2,042	41	195	13%	140	285
	Water	655	3	66	7%	69	45
	All	435	11	34	100%	1,035	450
Solid bulk	Road	37	1	1	93%	4,622	172
	Rail	473	16	19	2%	118	56
	Shipping	2,535	35	209	3%	130	329
	Water	538	3	58	2%	83	45
	All	121	3	8	100%	4,953	601
Semi-bulk	Road	114	5	3	85%	2,489	283
	Rail	198	17	7	10%	291	57
	Shipping	2,612	85	211	4%	108	282
	Water	534	3	58	1%	43	23
	All	220	9	12	100%	2,931	646
General freight A	Road	284	14	6	70%	2,048	581
	Rail	875	49	32	4%	130	114
	Shipping	2,941	56	149	25%	742	2,182
	Water	404	3	50	1%	20	8
	All	981	26	43	100%	2,940	2,885
General freight B	Road	213	13	4	77%	1,592	339
	Rail	369	37	14	3%	65	24
	Shipping	2,890	56	147	20%	415	1,200
	All	754	22	33	100%	2,073	1,563

Table D.14.   Multimodal transport model – Partial integration (PI) scenario 2005

Flow	Mode	Distance	Cost	Time	Modal share	Volume	Volume-km
Business travel A	Car	144	9	3	86%	2,711	390
	HST	620	111	7	1%	46	28
	Train	223	35	5	6%	174	39
	Air	954	276	7	7%	229	218
	All	214	31	3	100%	3,160	675
Business travel B	Car	113	6	2	89%	1,114	125
	HST	496	56	6	1%	19	9
	Train	187	20	4	7%	86	16
	Air	1,127	295	7	3%	35	39
	All	151	16	3	100%	1,253	190
Independent personal A	Car	96	2	2	89%	6,795	652
	Coach	90	14	5	1%	80	7
	HST	276	32	5	1%	74	21
	Train	96	13	3	9%	670	64
	Air	509	89	7	1%	41	21
	All	100	4	2	100%	7,660	764
Independent personal B	Car	78	1	2	87%	5,459	428
	Coach	90	14	5	2%	140	13
	HST	255	28	5	1%	45	12
	Train	86	12	3	10%	642	55
	Air	376	67	7	0%	12	4
	All	81	3	2	100%	6,298	511
Inclusive personal	Coach	140	13	5	40%	353	49
	Air	590	92	6	60%	531	313
	All	410	60	6	100%	884	363
Liquid bulk	Road	118	6	3	73%	753	89
	Rail	446	17	17	6%	67	30
	Shipping	2,007	41	194	14%	144	290
	Water	663	3	67	7%	69	46
	All	439	11	35	100%	1,033	454
Solid bulk	Road	38	1	1	93%	4,620	176
	Rail	443	15	18	2%	112	49
	Shipping	2,485	34	208	3%	134	333
	Water	539	3	58	2%	84	45
	All	122	3	8	100%	4,950	604
Semi-bulk	Road	116	5	3	85%	2,485	288
	Rail	194	17	7	10%	288	56
	Shipping	2,580	85	210	4%	113	291
	Water	542	3	59	1%	43	23
	All	225	10	12	100%	2,929	659
General freight A	Road	276	14	5	68%	1,996	552
	Rail	831	46	30	5%	151	126
	Shipping	2,891	54	148	26%	772	2,232
	Water	403	3	50	1%	19	8
	All	993	26	44	100%	2,939	2,918
General freight B	Road	211	12	4	75%	1,558	329
	Rail	358	35	13	4%	73	26
	Shipping	2,827	53	145	21%	440	1,244
	All	772	22	35	100%	2,071	1,598

Table D.15.   Multimodal transport model – Full integration (FI) scenario 2005

Flow	Mode	Distance	Cost	Time	Modal share	Volume	Volume-km
Business travel A	Car	137	13	3	84%	2,645	362
	HST	498	87	6	1%	42	20
	Train	220	31	5	6%	184	41
	Air	913	220	7	9%	291	265
	All	218	34	3	100%	3,160	688
Business travel B	Car	106	9	2	87%	1,096	116
	HST	425	49	6	2%	20	9
	Train	182	18	4	7%	91	16
	Air	1,026	229	7	4%	45	46
	All	149	18	3	100%	1,253	186
Independent personal A	Car	92	3	2	88%	6,755	623
	Coach	96	14	5	1%	83	8
	HST	266	31	5	1%	77	20
	Train	98	12	3	9%	690	68
	Air	512	75	7	1%	57	29
	All	98	5	2	100%	7,661	748
Independent personal B	Car	74	2	2	86%	5,421	402
	Coach	94	14	5	2%	146	14
	HST	247	29	5	1%	46	11
	Train	88	12	3	11%	667	59
	Air	385	58	7	0%	20	8
	All	78	4	2	100%	6,299	494
Inclusive personal	Coach	134	13	5	34%	300	40
	Air	595	78	6	66%	582	346
	All	438	56	6	100%	883	387
Liquid bulk	Road	96	6	2	72%	738	71
	Rail	419	17	16	7%	69	29
	Shipping	1,982	41	194	15%	149	295
	Water	659	3	66	7%	70	46
	All	430	11	35	100%	1,027	442
Solid bulk	Road	32	1	1	93%	4,583	147
	Rail	409	16	17	3%	144	59
	Shipping	2,457	35	207	3%	137	337
	Water	532	3	58	2%	88	47
	All	119	3	8	100%	4,952	590
Semi-bulk	Road	99	5	2	84%	2,480	246
	Rail	188	17	7	10%	294	55
	Shipping	2,541	85	209	4%	119	302
	Water	540	3	59	1%	44	24
	All	214	10	12	100%	2,936	627
General freight A	Road	217	13	4	63%	1,844	400
	Rail	846	46	31	8%	228	193
	Shipping	2,869	54	147	29%	841	2,412
	Water	410	3	50	1%	23	10
	All	1,027	27	48	100%	2,936	3,015
General freight B	Road	179	12	4	73%	1,509	270
	Rail	388	35	14	4%	84	33
	Shipping	2,837	54	146	23%	476	1,350
	All	799	23	37	100%	2,069	1,653

Table D.16. Multimodal transport model: Full integration with congestion charging (CC) scenario 2005

Flow	Mode	Distance	Cost	Time	Modal share	Volume	Volume-km
Business travel A	Car	129	20	2	83%	2,623	340
	HST	517	94	7	1%	45	23
	Train	229	32	5	6%	190	43
	Air	903	220	7	10%	303	274
	All	215	41	3	100%	3,160	679
Business travel B	Car	98	12	2	86%	1,084	106
	HST	430	50	6	2%	23	9
	Train	191	19	4	8%	100	19
	Air	995	225	7	4%	47	47
	All	145	22	3	100%	1,253	181
Independent personal A	Car	87	5	2	88%	6,730	587
	Coach	103	14	5	1%	89	9
	HST	270	32	5	1%	78	21
	Train	100	12	3	9%	706	70
	Air	507	75	7	1%	61	31
	All	94	6	2	100%	7,664	719
Independent personal B	Car	68	2	2	85%	5,385	368
	Coach	99	14	5	2%	154	15
	HST	249	29	5	1%	47	12
	Train	90	12	3	11%	691	62
	Air	381	58	7	0%	22	8
	All	74	4	2	100%	6,300	466
Inclusive personal	Coach	143	13	5	36%	318	45
	Air	602	80	6	64%	565	340
	All	437	56	6	100%	883	385
Liquid bulk	Road	87	5	2	71%	729	63
	Rail	422	17	16	7%	72	30
	Shipping	1,977	41	193	15%	152	300
	Water	661	3	67	7%	73	48
	All	431	11	36	100%	1,026	442
Solid bulk	Road	28	1	1	92%	4,551	129
	Rail	392	15	16	4%	180	71
	Shipping	2,452	35	207	3%	140	342
	Water	524	3	57	2%	94	49
	All	119	3	8	100%	4,964	591
Semi-bulk	Road	92	5	2	84%	2,474	228
	Rail	190	17	7	10%	299	57
	Shipping	2,539	85	209	4%	122	309
	Water	545	3	59	2%	45	24
	All	210	10	12	100%	2,939	617
General freight A	Road	192	12	4	60%	1,772	341
	Rail	835	46	30	9%	267	223
	Shipping	2,843	54	146	30%	869	2,469
	Water	448	3	53	1%	29	13
	All	1,037	28	49	100%	2,937	3,046
General freight B	Road	165	12	3	72%	1,484	245
	Rail	401	36	15	4%	92	37
	Shipping	2,825	54	145	24%	493	1,392
	All	809	23	38	100%	2,069	1,674

Table D.17.   Multimodal transport model: Sensitivity test – rail service quality improvement (RQI) to full integration scenario 2005

Flow	Mode	Distance	Cost	Time	Modal share	Volume	Volume-km
Business travel A	Car	132	21	2	79%	2,483	328
	HST	465	82	6	2%	68	32
	Train	186	26	4	11%	338	63
	Air	928	224	7	9%	272	252
	All	214	40	3	100%	3,160	675
Business travel B	Car	99	13	2	79%	993	98
	HST	399	46	5	3%	34	13
	Train	157	16	4	15%	185	29
	Air	1,053	233	7	3%	41	43
	All	147	21	3	100%	1,253	184
Independent personal A	Car	82	4	2	81%	6,202	510
	Coach	109	15	5	1%	113	12
	HST	265	31	5	2%	127	34
	Train	103	12	3	15%	1,147	118
	Air	488	73	7	1%	80	39
	All	93	6	2	100%	7,669	713
Independent personal B	Car	68	2	2	82%	5,172	350
	Coach	100	14	5	2%	156	16
	HST	249	29	5	1%	55	14
	Train	90	12	3	14%	896	81
	Air	382	59	7	0%	23	9
	All	74	4	2	100%	6,300	468
Inclusive personal	Coach	142	13	5	36%	316	45
	Air	595	79	6	64%	566	337
	All	433	55	6	100%	883	382
Liquid bulk	Road	82	5	2	65%	668	55
	Rail	408	16	16	15%	152	62
	Shipping	1,960	41	193	14%	139	272
	Water	659	3	66	6%	65	43
	All	422	11	34	100%	1,023	431
Solid bulk	Road	25	1	1	89%	4,392	110
	Rail	335	14	14	7%	338	113
	Shipping	2,418	35	206	3%	132	319
	Water	532	3	58	2%	82	44
	All	118	3	8	100%	4,944	586
Semi-bulk	Road	91	5	2	80%	2,341	213
	Rail	187	17	7	15%	439	82
	Shipping	2,530	85	209	4%	114	289
	Water	541	3	59	1%	42	23
	All	207	10	12	100%	2,936	607
General freight A	Road	192	12	4	60%	1,766	339
	Rail	833	46	30	10%	281	234
	Shipping	2,841	54	146	29%	862	2,448
	Water	443	3	53	1%	29	13
	All	1,033	28	49	100%	2,937	3,033
General freight B	Road	163	12	3	70%	1,455	237
	Rail	396	35	14	6%	129	51
	Shipping	2,824	54	145	23%	485	1,369
	All	801	23	37	100%	2,069	1,657

The following tables present the cost, time and disutility savings per year, comparing each scenario with the 2005 base. They give a breakdown by factor and flow type. In other words, they provide the transport benefit details for each branch of industry and its use of passenger/freight transport. All savings are measured in terms of a year.

Table D.18.   Multimodal transport model: Partial integration (PI) scenario in comparison with base scenario at 2005

	Cost savings ('000 ECU)	Time savings ('000 ECU)	Cost and time savings ('000 ECU)	Savings in disutility ('000 ECU)
Commerce: business trips B	-720,254	290,751	-429,503	5,870
Communications: business trips B	-65,195	37,005	-28,190	27,108
Finance: business trips A	-331,639	-45,566	-377,205	-213,226
Other market services: business trips A	-1,174,138	367,521	-806,617	-346,407
Non-market services: business trips A	-263,043	1,391,385	1,128,342	1,506,460
All business trips	-2,554,269	2,041,096	-513,173	979,805
Inclusive personal trips	-344,949	-300,008	-644,957	-1,552,857
Independent personal trips A	-628,312	1,028,081	399,769	2,250,446
Independent personal trips B	-386,937	425,799	38,862	1,176,324
All personal trips	-1,360,198	1,153,873	-206,326	1,873,913
Coal and coking: bulk	99,082		99,082	
Petroleum products: liquid	56,619		56,619	
Metal ores: bulk	-2,079		-2,079	
Cement, etc.: semi-bulk	18,231		18,231	
Non-metallic minerals: bulk	-16,325		-16,325	
Chemicals: semi-bulk	8,316		8,316	
Metal products: semi-bulk	6,992		6,992	
All bulk freight	170,836		170,836	
Agriculture: general freight	1,240,759	-374,892	865,867	1,499,937
Heavy machinery: HVG	229,896	-79,731	150,165	325,795
Office machines: HVG	254,888	-100,561	154,327	364,757
Electrical goods: HVG	585,342	-282,602	302,740	850,097
Transport equipment: HVG	270,799	-118,553	152,246	387,702
Food and drinks: general	933,149	-277,692	655,457	1,292,787
Textiles: HVG	442,505	-204,337	238,168	621,139
Paper products: HVG	88,197	-47,658	40,539	138,394
Rubber and plastics: HVG	229,052	-127,878	101,174	339,648
Other manufactured products: HVG	123,508	-34,912	88,596	159,706
All general freight	4,398,095	-1,648,815	2,749,280	5,979,962

Table D.19. Multimodal transport model: Full integration (FI) scenario in comparison with base scenario at 2005

	Cost savings ('000 ECU)	Time savings ('000 ECU)	Cost and time savings ('000 ECU)	Savings in disutility ('000 ECU)
Commerce: business trips B	1,6312,991	2,981,516	19,294,507	19,975,306
Communications: business trips B	1,462,798	326,715	1,789,513	1,883,688
Finance: business trips A	2,255,694	1,913,640	4,169,334	4,471,551
Other market services: business trips A	29,786,611	7,083,354	36,869,965	37,927,570
Non-market services: business trips A	131,564	5,679,149	5,810,713	6,542,468
All business trips	49,949,658	17,984,373	67,934,031	70,800,583
Inclusive personal trips	6,820,477	258,391	7,078,868	8,172,166
Independent personal trips A	-8,165,812	4,643,756	-3,522,056	42,419
Independent personal trips B	-4,324,772	490,758	-3,834,014	-1,306,684
All personal trips	-5,670,107	5,392,906	-277,201	6,907,901
Coal and coking: bulk	52,970		52,970	
Petroleum products: liquid	-430,701		-430,701	
Metal ores: bulk	-22,668		-22,668	
Cement, etc.: semi-bulk	-916,715		-916,715	
Non-metallic minerals: bulk	-456,329		-456,329	
Chemicals: semi-bulk	-1,173,135		-1,173,135	
Metal products: semi-bulk	-591,240		-591,240	
All bulk freight	-3,537,818		-3,537,818	
Agriculture: general freight	-591,428	-2,7093,00	-3,300,728	-237,223
Heavy machinery: HVG	-131,693	-461,972	-593,665	-19,209
Office machines: HVG	-220,715	-611,696	-832,411	-84,496
Electrical goods: HVG	-460,802	-1,476,740	-1,937,542	-152,500
Transport equipment: HVG	-208,590	-604,138	-812,728	-74,236
Food and drinks: general	-1,129,271	-1,864,116	-2,993,387	-527,868
Textiles: HVG	-353,287	-1,353,826	-1,707,113	-141,165
Paper products: HVG	-95,697	-246,017	-341,714	-35,285
Rubber and plastics: HVG	-199,005	-662,738	-861,743	-75,346
Other manufactured products: HVG	-71,012	-267,994	-339,006	-19,241
All general freight	-3,461,500	-10,258,536	-13,720,036	-1,366,569

Table D.20. Multimodal transport model: Full integration with congestion charging (CC) scenario in comparison with base scenario at 2005

	Cost savings ('000 ECU)	Time savings ('000 ECU)	Cost and time savings ('000 ECU)	Savings in disutility ('000 ECU)
Commerce: business trips B	11,775,488	4,246,125	16,021,613	17,112,213
Communications: business trips B	824,577	485,764	1,310,341	1,462,689
Finance: business trips A	-749,552	3,208,122	2,458,570	2,897,019
Other market services: business trips A	20,032,943	12,310,566	32,343,509	33,769,828
Non-market services: business trips A	-8,432,354	8,603,610	171,256	1,274,243
All business trips	23,451,102	28,854,186	52,305,288	56,515,992
Inclusive personal trips	6,512,769	251,615	6,764,384	7,257,801
Independent personal trips A	-20,004,853	8,447,681	-11,557,172	-6,697,116
Independent personal trips B	-9,856,670	399,035	-9,457,635	-5,747,171
All personal trips	-23,348,754	9,098,331	-14,250,423	-5,186,486
Coal and coking: bulk	67,247		67,247	
Petroleum products: liquid	-514,868		-514,868	
Metal ores: bulk	-19,258		-19,258	
Cement, etc.: semi-bulk	-1,293,897		-1,293,897	
Non-metallic minerals: bulk	-556,396		-556,396	
Chemicals: semi-bulk	-1,743,550		-1,743,550	
Metal products: semi-bulk	-859,563		-859,563	
All bulk freight	-4,920,285		-4,920,285	
Agriculture: general freight	-1,250,679	-3,386,868	-4,637,547	-871,659
Heavy machinery: HVG	-366,080	-616,828	-982,908	-231,751
Office machines: HVG	-483,722	-768,337	-1,252,059	-318,447
Electrical goods: HVG	-1,095,211	-1,940,743	-3,035,954	-748,797
Transport equipment: HVG	-515,228	-801,406	-1,316,634	-351,908
Food and drinks: general	-2,220,317	-2,517,960	-4,738,277	-1,533,951
Textiles: HVG	-647,914	-1,674,742	-2,322,656	-428,009
Paper products: HVG	-207,646	-319,901	-527,547	-135,502
Rubber and plastics: HVG	-444,132	-851,414	-1,295,546	-304,465
Other manufactured products: HVG	-150,831	-336,802	-487,633	-96,100
All general freight	-7,381,760	-13,215,001	-20,596,761	-5,020,589

Table D.21. Multimodal transport model: Sensitivity test – rail service quality improvement (RQI) to full integration scenario in comparison with base scenario at 2005

	Cost savings ('000 ECU)	Time savings ('000 ECU)	Cost and time savings ('000 ECU)	Savings in disutility ('000 ECU)
Commerce: business trips B	12,575,357	3,979,517	16,554,874	28,463,860
Communications: business trips B	925,677	461,413	1,387,090	2,943,958
Finance: business trips A	-540,696	3,623,484	3,082,788	7,947,702
Other market services: business trips A	20,911,032	14,004,593	34,915,625	50,250,244
Non-market services: business trips A	-7,554,448	10,106,217	2,551,769	14,964,308
All business trips	26,316,922	32,175,223	58,492,145	104,570,072
Inclusive personal trips	6,936,973	490,238	7,427,211	8,317,850
Independent personal trips A	-21,892,712	6,020,381	-15,872,331	-55,556,433
Independent personal trips B	-10,922,308	1,216,979	-9,705,329	-4,069,466
All personal trips	-25,878,047	7,727,598	-18,150,449	-51,308,049
Coal and coking: bulk	121,838		121,838	
Petroleum products: liquid	-348,018		-348,018	
Metal ores: bulk	-10,632		-10,632	
Cement, etc.: semi-bulk	-1,651,662		-1,651,662	
Non-metallic minerals: bulk	-293,848		-293,848	
Chemicals: semi-bulk	-1,891,302		-1,8913,02	
Metal products: semi-bulk	-1,039,245		-1,039,245	
All bulk freight	-5,112,869		-5,112,869	
Agriculture: general freight	-1,194,471	-3,149,412	-4,343,883	-680,147
Heavy machinery: HVG	-389,146	-572,573	-961,719	-119,099
Office machines: HVG	-508,071	-713,310	-1,221,381	-182,167
Electrical goods: HVG	-1,165,954	-1,792,317	-2,958,271	-420,051
Transport equipment: HVG	-539,494	-741,698	-1,281,192	-200,900
Food and drinks: general	-2,192,985	-2,318,568	-4,511,553	-1,285,009
Textiles: HVG	-690,698	-1,546,450	-2,237,148	-231,356
Paper products: HVG	-235,420	-294,070	-529,490	-71,159
Rubber and plastics: HVG	-474,670	-784,862	-1,259,532	-172,007
Other manufactured products: HVG	-157,125	-315,370	-472,495	-50,576
All general freight	-7,548,034	-12,228,629	-19,776,663	-3,4124,71

Bibliography

Aberle, G., *The social benefits of long distance transport of goods,* International Road Transport Union Report, Geneva, Giessen, 1993.

ACT Consultants, Institut für Raumplanung Universität Dortmund, Marcial Echenique & Partners, *The regional impact of the Channel Tunnel throughout the Community,* ACT Consultants, Report for the European Commission (DG XVI), Paris, 1992.

Airport Council International, 'Airport Council International, Annual Worldwide Airports Traffic Report 1996', Geneva, 1997.

Allsopp, C (ed.), 'Transport' (monographic issue) Oxford Review of Economic Policy, Vol. 6, No 2, Oxford University Press, Summer 1990.

Baum, H., 'Government and Transport Markets', in *European Transport Economics,* ECMT 1953–1993, edited by J. Polak and A. Heertje, Blackwell, Oxford, UK, Cambridge, USA, 1993.

Bayliss, B., *Road Freight Transport in the Single European Market,* Report of the Investigating Commission chaired by Brian Bayliss, Brussels, European Commission (DG VII), July 1994.

Bayliss, B., 'L'impatto del mercato unico sui sistemi nazionali dei trasporti: regolazione e concorrenza', in *Mercato Unico e Trasporti: il sistema italiano nell'integrazione europea,* Centro Studi Federtrasporto, 1995 Report, pp. 59–93, SIPI Publisher, Rome, 1995.

Bell, P. and Cloke, P., *Deregulation and Transport: market forces in the modern world,* David Fulton Publisher Ltd, London, 1990.

Ben-Akiva, M. and Lerman, S.R., *Discrete choice analysis: theory and application to travel demand,* MIT Press, Cambridge, Mass, 1985.

Bognetti, G. and Fazioli, R., 'Public Utilities and the Internationalisation of Economic Systems', in 'Annais of Economic and Cooperative Economics', Vol 68, No.3, CICIEC International, Lieges, September 1997.

Brittain, L., *Europe: the Europe we need,* Hamish-Hamilton, London, 1994.

Button, K., 'Environmental externalities and transport policies', *Oxford Review of Economic Policy,* Vol. 6, pp. 61–74, Oxford University Press, Oxford, 1990a.

Button, K., 'The Missing Networks: European Aviation', NECTAR Report, Department of Economics, Loughborough University, 1990b.

Button, K., *Transport and Road Pricing: Analysis of International Experiences,* Proceedings of the Conference in Bologna, October 1995.

Carbajo, J., *Regulatory Reform in Transport: some recent experiences – A World Bank Symposium,* The World Bank, Washington DC, 1993.

CER (Community of European Railways), 'The financial improvement of the European railways. The burden of the past debt', Report, Brussels, December 1995.

Civil Aviation Authority, CAA London Airport Survey, London , various years.

CNR Progetto Trasporti, *Sistemi di trasporto merci e/o passeggeri: procedura per l'analisi dei costi di investimento e di gestione e l'analisi economica e finanziaria,* Transystem Trasporti Intermodali Spa, Milan, 1985.

CONFETRA, EUROTRANSPORT 93, Proceedings of the Conference 'Competitività dell'autotrasporto in Francia, Germania, Italia, Olanda, Regno Unito', Verona, 11 November 1989.

Conseil Général des Ponts et Chaussées, *Nouvelle étude de l'imputation des coûts d'infrastructure de transports,* Paris, 1990.

Davison, L., Fitzpatrick, E. and Johnson, D., *The European Competitive Environment: text and cases,* Butterworth-Heinemann Ltd, Oxford, 1995.

De Jong, G. and Gommers, M., *Value-of-time in freight transport in the Netherlands from stated preference analysis*, Proceedings of the Sixth World Conference on Transport Research, Lyon, 1992.

Deregulierungkommission, *Marktöffnung und Wettbewerb: Deregulieren als Programm?* Report of the Independent Commission set up by the German Federal Government for the reduction of regulations against the market, Vol. 1: Transport and Insurances, Bonn, March 1990.

Dial, R.B., 'A probabilistic multipath traffic assignment algorithm which obviates path enumeration', *Transportation Research,* No. 5, 1971, pp. 83–111.

Domencich, F.A. and McFadden, D., *Urban travel demand: a behavioural analysis*, North-Holland, Amsterdam, 1975.

Douglas, N.J., *A Welfare Assessment of Transport Deregulation,* Gower, Aldershot 1987.

ECMT, *Private and Public Investment in Transport*, 81st Round Table, Paris, 1990a.

ECMT, *Deregulation of Freight Transport*, 84th Round Table, Paris, 1990b.

ECMT, *Privatization of Railways*, 90th Round Table, Paris, 1990c.

ECMT, *European Transport Economics,* edited by J. Polak and A. Heertje, Blackwell, Oxford UK, Cambridge USA, 1993a.

ECMT, *Statistical Trends in Transport 1965-1989*, Paris, 1993b.

ECMT, *Combined Transport*, Hearing of Combined Transport Organizations and Companies, Paris, 1995a.

ECMT, *European Transport Trends and Infrastructural Needs*, Paris, 1995b.

ECMT, *The Role of the State in a Deregulated Transport Market*, 83rd Round Table, Paris, 1995c.

ECMT, *Transforming the structure of the Freight Transport Sector*, 99th Round Table, Paris, 1995d.

ECMT, *Why do we need railways?* Papers of the International Seminar, Paris, 19–20 January 1995e.

Economist, Rail privatization (in the UK): slow train to success, p. 31, 3–9 February 1996.

Ernst & Young, *Transport Infrastructure, Business Costs and Business Location,* April, 1996.

Ernst & Whinney, 'The cost of non-Europe: Border-related controls and administrative formalities: an illustration in the road haulage sector', in *Research on the 'cost of non-Europe': Basic Findings*, Vol. 4, Office for Official Publications of the EC, Luxembourg, 1988.

Eurocontrol, *EATCHIP: 5 Years of Progress,* Brussels, Bureau GS.4, 1996.

European Commission, *The 'cost of non-Europe': Border-related controls and administrative formalities – an illustration in the road haulage sector*, Office for Official Publications of the European Communities, Luxembourg, 1988.

European Commission, 'Cost-benefit and multicriteria analysis: road transport. Converted action 1-1', EURET, DG VII, Brussels, 1994a.

European Commission, *EURET Final Report: Cost-Benefit and Multi-criteria Analysis for New Road Construction, EURET/385/94*, Brussels, DG VII, 1994b.

European Commission, 'Fifth Periodic Report on the Social and Economic Situation and Development of the Regions of the Community', COM(94) 322 final, Office for Official Publications of the European Communities, Luxembourg, 1994c.

European Commission, *Réseaux Transeuropéens, Tableau de Bord*, Version 1.3, Brussels, 1995a.

European Commission, *'Towards Fair and Efficient Pricing in Transport – Policy options for internalizing the external costs of transport in the European Union'*, Green Paper, COM(95) 691, Office for Official Publications of the European Communities, Luxembourg, 1995b.

European Commission, 'A Strategy for Revitalizing the Community's Railways', White Paper, COM(96) 421, Office for Official Publications of the European Communities, Luxembourg, 1996a.

European Commission, *Economic Forecasts 1996–1997*, Brussels, DG II, Spring 1996b.

European Commission, *Medium Term Projections 1996–2000: Technical note from the Commission services,* Brussels, DG II, June 1996c.

European Commission, *Réseaux Transeuropéens, Tableau de Bord*, Version 1996.1, Brussels, 1996d.

European Commission, *Single Market Review*, Vol. II.2, Impact on services: Air transport, Office for Official Publications of the European Communities, Luxembourg, and Kogan Page . Earthscan, London, 1997a.

European Commission, *Single Market Review*, Vol. II.5, Impact on services: Road freight transport, Office for Official Publications of the European Communities, Luxembourg, Kogan Page . Earthscan, London, 1997b.

European Logistics Association, *Logistics Excellence in Europe: 1,000 companies reveal their problems, needs and solutions*, Report by A.T. Kearney Inc. 1993.

Eurostat, *Carriage of goods 1991 road*, Office for Official Publications of the European Communities, Luxembourg, 1994.

Eurostat, *Carriage of goods 1991 rail*, Office for Official Publications of the European Communities, Luxembourg, 1996.

Eurostat, *Communications on the nomenclature of products used in the input-output tables*, Luxembourg, January, 1996.

Eurostat, *External Trade by Mode of Transport 1992*, Office for Official Publications of the European Communities, Luxembourg, 1994.

Eurostat, *National Accounts ESA: Input-Output Tables 1980*, Office for Official Publications of the European Communities, Luxembourg, 1986.

Eurostat, *Input-Output Tables Database*, Office for Official Publications of the European Communities, Luxembourg, January, 1995.

Fazioli, R. and Amelotti-Eicher, A., *Integrazione europea e ristrutturazione del settore ferroviario. Alcune esperienze a confronto*, Economia Pubblica, Milan, 1995.

Financial Times Survey, *Business Air Travel*, 30 April 1996.

Financial Times Survey, *The World Shipping Industry*, 4 June 1996.

Fowkes, T. and Preston, J., 'Novel approaches to forecasting the demand for new local rail services', *Transportation Research*, No 4, Vol. 25A, 1991.

Fridstrøm, L. and Madslien, A., *Own Account or Hire Freight: a stated preference analysis*, Institute of Transport Economics, Oslo, 1994.

FTA, 'Time Sensitivity Distribution', *Freight Matters*, 1/95, Tunbridge Wells, Kent, 1995a.

FTA, 'Vehicle Utilization', *Freight Matters*, 3/95, Tunbridge Wells, Kent, 1995b.

Galenson, A. and Thompson, L.S., 'Forms of Private Sector Participation in Railways', Report, Environmentally Sustainable Development Staff – Transportation, Water & Urban Development Department, The World Bank, December 1993.

Glaister, S., Starkie, D. and Thompson, D., 'The Assessment: Economic Policy for Transport.' *Oxford Review of Economic Policy*, Vol. 6, pp. 1–21, Oxford University Press, Oxford, 1990.

Gómez-Ibañez, J. and Meyer, J., *Going private: the international experience with transport privatization*, The Brookings Institution, Washington DC, 1993.

Good, D.H., Roller, L.H. and Sickles, R.C., 'US airline deregulation: implication for European Transport', *The Economic Journal*, No.103, pp. 1028–1041, July 1993.

Hau T.D., *Congestion charging mechanisms for roads: an evaluation of current practice*, Transport Division Infrastructure and Urban Development Department Working Paper, The World Bank, Washington DC, 1992a.

Hau T. D., *Economic fundamentals of road pricing*, Transport Division Infrastructure and Urban Development Department Working Paper, The World Bank, Washington DC, 1992b.

High Level Group, The, 'The European High Speed Train Network', report of the secretariat of the High Level Group on High Speed Europe, Brussels, 1995.

HM Treasury UK, *Communications on Treatment of Transport Costs in Input-Output Tables*, London, 1996.

Hylén, B., 'The separations of operations from infrastructure in the provision of railway services. The Swedish Experience', in ECMT, restricted circulation for 103rd Round Table, Paris, January 1996.

IRU (International Road Transport Union), *Handbook of International Road Transport*, Geneva, 1994.

ITS (Institute for Transport Studies), *Segmentation of the travel market in London: estimates of elasticities and values of travel time*, ITS Working Paper 345, University of Leeds, 1993.

Jones-Lee, M., 'The Value of Transport Safety', *Oxford Review of Economic Policy*, Vol. 6, pp. 39–61, Oxford University Press, Oxford, 1990.

Justus-Liebig University of Giessen, *The Social Benefits of the Long-distance Road Transport of Goods*, Giessen, 1993.

Kågeson, P., *Getting the Prices Right: A European Scheme for Making Transport Pay its True Costs*, European Federation for Transport and Environment, Stockholm, 1993.

Kat, J., Mayer, C. and Thompson, D., *Privatization & Regulation – The UK Experience*, Claredon Press, Oxford, 1989.

Krugman, P., *Geography and Trade*, MIT Press, Cambridge, Mass, London, 1992.

Krugman, P., *Development Geography and Economic Theory*, MIT Press, Cambridge, Mass, London, 1995.

Larsson, S. and Ekstrom, A., 'The case of the Swedish Railways', in *Privatization of Railways*, 90th Round Table , ECMT, Paris, 1993.

Leontief, W., *Input-Output Economics,* Oxford University Press, Oxford, 1986.

Moyer, N.E. and Thompson, L.S., *Options for Reshaping the Railway,* Transport Division Infrastructure and Urban Development Department Working Paper, The World Bank, Washington DC, 1992.

MVA, GVC, Owen Williams and TRT Trasporti e Territorio, 'Scenarios for Road Transport', APAS Report prepared for the European Commission (DG VII), Brussels, December 1995.

Nash, C., *The separations of operations from infrastructure in the provision of railway services. The British Experience*, in ECMT, restricted circulation for 103rd Round Table, Paris, January 1996.

Nash, C. and Preston, J., 'The (rail) policy debate in Great Britain', in *Privatization of Railways,* 90th Round Table, ECMT, Paris, 1993.

Netherlands Economic Institute, 'Inland Waterway Tariffs and Cost Structure', Transport Department, Rotterdam, 1996.

Newbery, D., 'Pricing and Congestion: Economic Principles Relevant to Pricing Roads', *Oxford Review of Economic Policy*, Vol. 6, pp. 22–38, Oxford University Press, Oxford, 1990.

Newbery, D., 'The case for a Public Road Authority', *Journal of Transport Economics and Policy*, Vol. XXVIII, No 3, London, September 1994.

Nijkamp, P. and Vleugel, J.M., *Missing Transport Networks in Europe,* Averbury, Aldershot-Brookfield USA-Hong Kong-Singapore-Sidney, 1994.

OECD, *Infrastructure Policies for the 1990s,* Paris, 1993.

Peeters, C., Verbeke, A., Declercq, E. and Wijnolst, N., *Analysis of the Competitive Position of Short Sea Shipping: Development of Policy Measures,* Delft University Press, Delft, 1995.

Petretto, A., *La regolamentazione dei prezzi e della qualità,* Franco Angeli, Milan, 1991.

Ponti, M., *Organization of Transport Markets,* Proceedings of the XIII Symposium ECMT – *New Problems*, *New Solutions*, Luxembourg, 9–11 March 1995.

Ponti, M. and Assanti, F., 'Le Ferrovie dello Stato: un possibile modello dei rapporti principale-agente', *Archivio di Studi Urbani e Regionali*, No 52, 1995.

Preston, J.M., 'Railway trends exhibit east-west split', *Railway Gazette International,* pp. 450–451; July 1996.

Planning and Transport Research and Computation (PTRC), *Financing Transport Infrastructure,* edited by S. Farrel, London, 1994.

Quinet, E., 'Transport between Monopoly and Competition: Supply Side and Markets', in *European Transport Economics,* ECMT 1953–1993, edited by J. Polak and A. Heertje, Blackwell, Oxford, 1993.

Rohr, C. and Williams, I.N., 'Modelling the regional impacts of the Channel Tunnel', *Environment and Planning B: Planning and Design,* No 21, 1994, pp. 555-567.

Rothengatter, W., 'Externalities of Transport', in *European Transport Economics,* ECMT 1953–1993, edited by J. Polak and A. Heertje, Blackwell, Oxford, 1993.

Round Table of European Industrialists, *Need for renewing transport infrastructure in Europe: Proposals for improving the decision-making process,* Brussels, 1990.

Schwanhäusser, W., *Can operations be separated from the network in the provision of railway products?* in ECMT, restricted circulation for 103rd Round Table, Paris, 1996.

Sheffi, Y., *Urban Transportation Networks,* Prentice-Hall, Englewood Cliffs, NJ, 1985.

Sviden, O., *Scenarios: On Expert Generated Scenarios For Long Range Infrastructure Planning of Transportation and Energy Systems,* Linkoping University, 1989.

Transroute-ISIS, Heusch Boesefeld and A.T. Kearney, 'EC Motorway Network Perspectives: 2010 Horizon', Lyon, February 1992.

TRT (Trasporti e Territorio), *Politiche tariffarie nel trasporto ferroviario delle merci: un confronto europeo,* Milan, 1994.

UK Department of Transport, *New Opportunities for the Railways: the Privatization of British Rail,* Report of the Minister for Transport to the British Parliament, HMSO, London, July 1992a.

UK Department of Transport, *Transport Statistics Great Britain 1992,* HMSO, London, 1992b.

UK Department of Transport, *Pricing for Better Motorways,* White Paper of the British Government about the introduction of motorway tolls, HMSO, London, 1993a.

UK Department of Transport, *National Travel Survey 1989/1991. Transport Statistics Report,* HMSO, London, 1993b.

United Nations Economic Commission for Europe, 'Census of Motor Traffic on Main International Traffic Arteries', Transport Division (Geneva), New York, 1993.

Widlert, S. and Bradley, M., *Preferences for freight services in Sweden,* Proceedings of the Sixth World Conference on Transport Research, Lyon, 1992.

Williams, I.N., 'A model of London and the South East' in *Environment and Planning B: Planning and Design,* Vol.21, No.5, 1994.

Williams, I.N. and Echenique, M.H., 'A regional model for commodity and passenger flows', *Proceedings of the PTRC Summer Annual Meeting,* 'Planning and Transport Research and Computation' (PTRC), London, 1978.

Wilson, A.G., Coehlo, J.D., MacGill, S.M. and Williams, H.C.W.L., *Optimization in Location and Transport Analysis,* Wiley, Chichester, 1981.

Winston, C., 'Economic Deregulation: Days of Reckoning for Microeconomist', *Journal of Economic Literature*, September 1993.

World Bank, *World Development Report 1994: Infrastructure for Development*, Oxford University Press, Oxford, 1994.